A MEMOIR

LETTERS, AND DIARY

OF THE

REV. HENRY S. POLEHAMPTON, M.A.

FELLOW OF PEMBROKE COLLEGE, OXFORD,

CHAPLAIN OF LUCKNOW.

EDITED BY THE

REV. EDWARD POLEHAMPTON, M.A.

AND THE

REV. THOMAS STEDMAN POLEHAMPTON, M.A.

FELLOWS OF PEMBROKE COLLEGE, OXFORD.

SECOND EDITION.

LONDON:
RICHARD BENTLEY, NEW BURLINGTON STREET,
Publisher in Ordinary to Her Majesty.
1858.

In the interest of creating a more extensive selection of rare historical book reprints, we have chosen to reproduce this title even though it may possibly have occasional imperfections such as missing and blurred pages, missing text, poor pictures, markings, dark backgrounds and other reproduction issues beyond our control. Because this work is culturally important, we have made it available as a part of our commitment to protecting, preserving and promoting the world's literature. Thank you for your understanding.

LUCKNOW.—The City Church during the Siege.

The grave in the front of the sketch, with three small shrubs at the foot, shows where Mr. Polehampton was buried. At his feet lies Major Banks, and at his head Sir Henry Lawrence.

LONDON:
R. CLAY, PRINTER, BREAD STREET HILL.

DEDICATION.

TO THE

REVEREND RICHARD OKES, D.D.

PROVOST OF KING'S COLLEGE, CAMBRIDGE.

Dear Mr. Provost,

We trust you will excuse the liberty we take in venturing to dedicate our book to you.

Among our brother's many friends, and our own, it is impossible for us to find one, to whom the dedication is so justly due as to yourself.

For you were his father's friend; to your interest and good word he owed his Indian appointment; and one of his brothers owes to your untiring friendship almost everything he has possessed, or does possess, in life.

If our brother's name was not eminent, it was only not so, because he was so soon summoned from his labours. His life was short, but it was a noble life; for with all the straightforward simplicity and energy of his being he laboured to do his duty to his God and to his country.

Therefore, if we do not dedicate to you the life of an eminent man, we yet offer that of an honest and a good one; and we would fain hope that, when you have added the perusal of our story to what you already know of its subject, you will not disdain our offering.

We have added some mention of the noble woman, who cheered and sustained our brother's living and dying hours, and who, bravely battling with her own overwhelming sorrows, tenderly ministered to the death-beds of many a sufferer in that period of trial and woe.

We feel confident that such mention of her will not cause our book to be less favourably received by you.

We have the honour,

DEAR MR. PROVOST,

To remain, with sincere respect and affection,

Your obliged and faithful Servants,

THE EDITORS.

CONTENTS.

MEMOIR.

Preface—Birth—Eton—Entrance at Pembroke College, Oxford—Iffley Lasher—Gallant Act—Boating—University Boat—St. David's—Ordination—Letter on Ordination—First Sermon—Its application to his Spiritual Life—1848, Greenford—Letter on the close of 1848—Appointed Curate of St. Chad's, Shrewsbury—St. Aldate's, Oxford—Ministry at St. Chad's—Testimony of Colleague—Cholera—Preaching—Parochial Visits—Anecdote—Engagement—Appointed to a Chaplaincy in Bengal—Letter to his Mother—Marriage—Letter—Visit to Greenford, &c.—Letter from Oxford—Boat-race—"Pewter-pot"—Testimonial from Parishioners of St. Chad's—Farewell Sermon—Departure for India—Devotion to his Work—Oudh Mission—Cholera in the 52d Regiment—Fever—Anecdote—Preparation for Death—Tennyson and Longfellow—Testimonial from 52d—Letter from Captain Fletcher Hayes—Testimonies of the Bishops of Calcutta and Madras—The coming of the End—Siege of Lucknow—Death—"Perfect Peace"—Hymn—Southey's Poem on Heber's Portrait—Mrs. Polehampton—The Lucknow Nurses . . . . P. 1

Notes to Memoir 35

LETTERS.

1856—*January 11th.*—The Voyage—Southampton—Parting—First Dinner on board the PERA—Engine breaks—Anxiety—Lisbon—Quarantine—Death on board—Funeral at Sea—The PERA—The Boats 37

January 16th.—Quarantine—View of Lisbon—Divine Service on board—Sermon on the Danger of the Voyage—Out of Quarantine—Visit to Lisbon—Madame Bolt's Hotel—Lionizing—Churches—Incident in St. Roque—Houses—Costumes—Table d'hote—Belem Monastery—Life on board 44

CONTENTS.

January 23d.—Voyage resumed—Sea-sickness—Gibraltar—Sierra Nevada—Open Ports—Dinner in a heavy Sea—Clergy on board—Principal Kay—Mr. Stewart—Prospect of future re-union. P. 52

January 24th.—Malta—English Church at Valetta—A pleasant Meeting—Maltese Divers—St. Paul's Voyage—Alexandria—Eastern Bazaars—Eastern Dresses—Nubians—Railway to Cairo—Dragoman—" Recollections of Arabian Nights "—The Desert—Thunderstorm—Desert Horses—Suez—Peninsula and Oriental ship *Hindostan*—" When Israel came out of Egypt "—Impression of the Route 57

February 18th.—Passengers in *Hindostan*—Dr. Kay—The Red Sea—Ceylon—Native Boats—The American Captain . . . 66

March 8th.—The River Hooghly—Datchet—Pilots—Quicksands—Garden Reach—Domestic Architecture—Spence's Hotel—Old Friends—Freshman's Hindostanee—Bishop's College—Chapel—Daily Life in Calcutta—The Course—Shops—Native Quarters—" Beating down"—Appointment to Lucknow—Sermon in Cathedral—Calcutta Cathedral—Heat—" The Eastern Lily gathered." 69

April 7.—Fireflies—Cicala—Want of Turf—Departure from Calcutta—French Settlements—Gharree—The Dâk-Bungalow—Tough " Murghis "—Benares—Mr. Verrett—Company's College—Allahabad—Old Friends—Eastern Present—Mr. Spry—Cawnpore—Mr. Moncrieff—Lucknow—Parishioners—Lady Outram—Description of Chaplain's House—Congregations—Field of Labour—Schools—Civility of Natives.—Religion in 52nd Regiment . 79

May 2d.—Description of a Drive through Lucknow—Elephant—Bheesties—Bullock Vans—Nawaub's House—Fakeer—Mosque—Hindoo Temples—Costumes—Digression—Barracks—Divine Service in open air—Hospital—Prayer-meeting of 52nd Regiment—Residency Church—Annexation—Bat-hunt—King of Oudh's Wives—Schools—Martinière—General Martin—Bell's Life—Oxford and Cambridge Boat-race—Servants—Expenses . . . 89

June 17th.—Old Reminiscences—Pontesbury Brook—" 4th of June " in Lucknow—Dress for India—Horses 102

June 30th.—Roman Catholic Priest—Friends—Cholera in 52nd Regiment—Mrs. Block 104

July 18th.—Cholera—Mr. Augustus Chauncey—His Death—Peace of the Righteous in Death—" Be ye also ready "—Happiness in his Work—Mooltan—Chloe—Stag-hunt in Compound—Goats—

CONTENTS.

"Call the cattle home"—Rains—Bis Cobra—Christenings—Fruits—Baboo—Baptism of Mussulmaun—Dr. Naismith—Timid Believers—Hope of future Missions—"Look forward" . . P. 107

August 2.—Rowing to the Train—Collision in the Streets of Lucknow—Captain Fletcher Hayes, M.A. 122

September 3. (From Mrs. Polehampton)—Mr. Polehampton's Illness Kindness of Mr. Gubbins 124

September 20.—Origin of Fever—Confinement to Hospital—Over-exercise—Running by the Buggy—"The Lucknow Four"—Delirium—Marmion—Removal to Mr. Gubbins'—Bengal Leeches—Lessons of Sickness—The Mohurrum—Arrest of Rajah—Tiger-shooting—Captain Dashwood—Chesterton—Good Resolutions—Comfort of Bible, Poetry, &c. 126

October 4.—Return to Duty—The Spavined Steed—Passion-flowers—Old Memories—Dried Flowers—The Darogha—Imaum-Barrah—Darogha bumptious 138

October 16.—Mrs. Fayrer—Position of Surgeons—Captain Macpherson—The Band—The Moosa Bagh—Flying Foxes—"Pilgrim's Progress"—Apollyon—Cleanliness of Lucknow—The Suburb—Dr. Anderson—Lieutenant Petrie—His Death—Brigadier Gray—Cobra di Capello—Drive by Night—Funeral of Lieutenant Petrie—Sermon to 52nd Regiment after Cholera—Choir—Captain Babington—Landowr—Music—Confirmation Candidates—Accident—Elephants 142

November 6.—Indian Horses—Resignation to God's Will—Inhumanity of Natives—The "Pariah"—Home-longings. . . . 155

November 7.—Dandie and Chloe—Custard Apples—Flowers—Native Costumes—Nazir. 157

December 7.—Cool Weather—The Bishop of Madras—Mr. Cuthbert's Sermon for the Oudh Mission—Confirmation—Consecration of Burial-ground—The Bishop's Sermon—His commendation of the Chaplain—Extract from Record Book—General Anson—Native Servants 160

1857. *January* 7.—Birth of Baby—His Illness—Baptism—Death—Funeral—A Mother's Grief—Disappointment—"Take heed that ye despise not one of these little ones"—Benoni 166

January 10.—Departure of 52nd Regiment—Final Service—Testimony to the Officers and Men—An agreeable Surprise . . 171

CONTENTS.

January 23rd.—Journey to Sultanpore anticipated—Mrs. Block—Insolence of Palki-bearers—Colonel Inglis—Irregular Cavalry—Letter to Colonel Campbell of 52nd—52nd Regiment . P. 173

February 16th.—Journey to Sultanpore—Palki-travelling—Bucksheesh—Mr. Ommanney—Mr. Block—Oudh Mission—Wedding—Description of Country—Return Home—Storm—Suwar—Journey to Seetapore—Mr. Christian—Sir Mountstuart Jackson—Peernuggur—Bareè—Religion of Lower Orders—Missionary Work 179

February 26th.—Baree—Robbers—Outbreak at Fyzabad . . 200

March 9th. (1.)—Hope of a Fellow-Labourer—Christmas Decorations—Strawberries—Waterloo Wheat—Pomegranates—Oranges. 202

March 9th. (2.)—Brigadier Gray—32nd Regiment—Eton Men—Treasure in Heaven 205

March 9th.(3.)—Preaching—Dust-storm—Unhealthiness of India 207

March 24th. — Sad Memories — Fruits — Flowers — Mr. Harris—Chloe garlanded—Peshawur—Murder of Mr. Boileau—Fuzzl-Ali—Burial of Mr. Boileau 210

April 6th.—Sir Henry Lawrence—The Lawrence Asylum—Fête in the Martinière—Harmoniums—Colonel Edwardes—Shrewsbury Men, Evans and Jones—Burning of Dr. Wells' Bungalow—Recipe for keeping a House cool—Clay Models—Books 217

April 17th.—Death of Fuzzl-Ali—The Darogha—Daguerreotypes—Picture of Baby—Death of Captain Wildig 223

April 30th.—Journey to Durriabad—Ghosts—Haunted House—Dr. Stedman — Hostile Feelings of the Sepoys—King of Oudh's Troops 226

May 12th.—Twelfth of May—Burning of Bungalows—Mutiny of 7th Irregulars—The Bishop of Derry at the Boyne—Mutineers quelled—Crimean Widows—Smallness of European Force—Beechey Sahib—Native Artillery—Oxford and Cambridge Boat-race—Ladies brought in to the Residency—Description of Residency—Mr. Schilling appointed to command at the Martinière—Precautions for Self-Defence—Sir H. Lawrence's Opinion of the Outbreak—32nd Regiment—Causes of Disturbance—Our Duty to preach the Gospel in India 230

May 28th, 1857.—Lady Outram's Escape from Allygurh—Alarm—Flight to Cantonments—Residency—Cawnpore—Last Sermon in Cantonments Church—Final Retirement to City Residency—Soldiers' Opinion of Sir Henry Lawrence—List of Guests at Mr. Gubbins' House—Captain Forbes—End of last Letter . . . 247

CONTENTS. xiii

DIARY OF REV. H. S. POLEHAMPTON.

Ascension Day.—Trust in God—Visits to the Soldiers—Church Services—City Residency—Traitors—Last Visit to Baby's Grave—Prayers on the Roof—Death of Brigadier Handscomb—Death of Captain Grant and Ensign Raleigh—Anxious Night—Dangerous Drive—Difficult Questions—Fortification—Murder of Captain Hayes, Lieutenant Barbor, and Mr. Fayrer—Cawnpore—Fugitives from Seetapore—Death of Colonel Birch—Death of Captain Gowan—Escape of Sergeant Abbott—Good Behaviour of the Country People—Rising at Durriabad—Secrora—Mutiny of Military Police—Letter from Captain Orr—Letter from Sir Mountstuart Jackson, Bart.—Major Marriott—Murder of Officers—Major Gall—His Death—Sultanpore—Murder of Riding-Master—Muchee Bawn—Prisoners—Sir Hugh Wheeler—The Diggins—Service at Cantonments—Chloe—Brigade Mess—False Intelligence of the Capture of Delhi—Allahabad—Ramsay the African—Service at Brigade Mess—Evans, of the Abbey Foregate—Fall of Cawnpore—Baptism of Baboo—Chinhut—Beginning of Siege—Grave-digging—Retirement from Muchee Bawn—Mrs. Polehampton, Mrs. Gall, and Mrs. Barbor volunteer as Nurses—Sir H. Lawrence wounded—Death of Mr. Ommanney—Death of Sir H. Lawrence—Mr. Polehampton wounded—"Mors janua vitæ"—False Alarm—Futtehpore—List of Wounded Officers—Finis 256

LETTERS OF MRS. POLEHAMPTON.

LETTER I.—Mr. Polehampton's Death—Its perfect Peace—Text—Monument and Inscription 331
LETTER II.—Room in Hospital—Servants—Peter's Visit to Cantonments—Miss Birch—Atmosphere of Hospital—Flies—Patience of Sufferers—Miss Palmer's Death—Maggie Macdonough—Mrs. Gall and Mrs. Barbor — Begum Kotee — Evening Walks — Colonel Palmer and Mr. Harris—Divine Service—Visit to the Residency—Baboo Jadub Chundar—His Letter—Mrs. Bartrum—Cooking under Difficulties—Return to Hospital Work—Private Life—"The most precious hour"—Leaving Lucknow—Precious Things—Harmonium—Widows—Wounds 334

CONTENTS.

DIARY OF MRS. POLEHAMPTON.

Last Visit to Churchyard—Wearied Horses—Secundra Bagh—Kindness of Officers—Muchli Bagh—Skirmish—Death of Ensign Dashwood—Kitmutgar—Death of Sir H. Havelock—Mr. Jackson—Letter from Sir Mountstuart and Miss Jackson — Cawnpore Besieged—Dangerous Sketching—The Scene of the Massacre—Nana's Proclamation—Desolation—Kindness of Captain Green—The Chapel—Relics of Cawnpore—Amputation—Chimia—Allahabad—"Heroine"—Mr. Gubbins—Rash Walk—Mr. Erskine—School—Thanksgiving Service—Visit to the Hospital-Tents—Letter from Archdeacon Pratt—Rumours from Lucknow—Death of Mr. Inglis—Letter from Dr. Kay—Letters from Home—The Prisoners in Lucknow—Departure from Allahabad—Chunar—Benares—Mrs. Orr and Miss Jackson—Ghazeepore—Buxar—Boliah Flats — Captain Edgell—Dinapore—Mr. Burge—Death of a Chaplain—Coolna—Sunderbunds—Arrival in Calcutta—The *Himalaya*—Kindness of Lady Canning—Dr. Kay—Death of Mrs. Bartrum's Baby—Funeral—Preparations for Departure—Finis 350

EXTRACTS FROM SERMONS PREACHED IN INDIA 379

APPENDIX 397

CHRONOLOGICAL TABLE OF THE CHIEF EVENTS MENTIONED IN THIS BOOK.

Birth of the Rev. H. S. Polehampton	1824.	Feb. 1st.
His Ordination—Deacon	1848.	June 18th.
His Ordination—Priest	1849.	
Appointment to a Chaplaincy, H.E.I.C.S.	1855.	September.
Marriage	—	Oct. 10th.
Departure for India	1856.	Jan. 4th.
Arrival at Calcutta	—	Feb. 24th.
Arrival at Lucknow	—	March 26th.
Cholera in H.M. 52nd Regiment	—	June—Aug.
Mr. Polehampton's dangerous Illness	—	Aug. & Sept.
First suspicions of Rebellion at Lucknow	—	September.
Bishop of Madras's Visitation, Confirmation, &c.	—	November.
H.M. 52nd Regiment leaves Lucknow and H.M. 32nd Regiment arrives	—	Dec. 27th.
Birth of Mr. Polehampton's Child	—	Dec. 30th.
Death of Child	1857.	Jan. 3rd.
Mr. Polehampton visits Sultanpore	—	Jan. 30th.
Mr. Polehampton visits Seetapore	—	Feb. 10th.
Mutiny at Fyzabad	—	February.
Murder of Mr. Boileau by Fuzzl Ali	—	March.
Arrival of Sir Henry Lawrence as Chief Commissioner	—	April.
Dr. Wells' Bungalow burnt	—	April 5th.
Mutiny of the 7th Irregular Infantry at the Moosa Bagh	—	May 3rd.

CHRONOLOGICAL TABLE.

Ladies, &c., retire to the City Residency	1857.	May 25th.
Mutiny of 71st Native Infantry, 7th Cavalry, &c., in Cantonments	—	May 30th.
Mutiny at Shahjahanpore	—	May 31st.
Murder of Capt. Hayes, &c.	—	June 1st.
Mutiny at Seetapore	—	June 1st.
Mutiny at Mohumdee	—	June 3rd.
Seetapore fugitives arrive at Lucknow	—	June 4th.
Murder of Mohumdee fugitives	—	June 5th.
Mutiny at Durriabad	—	June 9th.
Secrora fugitives arrive at Lucknow	—	June 9th.
Mutiny of the Military Police	—	June 12th.
Battle of Chinhut: beginning of Siege	—	June 30th.
The Muchee Bawn abandoned	—	July 1st.
Mrs. Polehampton, &c. volunteer as Nurses	—	July 1st.
Death of Sir Henry Lawrence	—	July 4th.
Mr. Polehampton wounded	—	July 8th.
His Death	—	July 20th.
The First great Attack on the Residency	—	July 20th.
Death of Major Banks	—	July 21st.
Letter arrives from General Havelock	—	July 25th.
The Second great Attack	—	Aug. 10th.
The Third great Attack	—	Aug. 18th.
News of General Havelock's Retreat	—	Aug. 29th.
The Fourth great Attack	—	Sept. 5th.
Arrival of Generals Outram and Havelock	—	Sept. 25th.
Arrival of Sir Colin Campbell	—	Nov. 17th.
Lucknow abandoned	—	Nov. 19th.
Death of General Sir H. Havelock	—	Nov. 23rd.
The Ladies reach Allahabad	—	Dec. 7th.

The Hospital of Lucknow Residency, formerly the Residency Banqueting Hall.

The two windows on the ground-floor, between which is a †, are those of the room in which Mr. Polehampton was wounded, and in which he died.

CYTOTAXONOMY OF ZINNIA

MEMOIR

OF THE

REV. HENRY STEDMAN POLEHAMPTON.

IN sending into the world another book bearing reference to the memorable siege of Lucknow, we feel called upon to say a few prefatory words as to our design. And this is the more necessary, since the subject of the following Memoir was not one of those who, favoured by opportunity or endowed with brilliant talents, have won for themselves a famous name. Our brother was indeed placed in a very important station among the besieged, being one of two ministers of the Church of England, whose special duty it was to comfort the mourner, to prepare men for death, to animate all with trust in the Lord of Hosts, in a season of extreme peril. But he was called away to his rest early in the siege; and on his fellow-labourer, Mr. Harris, fell the burden and heat of that long, weary day of trial. His Diary, a portion of which we now publish, cannot, therefore, pretend to vie in interest with those of others, or to furnish a history of the doings and sufferings of that heroic garrison. He was, however, one whom many in England and in India had learned to regard with deep affection. He had numerous friends at school and college, now widely scattered through the world, and many parishioners to whom his brief ministry had been greatly blessed; and not a few of these have asked us to tell them somewhat of his life after he was, in God's providence, removed from them to a distant and more arduous field of labour. At their instance, we at first thought of printing, for private circulation, a few of his letters, and some extracts from his Diary; but, when we came to examine the materials before us, we found so much which appeared likely to interest the public, that we determined to enlarge our plan, as we have now done. They, who knew and valued our brother, will be glad to read, in his own words, the record of his later years; and will love to recognise many an allusion to past hours and scenes, in which they were themselves present, and to find that distance had no power to change that frank, hearty nature, which they admired in boyhood and early manhood. And, we believe, many who did not know him will have pleasure in tracing the steps by which a character was formed, singularly adapted for the work assigned to him in India;—a work, it must be remembered, of no slight difficulty, viz. to influence for good, and to lead heavenwards, rough, untutored soldiers, and others who are exposed to strong temptations, in a land where Christianity has been too much kept out of sight. For such a post men are needed, who recommend religion by their example, no less than by their words: who, without laying aside in any degree the dignity of their sacred profession, can enter into all the feelings and sympathise with the peculiar trials of their flock; who can meet danger with the spirit of a soldier, and speak of a courage to which they are no strangers themselves, and of a power of endurance which, in reliance on their God, they well know how to practise.

That he, to whose memory this volume is dedicated, was well fitted for such arduous duties, many have borne witness. And we trust that this record of his short life may both promote, in some measure, the glory of God, who alone made him what he was, and may show, for the encouragement of others, how dear and influential a man may become, who, without shining abilities, or high station, or wealth, resolves, by the help of the Holy Spirit, to do his duty steadily and unassumingly in his appointed sphere.

We have inserted some specimens of our brother's preaching in India; the last Sermon serving to show the spirit in which our countrymen prepared to meet the storm which, in 1857, burst over them with such fearful violence.

HENRY STEDMAN POLEHAMPTON was born February 1, 1824, at Greenford, Middlesex. His father, the rector of that parish, was the Rev. Edward Polehampton, M.A., formerly Fellow of King's College, Cambridge. His mother was the younger daughter of the Rev. Thomas Stedman, M.A., vicar of St. Chad's, Shrewsbury. In 1832, at the age of eight years, he was admitted on the foundation at Eton College. Of his boyhood there is little to remark. He was always of a peculiarly fearless, honest nature, much liked by his companions, and more attached to those manly sports of swimming, boating, and cricketing, for which Eton is famed, than to the studies of Greek and Latin. He imbibed, however, no slight taste for literature and scholarship, especially poetry: while, at the same time, he became a stout swimmer, a good "oar," and, before he left Eton, was the first choice out of the "Eleven," in which, on one occasion, he played in the Public School Matches at Lord's cricket-ground. Thus, not unfitted for its various pursuits, he entered the University of Oxford in 1842, as Scholar of Pembroke College, on the foundation of Richard Wightwick, with whom, by the mother's side, he was connected. He passed the University examinations with credit, but did not become a candidate for honours. His career, however, was far from uneventful, or without usefulness. Every one acquainted with public-school or College life is aware that its advantage is by no means confined to scholarship. The training of the heart is no less important than that of the intellect; and the intercourse of mind with mind, at an age when character is easily moulded to good or evil, gives to University-life a value, which no other education so well supplies. Henry Polehampton both gave and took impressions.

In the highest matters he would in after-life acknowledge the obligations under which he lay to more than one of the circle in which he moved at Oxford; and several have told us of the silent influence which his upright character had upon them.

In 1845 a circumstance occurred, which raised him rapidly in the good opinion of all. It will be remembered by Oxford men of that date, that one day, during the summer term, two students of Christ Church, Messrs. Gaisford (son of the Dean) and Phillimore, were drowned in Sandford Lasher. One of them had sunk while bathing, and his companion lost his life in the gallant attempt to save him. Two days after this sad event, Henry Polehampton and another member of the College had gone down the river. On their return, they saw, from Iffley Lock, a number of persons collected round the Lasher (a bathing-place, which was then as dangerous as Sandford), evidently in great agitation. Approaching to learn the cause, Henry found a man, in the most perilous part of the stream, on the point of drowning; while his brother, having in vain tried to assist him, had been compelled to relinquish the effort, and no one else seemed inclined to hazard the rescue. Without a moment's hesitation Henry plunged in, and with much presence of mind and at considerable risk swam to the drowning man, and succeeded in conveying him safely to the shore. The University rang with applause, and the Royal Humane Society at its next meeting awarded him the silver medal, " ob civem servatum." He always spoke of this circumstance with much modesty, asserting (which was perfectly true) that he *could not* have acted otherwise; at the same time, convinced of the imminent danger to which they had both been exposed, he in future lost no opportunity of practising various methods to prepare himself for any similar emergency.

The uniform success of the College-boat during his captaincy proved at once his energy and his influence over men; and none of his old friends, or others who admire the manliness of English youth, will consider a passing allusion to this subject out of place in his Memoir. In 1846 he was chosen to row in the University boat in the match with Cambridge, the latter being the winners of a well-contested race.

But he had now to fit himself for more serious

labours. He spent the long vacation of 1846 at St. David's, reading with a friend and tutor (the Rev. George W. Watson, of Merton College) for his degree. Nor was that period unproductive of good: for he joined the rest of the party in strenuous efforts to restore the ancient cathedral, in which object they were to no small extent successful. Having taken his B.A. degree in November, he began earnestly to prepare for Holy Orders; and on Trinity Sunday, 1848, was ordained Deacon at Cuddesden by Dr. Wilberforce, Bishop of Oxford; his Fellowship at Pembroke furnishing a title. It was a bright summer morning; and one of his brothers, who was waiting in the churchyard to see the procession pass from the Bishop's palace to the church, will never forget the impressive scene. Many a face was there animated with high resolve to do and suffer, if need were, in the cause of the Great Master, whose servants, in an especial sense, they were presently to become. The manly countenance of the subject of this Memoir is still before him; serious, humble, earnest, with a peculiar expression, which those who have seen him in moments of importance will easily recal. And then the Ordination itself, as performed by

Bishop Wilberforce with intense feeling and solemn simplicity, is not readily forgotten by any who have ever witnessed it. The effect of the ceremony on Henry Polehampton will be best gathered from the following letter which he wrote to his mother.

Pembroke College, June 19, 1848.

MY DEAR MOTHER,

I received your letter this morning, and thank you sincerely for your good wishes for my welfare. God grant they may all be fulfilled. And now I will enter into some particulars of my examination and ordination. The examination commenced on Thursday morning at ten at the palace at Cuddesden. There were about forty candidates. We had three papers on Thursday, beginning with a piece of English to turn into Latin prose. Then a paper of "Pastoral" questions, for which we had two hours given; and for the next, of Old Testament history, three hours; so that we had six hours that day. The next day there were two papers and a sermon— six hours again—and about thirty minutes of *vivâ voce* for each of us (this last being spread over the three days). On Saturday we had only one paper, on Ecclesiastical History. We had to be in chapel every morning at ten and every evening at six, and the Bishop gave us a beautiful extempore address every evening, after the second lesson, and on Saturday delivered his Charge, a most valuable one. His hospitality really was almost too great. For every one of the forty candidates who chose, there was a bedroom provided, either in the palace or in the village. . . . He speaks with wonderful fluency and deep feeling.

The Ordination was held yesterday in the parish church at Cuddesden. We had to walk in procession from the palace to the church in our surplices and hoods; the deacons (that were to be) first; then the priests, then the bishop and archdeacon, the two chaplains and the preacher. The sermon was preached by the Rev. J. E. Austen Leigh, Rural Dean, and then all the candidates walked up into the chancel, and the Ordination Service began. It is deeply interesting; and it is impossible for the oldest spectator not to be struck by the impressiveness of it. That part, where the Bishop desires the prayers of the people, just before he ordains the priests, and there is entire silence kept in the church for about five minutes, while every one (I hope) prays inwardly, is quite awful; and then it is so beautifully broken by the hymn, "Come, Holy Ghost, our souls inspire." It is the most thrilling, soul-stirring ceremony I ever witnessed, or, as in this case, took part in. Laying aside the solemnity of the thing, the chancel, at the time of the Bishop's laying on his hands and invoking the Holy Spirit, would make a splendid picture. I wish you had been there to see and hear. It is the custom for one of the newly-ordained deacons to read the Gospel; and the one to whom the Bishop gave it was so nervous and excited that he broke down in the middle, though it is only about eight lines long, and made two or three attempts to start again unsuccessfully; at last he managed to go on, but burst into tears before he got through it. It was the most painful thing I ever saw.

Well, my dear Mother, it is now all over, and I hope I shall never break the solemn vows which I made before God in Cuddesden church, but be an altered and a better man, for which I desire your prayers.

Ever your affectionate Son,
· HENRY S. POLEHAMPTON.

On the following Sunday morning he preached his first sermon in the parish church of Headington, near Oxford, the home of some of his oldest and dearest friends, who had been present at his ordination. His text, little as we who heard him thought, perhaps, at the time, was singularly applicable to his own spiritual and ministerial life. It was from St. Mark iv. 26— 29: " And he said, So is the kingdom of God, as if a man should cast seed into the ground; and should sleep, and rise night and day, and the seed should spring and grow up, he knoweth not how. For the earth bringeth forth fruit of herself; first the blade, then the ear, after that the full corn in the ear. But when the fruit is brought forth, immediately he putteth in the sickle, because the harvest is come." The seed, which had been sown in him in infancy, though hidden occasionally for a while, had ever been gradually developing. The earnest, reverent manner, in which, as a little boy, he used to repeat the hymns chosen with singular taste and judgment by his governess, whom, through life, he regarded with the sincerest affection; the frank, open nature, which at school scorned deceit; the fact, witnessed by one of his College friends, that, without any obtrusion of religion, he was always to be found on the side of right and holiness; these were progressive steps in the growth of that Divine plant, the seeds of which the great Sower had cast into the field of his heart. But it was more obvious in his ministry. Very silent, very imperceptible to those who saw him from day to day, but very real, was his advance from more to more. The dews of grace, and the rays of the Sun of Righteousness, were taken up by continual degrees into his being. He never from the first concealed in his teaching the great doctrine of Christ crucified. He never placed, or allowed his hearers unwarned to place, confidence on anything but the atonement of his Lord; but, as his ministry went forward, and he gained more extensive experience, all his statements were more carefully guarded, and his aim at simplicity of preaching became more definite. The blade promised fair at his ordination, and in his ministry at Shrewsbury the ear developed, and the full corn began to appear. As he said in that first sermon at Headington :—" The care " of God is evident, in that the husbandman " is not obliged to prop up the corn in the " field, as he does other plants; but by the " operation of the God of nature it stands, " receiving fresh supplies of strength to support " the full corn in the ear, when that becomes " hard and heavy;" so, as he grew in grace, he felt, with ever increasing force, that God's power alone could sustain him; and that it was as needless as it was useless to rest on any strength but upon Christ.

For a few weeks in the summer of 1848, he had charge of the parish of Greenford, the place of his birth. Thus it happened, that he occupied for a while the pulpit of his father, as he did afterwards that of his grandfather. The rest of the year was employed in tuition; but, much as he liked boys, and successful as he was in gaining their affection, he was always longing to be engaged in his own chosen and sacred profession. The following letter, addressed at the end of the year to his mother, is not without interest.

Burton Street, Eaton Square,
December 31, 1848.

My dear Mother,

I cannot let the old year go and the new one begin without writing a line to let you know that you have been much in my thoughts this day; and to express the wish that every blessing of health, reason, comparative freedom from care, and whatever else God's providence has poured out upon you, may be continued and multiplied during the year which you will have begun before you receive this.

For myself, I cannot but consider the past year as one of the most important of my life; for in it I was called to that profession which has been my deliberate choice, and which I hope I shall at least never disgrace. For you it has been one of much anxiety nor have I been without my troubles; but we may both say that our blessings have so far outnumbered our troubles, as to make us almost forget the latter, if we duly appreciate the former.

Ever your affectionate H. S. P.

At Easter, 1849, he was appointed to the assistant-curacy of St. Chad's, Shrewsbury, of which parish his grandfather, the Rev. Thomas Stedman, had formerly been for more than forty years vicar. Soon afterwards, the College presented him to the Rectory of St. Aldate's, Oxford; but finding after his institution that he could not, as had been thought, hold that living with his Fellowship, he resigned it, and settled diligently to his work in Shrewsbury. A call was soon made on his energies and courage, to which he proved fully equal. During the absence of his colleague, the cholera broke out with much violence. The visitation of the sick and the burial of the dead in that populous parish fell almost entirely upon him; but no death-bed was uncheered by his kind face and earnest prayers. His labours at that season will not for many years be forgotten by the poor. "He was one," says a gentleman who knew him thoroughly, "who endeared himself to all with whom he came "in contact." "I have been told," writes the Rev. Henry Fletcher, then his fellow-curate, "in "more than one instance by the parishioners of "St. Chad, of the benefit they had derived from "his ministrations. One, a magistrate, who has "gone, I trust, to a better world, told me he "owed all his religious convictions, under God, "to his instructions. 'As a dying man,' he "said, 'I am indebted to him for peace of mind. "He knows how to give spiritual comfort, and

" God has blessed his exertions on my behalf.'
" I know also other instances, where he has been
" the means of removing religious doubts, and
" strengthening the souls committed to his charge.
" His preaching, as well as his visitation of the
" sick in the time of the cholera in 1849, will
" ever be remembered in St. Chad." This, it will
be observed, was at the beginning of his ministry, and to the close of his life similar testimony
was borne by others. The success of his preaching was due, no doubt, in some measure to
personal advantages. His voice was powerful
and very melodious; his reading careful, distinct,
and feeling; his manner in the pulpit quiet, but
thoughtful and fervent, and we believe he seldom
uttered a sentence which did not flow from his
heart as well as his lips. The secret of his influence in going from house to house was that,
wherever he went, he went as a friend. He was
no less courteous to the poorest than to the
richest of his flock, listening to their tales of distress with cheerful sympathy, and pointing out
their faults and sins with a tender seriousness.
The result was, that they loved as well as respected him; and all felt that they were dealing
with a gentleman as well as a faithful, plain-

spoken clergyman. We remember one anecdote, which he told us, which, if it causes a smile at the somewhat material notions entertained by untutored minds with reference to a future life, illustrates also the affection which his kindness inspired. An old man, to whom he had been able to speak peace in his dying hour, said to him, "Ah! sir, I am going first; but you will "follow, and we shall meet again; and won't "I flap my old wings, as I see you a-coming "through those gates of pearl!" We little thought how soon he would follow; but we doubt not that many will welcome him with joy into that kingdom, to which he so faithfully taught them the way.

In 1852, Mr. Polehampton became engaged to his future wife; Emily, youngest daughter of C. B. Allnatt, Esq., of Shrewsbury, barrister-at-law. After waiting three years and seeing no prospect of obtaining preferment in England, he offered his services to the Directors of the East India Company, and was soon able to write as follows to his mother.

Chesterton, September 2, 1855.
MY DEAREST MOTHER,
You will be, like me, half glad, half sorry to hear that I have this evening received a letter from the

Provost of King's, inclosing for me, from Mr. Butterworth Bayley, the offer of a Chaplaincy in the Bengal Presidency. Of course I shall accept it. A gentleman, to whom he gave a chaplaincy about six months ago, and who was on the point of going out, has been obliged to resign it, and thus has enabled Mr. Bayley, at the Provost's instance, to give me the appointment. Bengal is Henry Salt's Presidency, which so far will be well for Emmie. She takes it very quietly. I have no manner of doubt that she will cleave firmly to me, and will go where I do. It will be a bitter trial for her, and for me, and for all of us; but we must remember how many of all ranks are every day being subjected to the same trial, and that all these things are ordered for us by God, in whose hands we are, whether in India or in England. I must start within six months after the appointment is made. I shall have plenty to think of, and to do now. It is strange that my father heard of his living here. Martha, my aunt's old servant, has been staying here. She was present when the news of Greenford came to my father, in 1821. I wish my appointment was a parish in England; but I am most thankful for what I have got. Anything is better than going on for an indefinite number of years with my engagement.

Ever your affectionate Son,
HENRY S. POLEHAMPTON.

He was married, by his brother Edward, in St. Chad's church, on the 10th of October, and at once began to prepare for his departure. He first, however, visited the places where so much of his life had been passed, and which were all very dear to him, Greenford, Eton, and Oxford. The subjoined letters will not be without interest, showing as they do in so many ways the character of the man.

Shrewsbury, October 31, 1855.

MY DEAR EDWARD,

I will now tell you as briefly as possible what we did while we were out. On Monday we went to Eton, and stayed with the Marriotts, who were very kind and hospitable. On Tuesday morning we went to St. George's to service, and then lionized Windsor, and afterwards Eton College. On Wednesday, after breakfast, we went to Hanwell by train. It was a fine day, so we walked across the fields to Greenford. When we got into the village, I showed Emmie where the Randolphs, Huddlestones, &c. lived, and we went down the hill to Sayer's [the parish-clerk in his father's time, and since]. He knew me at once, and we then went to the church. Besides its interest to me, there is a great deal to see there in the way of old brasses. I showed Emmie the register-book, with one of our births on every other page. Sayer pointed out the window which my father made, or rather began, with a pickaxe. He wanted the poor, who sat under the gallery, to have more light. The churchwardens said there was enough. My father answered, there was not. They said there should not be another window; he said there should. They got peremptory; "upon which," said Sayer, "Mr. Polehampton says, says he, 'Brown, bring me "the peck;' and he hits it into the wall, and picks out four or five great stones; and says he, 'There, now, my boys, I've made a beginning; you go on; never mind what anybody says, and do you make a finish of it.'" So there the window is, and the poor of Greenford can see to read their Bibles. On going out of the church, we looked with great interest at our vault. I wish there was a monument in the chancel to all of our family who have died. A brass plate well done would be best. Old Mrs. Woodman has been dead some time, and the family is broken up.

When we got to the rectory, we found that Mr. Middleton was away, and that his *locum tenens* was a Mr. Ward, who had been an East Indian Chaplain for twenty-five years, and Archdeacon of Bombay. He said he had never had a headache in twenty-five years' life in India. He gave me many useful hints, as his wife did Emmie. They let us ramble all over the house; I had never been up-stairs since I left the house when I was nine years old, but I knew every room and every cupboard. It was *very* interesting to me; I could hardly help crying over and over again. There was the room next to my father's, where we used to sleep, and through which I remember, first, my mother rushing to Miss Ansell on the morning of my father's death. And the school-room, where you would not let me eat any breakfast that morning; and I, whose appetite was much as usual, felt rebuked by you, and thought that I too ought to feel as you did. The bed in my mother's room stood in the same place in which I always remembered it; and it was upon one side of it, in that place, that I remember kneeling on the bed, and looking down on my dead father's face. I remember a thousand things connected with every room; and I would have given anything to have stopped there hours by myself, but that could not be. We went into the garden, which was looking very nice; but I should have liked to stop there too, and get behind the bushes, where we used to play and make houses among them, when we were children. However, I am too apt to muse on the past: I must wake up now, and work hard, in the short time I have left me in England, and make provision for the future.

We walked up the village again, where I had ordered a fly to be waiting for us at Hunt's. He was looking very well, and asked after you. We drove back to Hanwell, and called on the Haffendens. Mr. Haffenden was very kind. A dog, something like your old setter "Shot," followed me, and Mr. Haffenden asked if he was one of the old "Shot" breed! We then returned to Eton. As we walked through College, the masters were just going into five o'clock school, and I shook hands with Balston and Yonge, and also with Wolley, whom I introduced to Emmie. On Thursday we lionized College, chamber, the schools, and everything; and I suppose I did so very minutely, for I tired Emmie dreadfully, though she was much interested. In the evening I went and saw Cheales, whom I had only just discovered to be in Eton. With Marriott's leave, I asked him to breakfast next morning. He came, and was most agreeable; he and Emmie got on capitally together, and he would come to Slough with us, and see us off by the train. He is a first-rate fellow, and so is Marriott. Nothing could be nicer than our stay there. We got to Oxford at six. Swabey came to call next day; we walked through Oxford with him to his church, and then went to Headington. I am glad to be at home again; but I should have liked to stay in Oxford—it looked so beautiful. Of course I mean to come up to the Bursars' dinner in November.

Ever your affectionate Brother,
HENRY S. POLEHAMPTON.

Shrewsbury, November 12, 1855.

MY DEAR EDWARD,

On Saturday, after your departure [from Oxford], I went up to Headington and lunched there. . . . . They took a most affectionate farewell. It was almost too much for me. I love them as my own brothers and sisters. . . . . God bless them all ! . . . . I walked down to Oxford and went straight to the University barge. I will now tell you of the scratch four-oar races in which I had determined to have a last pull for auld lang-syne. We did not get the same boat as the day before, which is about the fastest on the Oxford river. That which fell to our lot was not a bad one, but certainly inferior to that which we had the previous day. We had the towing-path side, and I was not without hope that we should come in first. Pinckney, a University eight-man, was stroke of the boat on the Oxfordshire bank; Denne, another University eight-man, of that in the middle. Pinckney's crew was a remarkably good and strong one; ours was decidedly the smallest—I being the biggest and heaviest man in it, and I am only eleven stone ten.

Well, we all three went off at a most rattling pace, and kept close together—Pinckney's boat rather leading up to the point below Saunders' Bridge. Here I could see that, in spite of all we could do (and our men pulled with immense pluck), the outside boat was drawing ahead. The middle boat was, if anything, a little ahead too. However, we got on a "spurt," and gradually worked away from Denne's boat, coming in, eventually, about a length ahead of it; the leading boat being, I believe, a trifle more than that ahead of us. It was not bad for a boat with a married man, of thirteen years' standing, just come up from grass, to come in second of nine really good fours. We have won pint-pewters, which is a great satisfaction to me. The first boat gets *quarts;* I prefer the *pints.* I shall take mine out to India, having the names engraved on it. I am rather proud of my feat. My right arm is still stiff. I thought I must have looked very much "done;" as I was after Saunders' Bridge. But one or two men, who ran, told me I was not nearly so much done as our stroke. * * * *

Your affectionate Brother,

HENRY S. POLEHAMPTON.

No slight interest attaches to the pewter-pot alluded to above. During his illness, Henry used it constantly, and in the siege, for whatever he drank: it was the last vessel which touched his dying lips; and, after his death, his wife used it in her noble ministrations to the sick and wounded, and it is one of the few relics she preserves of him whom she loved and tended with such unwearied love.

We must now pass on to tell of his last days in England. It was not likely that his parishioners would suffer him to depart without some expression of their regret and affection. Accordingly, a numerous party assembled in St. Chad's school-room, to present him with a purse containing eighty guineas, and a silver tea-pot, on which was engraved the following inscription :—
"Presented, with a purse of eighty guineas, by the parishioners of St. Chad's, Shrewsbury, to the Rev. Henry Stedman Polehampton, M.A., in token of their regard.—Christmas, 1855." It was offered, in the name of the subscribers, with a warm-hearted address, by the Rev. John Yardley, the kind vicar of the parish. It also was preserved in the siege, and remains in Mrs. Polehampton's possession.

On Sunday, December 30th, at the evening service, he took leave of those among whom he had now ministered for more than six years, in a sermon on Romans xii. 5 : " We, being many, are one body in Christ, and every one members one of another." On the 2d of January, 1856, he and his wife left Shrewsbury and began their journey to Southampton. It need not be said what a painful day it was. At more than one station on the route, tokens of affection awaited him. At Birmingham, one of his oldest friends and schoolfellows was waiting to bid him " God speed!" with a copy of Henry Martyn's Life in his hand; no unfitting present for one who was to follow in that good man's steps. At Reading were others, whom he deeply loved. At Basingstoke we met him, and, after two days spent at Southampton, accompanied him to the ship, "sorrowing" indeed, but little anticipating that we "should see his face no more." They sailed on Friday, January 4th, in the *Pera*.

And now but little remains for us to tell. A graphic account of the voyage, of the journey to Lucknow, and of their Indian life, will be found in the Letters and Diaries of Henry and his wife, which form the greater portion of this volume. We will not weaken the effect of their tales by comments of our own. Upon one or two points, however, we must briefly dwell.

From his first arrival in India, feeling that by the goodness of God he had now obtained his chief earthly wishes—a wife, to whom he had long been tenderly attached—an income sufficient to place him beyond the reach of pecuniary anxiety, and a noble sphere of duty, which would require all his energies—he resolved to devote himself with his whole heart to his Master's work. He wished much to be able to spread the knowledge of Christ among the heathen; and with this view he preached and spoke publicly and privately in Lucknow, Sultanpore, and Seetapore, on behalf of the Oudh Mission. This Mission, for the present unhappily suspended, will, it is to be hoped, when the country is at length pacified, be vigorously resumed. He had, however, some success among the natives, one instance of which will be read with interest in his letters and his wife's diary, viz. the conversion to Christianity of the Baboo, Jadub Chundar.

But his principal exertions were among the soldiers of H.M. 52nd Regiment; and the unwearied care with which he attended to them, during a severe visitation of cholera in the summer of 1856, produced an illness, from which he with difficulty recovered, and which probably left permanent ill effects on his naturally strong constitution. We allude here to this illness, fully described in his own letters, for the sake of mentioning one or two interesting facts which he has omitted. He himself tells how the near sight of death deepened his seriousness, and caused him to form fresh resolutions to serve God. The following anecdote shows how graciously, in answer to a simple prayer, God was pleased to remove from him all fear of death, and so to fit him for the trials of the ensuing year. At half-past twelve o'clock on the night of Wednesday, August 27th, 1856, he called his wife and requested her to write these touching sentences:—" As I was lying on my bed about " two hours ago, trying to reap some benefit " from a sleeping-draught, it suddenly came into " my mind to pray these words:—' I desire to " be a little child—a learner in Christ's school.' " Immediately there came over my whole frame " a perfect peace and tranquillity indescribable " in words. I cared not whether I slept or lay " awake, lived or died. I could only call it " perfect peace, perfect submission to the will of " God, perfect bliss."* " The peace of God which passeth all understanding," whose channel

* See note to Memoir.

he had been permitted to be to so many a dying soldier, was thus mercifully granted to him in the hour of his sorest need. Truly, he who had watered others was watered also himself.

He tells in one of his letters how at this time he delighted to recal to memory the hymns of his childhood. He would also ask his wife to read to him selections from the poems of Tennyson and Longfellow, and expressed his intention of writing to the former poet, to thank him for the pleasure which his writings had always, but then especially, afforded him. It is at the desire of his widow that this fact is here mentioned, and it may not be unpleasing to those great poets, should these words meet their eyes.

The officers and men of the 52nd Regiment, when they left Lucknow, proved their appreciation of Mr. Polehampton's labours, by presenting him with a silver inkstand, and his wife with a harmonium. The harmonium remained safe in the church during the siege, and forms another of the few treasures which Mrs. Polehampton was able to bring to England. The subjoined letter from Captain Fletcher Hayes will be read with interest, both for the sake of the writer, himself not the least gallant victim of the mutiny, and for the testimony which it bears :—

Lucknow, September 5, 1856.

MY DEAR MRS. POLEHAMPTON,

. . . . We were both truly delighted to hear the cheerful accounts which you have given of your good husband. We have made daily inquiries after his health, but did not deem it right to intrude on you in your sadness. No one, who has been acquainted with him, or has witnessed his noble devotion to the poor soldiers in the late pestilence, can have failed to honour him for his zeal, energy, and true Christian labour for the good of his fellow-creatures; and most sincerely do I hope that by God's good blessing he may be speedily restored to his wonted health, and to resume his ministry among those, by whom he is so much respected and admired.

Believe me, with hearty prayers for your husband's rapid recovery, very sincerely yours,

FLETCHER HAYES.

Praise from such a man is of no slight value, and from all sides the same sentiments resounded. The Bishop of Calcutta (Dr. Wilson) had before, in his report to the Directors, expressed his warm approval; and the Bishop of Madras wrote in the same strain, adding, that unless an additional chaplain were speedily sent to assist him, he must give way under his exertions.

But the end was now not far off. The storm already began to threaten, and soon burst upon Lucknow. How he prepared himself and others to meet its fury, may be gathered from the sermon (the last he ever wrote), which he preached, when the tidings came of the outbreak at Delhi and Meerut. It is printed at the end of this volume. We need not speak here of the siege, or of his conduct in it. We need not repeat the testimony of the poor atheist, though gallant soldier, Deprat, who could see his goodness and its effects, though unhappily he could not be induced to seek the same peace from the same unfailing source.* And we are unwilling to say much of his death-bed, because we feel that there is a sacred privacy in the closing scene, which, though deeply interesting to friends, is not too publicly to be laid open. And he himself in his dying moments desired to be left quite alone with his wife and his God. We will not therefore draw aside the veil. Suffice it to say, that his illness was blest to others, while death brought, we cannot doubt, eternal joy to himself. An officer, who was wounded, and in the hospital at the same time with him,

* See Mr. Rees's "Siege of Lucknow," pp. 161 and 219.

said that, while he was dying, his cheerfulness and composure were the support and comfort of all the sick and dying around him! His dear wife speaks of "the perfect serenity and peace that were his throughout," so that it was even for her, in that hour of desolation, "impossible to feel anything but rapture in the thought of his having entered into his Master's joy." "Peace now and for ever," were his last words. Joy unspeakable to us who so dearly loved him, to think that peace is his everlasting state!

The seed had indeed "sprung up;" and "the full corn" had been seen "in the ear," and now the Lord "put in the sickle, because the harvest was come." The words of the favourite hymn of his boyhood, fitly end the Memoir of his Life :—

> "The pains of death are past;
> Labour and sorrows cease,
> And, life's long warfare closed at last,
> His soul is found in peace.
> Soldier of Christ! well done;
> Praise be thy new employ;
> And, while eternal ages run,
> Rest in thy Saviour's joy."

And surely there are none who will not forgive, if, in conclusion, we say a few words of our own loss. A noble, warm-hearted man can scarcely pass away (alas! how many such has England lost during the last two years!) without leaving a void difficult to fill. And if he be one whose duty and inclination alike prompt him to seek the eternal good of others, whose generous nature wins to itself the love of friend and stranger, of relative and alien, it cannot be but that by some pen, however feeble, words of affectionate farewell shall be traced.—The one was known widely, the other by but a comparatively narrow circle; but we cannot help thinking that the following lines, written by Southey on the death of Bishop Heber, will be thought by all who knew him (and all who knew loved also) applicable to our dear brother. The same thoughts rise in our minds, when gazing on Henry's portrait, which Southey so well expressed, when he looked on the picture of the more gifted, though not more honest, Heber:—

"Yes! such as these were { Heber's / Henry's } lineaments.
Such was the gentle countenance, which bore
Of generous feeling and of golden truth
Sure Nature's sterling impress."

"And what if there be those
 Who in the cabinet
 Of memory hold enshrined
 A livelier portraiture,

And see in thought, as in their dreams,
  His actual image verily produced?
  . Yet shall this counterfeit convey
To strangers, and preserve for after time,
All that could perish of him, all, that else
  Even now had passed away.
For he hath taken with the living dead
  His honourable place;
  Yea, with the Saints of God
His holy habitation. Hearts, to which
    Through ages he shall speak,
Will yearn towards him; and they, too, (for such
    Will be) who gird their loins
    With truth to follow him,
Having the breast-plate on of righteousness,
    The helmet of salvation, and the shield
    Of faith, they too will gaze
      Upon his effigy
    With reverential love,
  Till they shall grow familiar with its lines,
And know him, when they see his face in heaven.

* * * * *

    Hadst thou revisited thy native land,
      Mortality and Time
    And Change must needs have made
    Our meeting mournful. Happy he,
    Who to his rest is borne,
    In sure and certain hope,
    Before the hand of age
    Hath chilled his faculties
Or sorrow reached him in his heart of hearts!
  Most happy, if he leave in his good name
    A light for those who follow him,
    And in his works a living seed
    Of good, prolific still.

"Yes! to the Christian, to the Heathen world,
  Heber }
  Henry } , thou art not dead, thou canst not die !

> Nor can I think of thee as lost.
> A little portion of this little isle
> At first divided us; then half the globe:
> The same earth held us still; but when
> Wert thou so near as now!
> 'Tis but the falling of a withered leaf—
> The breaking of a shell—
> The rending of a veil!
> Oh! when that leaf shall fall—
> That shell be burst—that veil be rent—may then
> My spirit be with thine!"

And may we not also say one word of her whom our brother has left behind, a pride and legacy to us, and, we may add, to England? To us she is unspeakably dear, because she was such a true and faithful wife to a brother, who during three and thirty years had wound himself closely round our hearts. But, when she lost him, she sought her comfort in ministering to the sick and wounded among that heroic garrison. "The honoured names of Birch, Polehampton, Barbor, and Gall," formed a sentence in Brigadier Inglis's despatch, which drew the admiring attention of thousands, by whom Florence Nightingale and her companions were not forgotten. England, which loves to honour the deeds of her men, will not forget those of her women. May God bless and comfort those who so nobly comforted others!

NOTES TO MEMOIR.

NOTE I.

From the REV. HENRY BLUNT'S *Posthumous Sermons,*
vol. iii. p. 167.

"I have been upon a sick and, as I believed, a dying bed. I have stood upon the brink of a fathomless eternity, and I have looked fearfully down upon that place of torment, whither my own sins and iniquities would long since have carried me: and at that awful hour there was One who stood by me in the watches of the night and whispered strong consolation; there was One who said, 'There is therefore now no condemnation to them who are in Christ Jesus; I have drawn the sting of death; I have robbed the grave of its victory; I have satisfied the offended justice of God for your sins; fear not.' Shall any tell you this is a *delusion?* Shall they tell you that *imagination* dried the mourner's tears, and delivered the tempted out of temptation, and made a bed of pain a bed of peace? Let them tell the starving man that imagination can feed him; tell the drowning man that imagination can rescue him; tell the dying man that imagination can heal him: but let them not tell the Christian that he could mistake the felt Presence, the abiding, comforting, supporting Presence of his Lord for anything earth or hell can feign. He feels in his heart of hearts that it is the truth of God."

Note II.

The Parishioners of St. Chad's have placed in the chancel of their church a marble tablet to Mr. Polehampton's memory, with an inscription from the pen of the Rev. B. Kennedy, D.D., Head Master of Shrewsbury School.

LETTERS

OF

THE LATE REV. HENRY S. POLEHAMPTON.

                          Lisbon Harbour,
                          January 11th, 1856.

MY DEAREST MOTHER,

You will wonder at the address on this sheet, and well you may! I will, however, without giving you any further explanation at present, tell you all that has happened to us since I left you at Shrewsbury. On Friday, at 11, this day week, Edward and Tom went with us from Southampton on board the *Pera*, which was lying about a mile out. Edward went with me to my cabin, and helped me to stow everything away. He was immensely useful, showing me where to put the things, which I should want for immediate use, of which I had no idea. There are no drawers, or anything equivalent to them, in the sleeping cabins: so everything I want is put under my mattress,—books, shirts, writing-case, dressing-case, &c. Some other things are in a small portmanteau under the berth.

Well, as I daresay you know, Edward and Tom remained with us on board until we sailed, about two hours. The mails then came out, and they were obliged to return in the steamer which brought them. I took a shot at Tom with an old spectacle-case, as he stood on the deck of the small steamer alongside, with which I hit him in the neck. I saw him pocket it; and I daresay he will keep it as a relic! We all felt parting very deeply: but we said little about it; for words on the subject would probably have caused an outburst of sorrow from one or other of us, which was just then of all things to be avoided. I looked after Edward and Tom as long as I could see them; Edward was standing on the quarter-deck with his plaid wrapped round him, waving his cap, and Tom exposed to the rain in nothing but a frock-coat. I hope he didn't catch cold.

Almost directly after they left dinner was announced, and we went to it with what appetite we might; which, just after parting, and with sea-sickness in immediate prospect, was not, as you may imagine, very great. We went very steadily till we got nearly to the Needles, and then, just towards the end of dinner, the ship began to roll. Seats at the table were vacated rapidly one after the other. . . .

. . . . On Sunday night the ship's engines suddenly stopped, and, feeling stronger, I went on deck, to ascertain the reason. This was the first time I had been out of my cabin since Friday night. I found that one of the engines had broken down, and that there was no chance of its being repaired. Previous to this the jib-boom had given way. We lay by for six or seven hours, and then went on with very diminished speed. Almost ever since we left Southampton there had been a good deal of sea, and now we were well into the Bay of Biscay, and were rolling tremendously. However, I managed to stay on deck for two hours on Sunday night, the sea having moderated a little. On Tuesday I was quite strong, and could walk about, in spite of the heaviest rolling and pitching. All Monday we made very little way, not going, on an average, more than six knots an hour, whereas we ought to have gone twelve. On Tuesday we lost another spar, the fore-try-sail-mast; the ship leaked a good deal, and I found, by talking to the sailors at night, that they were really getting very anxious. I talked for some time to an old quartermaster on Tuesday night. He said, " We shall do well enough, Sir, if the masts hold, and the other engine does not break; but, you see, it's a new ship, and we can't depend on anything: and, if the other engine goes, why, God help us!" I found out afterwards that the reason why the sailors were so anxious was that the wind was blowing on shore, that is, we were on a lee-shore, though a good way—about forty miles—from it. But they feared that, if the other engine failed, we should drift on to it; and the ship's being leaky, too, seemed to alarm them. You may imagine that all this made me feel very anxious, especially as, in case of danger, I should have not only myself to look after, but two others. I spent nearly all Monday and Tuesday nights on deck, for it was impossible to sleep. On Tuesday night things looked so bad that I seriously made up my mind and prepared myself for the worst (A). And now all the danger is over, and we are quietly lying in Lisbon harbour, I may say, I believe we were in a very critical state; a leaky ship, two spars gone, a heavy sea, the wind on shore,—quite enough to make one anxious. On Wednesday we were still to the northward of Lisbon. The wind got round ahead of us, and the captain determined to run for Lisbon to refit. He was obliged, however, to stand out to sea, before he could do so with safety. On Wednesday night the sea ran so high, that he believed that, if we reached Lisbon, we could not cross the bar at the mouth of the river: so he changed his course, and bore away for Vigo, which you will find just at the south of Spain. When we were about half way between there and Lisbon the wind changed again, and it was resolved to make another trial to reach Gibraltar; and this intention was kept up till yesterday evening: when, finding it impossible to make way against the head-wind, and the sea moderating, we ran for Lisbon once more; and, on waking this morning, were in sight of land. It was a lovely morning, the coast beautiful; we could see the hills of Cintra. Presently we came near the mouth of the Tagus, took a pilot on board, and came up abreast of the town, where we now lie. I fear we shall not be able to land; at all events, not at present: for a gentleman died on board on Wednesday night; and the Portuguese think we have cholera, or something dreadful, and so we are in quarantine with a yellow flag at the masthead.

This gentleman, an American, Dr. Carstairs, was, with his wife, on his way to Gibraltar to go to the south of Spain, for the benefit of his health. He was suffering from bronchitis, and this and sea-sickness supervening suddenly put an end to his life. This threw an additional gloom over the ship. We buried him at sea yesterday, at twelve;

On Wednesday night, on going to my cabin, I found them making his coffin just outside my door; and the last sounds which I heard that night, and the first on Thursday morning, were the taps of the hammer! The coffin was, on Thursday at noon, covered with a flag and carried on deck; Dr. Kay, the Principal of Bishop's College, Calcutta, and myself, preceding it. Dr. Kay read the service, excepting the Psalm, where we took alternate verses. At the words, "We therefore commit his body to the deep," they let the coffin fall, and, with a tremendous splash, it sank at once. It was blowing half a gale of wind at the time, and it was fortunate that both Dr. Kay, being an old voyager, and I, had our sea-legs.

The misery we have suffered in this crack ship the *Pera*, which was to have got to Malta in four days, but has taken seven in getting to Lisbon, passes all belief. I should not say *I* have suffered; for, barring two days' sea-sickness, and the anxiety consequent on Emmie's protracted illness, and the knowledge of the critical state we were in, I have enjoyed myself immensely. I like a gale of wind better than anything, so long as the wind is not contrary. It is a noble sight to see a fine ship like this, tearing through the sea with all sail set,—and no rolling or pitching affects me now. But all the ladies have suffered;

their cabins have leaked fearfully, and when the sea has washed over the ports it has come trickling through, till the beds of those who sleep under them have become very wet. . . . The *Pera* is really a noble ship; we have an excellent captain (Captain Soy), and are well officered, but she is new, and the rolling opened her seams. We ought, I am sure, to thank God most heartily that we had no storm, otherwise I do not believe I should have been writing to you now.

Emmie has just called me to her cabin to look out of the port at an old woman in a boat, who is asking her in Portuguese to buy some figs. God bless you, my dearest Mother! I know that we have your prayers, as you have ours.

Your affectionate Son, &c.

Notes to the above, from a letter written next day :—

(A.) "Went round and made a calculation of the capabilities of the boats. There were seven very good ones, which might hold nearly all the passengers and crew, but boats are bad things in a heavy sea, and there was a good deal of sea all the time. Made up my mind how to act in a case of emergency, and otherwise prepared myself for the worst. Did not say anything about it to Emmie and Ellen."——"Things looked so bad that before going to bed I thought it best to tell Emmie and Ellen that the ship was in a somewhat critical state, and that if anything went wrong, I would come to them at once, and that they were not to stir till I did. They took the intelligence very calmly."

> Peninsular and Oriental ship *Pera*, off Lisbon,
> January 16th, 1856.

My dearest Mother,

I think my last letter to you or Edward concluded about last Friday. We have been here ever since, and shall not sail again till Friday or Saturday next. We hoped to be let out of quarantine on Saturday, but such was not the case. Because we had had a death on board, although we sent certificates that it was from no sort of contagious disease, but from bronchitis of some years' standing, the absurd Portuguese authorities put us into quarantine; the effect of which was that none of us could land, and even workmen, who came to the ship from land, were obliged to remain on board till we were out of quarantine. All Friday, Saturday, Sunday, and part of Monday, in spite of the captain's exertions, we remained with the yellow flag flying at the masthead. There was nothing to be done, excepting to grumble and bear it. We were anchored just opposite to the unfinished palace of the Ajudha and the monastery of Belem, at the extremity of Lisbon. The buildings on shore looked exceedingly picturesque. The clearness of the atmosphere is wonderful. I wished for Mr. Stant, with his photographic apparatus; everything would have come out with great clearness. The right-hand bank of the river is covered by the buildings of Lisbon; above them rise steep hills, and far beyond them we can see, sixteen miles away, the heights of Cintra; for a description of which place see Byron's "Childe Harold." We read and wrote a good deal during the days we were in quarantine; and looked at the shore through telescopes, by means of which we could see oranges growing on the trees in the gardens. Some men came off with baskets of oranges fresh gathered; the leaves on them so fresh and beautiful! The worst of the quarantine was that we could not get the necessary repairs done to the machinery, because they would not let our men land to go to the foundry. I say *the worst;* but the worst, I fear, has to come, in our missing the steamer at Suez, and having to stay a fortnight at Cairo.

On Sunday we had service in the saloon at eleven o'clock. Mr. Stewart,* a friend of Tom's, who is going to the Holy Land, read prayers; I the lessons; and Dr. Kay preached. We had a very good congregation: none of the crew, however, attended; indeed there was no room for them. We clergymen went to the captain, and offered to give them a service in the forecastle; but he said that they were so busily employed in

* The Rev. J. Haldane Stewart, Rector of Millbrook, Hants.

necessary work, that it was impossible. We pressed it, but it was of no use. We had Evening Service at half-past seven, after tea. We had a better congregation than in the morning; and, besides the passengers, all the servants and the sailor-boys attended. Dr. Kay read prayers, Mr. Stewart the lessons, and I preached. I had not intended to say anything *particular* in my sermon about the danger we had been in, but had selected a sermon, which I thought suitable, because I believed that many of the passengers had been very much alarmed, and had probably in their fear of shipwreck and perhaps of death, made professions of penitence to God, and vows of amendment. The text was, " Godly sorrow worketh repentance unto salvation, but the sorrow of the world worketh death." The main drift of the sermon was to show that vows made in distress would never be fulfilled, if made merely through fear of death or disaster, and not from love of or in the strength of God. However, just before service, not five minutes before, General Armstrong, a passenger, came and asked me to make some particular reference in my sermon to the circumstances in which we had lately been. At the same time Dr. Kay told me that the captain wished him to use the service appointed for thanksgiving on account of salvation from shipwreck. It appears that Dr. Kay had proposed to the captain, when we first entered the Tagus, to have a Thanksgiving Service, but he would not then consent, I believe because he was afraid of alarming the passengers. So, under these circumstances, I was obliged to think over the heads of something to say; and at a place in my sermon where some expressions relative to escape from imminent danger gave me the opportunity, I introduced the subject of our late preservation, and spoke extempore for about five minutes. I am thankful to say that I was enabled to do so without hesitation, and in such a manner as to please the passengers generally, and, I trust, so as to do them some good also. On Monday morning, by " striking the iron whilst it was hot," we succeeded in establishing daily morning prayers in the saloon.

On Monday, about noon, a cheer on deck announced to us, who were reading below, that we were out of quarantine. We had expected five days more of it. We got up anchor and steamed three miles further up the Tagus, and anchored off the custom-house, where we now lie. After dinner, Emmie and I, having packed up a few things, took a shore-boat and went on shore. We found a boy at the custom-house stairs, who could speak a little English; so we hired him as a guide. We went first to the Hotel Braganza, where they were full. They recommended us to Madame Bolt's Hotel, which is on a hill, the highest point of Lisbon. Lisbon is on seven hills; the streets all up and down. You have to ring the bell at the hotels, at a gate like a college-gate in Oxford. Immediately on entering we perceived a smell like a stable, which pervaded the whole house, more or less, and which considerably annoyed us, and made us augur anything but good of Madame Bolt. However, she proved to be a very nice German woman, and her rooms, in cleanliness and comfort, all that could be desired. By keeping the windows a good deal open, we managed to keep the stable smell out of our rooms; but on the staircases it was unbearable. At the Braganza it was the same.

After breakfast next morning we sallied forth, accompanied at first by our guide; but we soon discarded him, for we found we could get on well enough by aid of our French, bad as it was. I could hardly get Emmie to speak a word: the only thing to be done was for her to tell me the sentences, when we wanted anything, and for me to speak them, which I did with an accent which literally "astonished the natives." The greater number, however, of the people could speak nothing but Portuguese. We went into some churches; they are all bad imitations of Roman architecture. All the old gothic churches were thrown down in the earthquake of 1755, and none now remain, excepting one at the monastery of Belem, in the suburbs of Lisbon. For an account of the earthquake, see my father's book, "The Gallery of Nature and Art," in which I read it when I was seven years old. I have a vivid recollection of a picture of a man kneeling at the foot of a statue of a saint, which is answering his prayers by kindly tumbling on his devoted head. The churches are poor and tawdry. I never saw such wretchedly dressed wooden dolls as the statues of the saints at the different altars are. In the church of St. Roque yesterday we saw a poor woman going round praying at all the altars. She seemed devotional enough; but it was not only absurd, but disgusting to me, to see her followed all round from altar to altar by her dog—a great brute, shaved like a poodle. He seemed quite used to it, stopped when she stopped, and went on when she did.

The streets of Lisbon are wonderfully striking. They are tolerably well-paved and clean. The houses are very high; mostly built of white stone. Some are covered from top to bottom with Dutch tiles of most beautiful blue patterns. Every window has its balcony, painted light green. The houses are tiled with great ridged tiles, like the Italian houses. They show manifest traces, in their Moresque architecture of the occupation of Spain and Portugal by the Moors for so many centuries. The people generally are dressed like unfashionable English and French. The common people keep up the old national dress; the women wear long brown cloth cloaks with capes, and white muslin handkerchiefs on their heads; the men, either knee-breeches, or loose blue trousers tied round their waists with red handkerchiefs, and large black sugar-loafed hats.

We wandered all over the town, and poked about everywhere, and had great fun. I don't think the Portuguese are half such devoted Romanists as the Belgians. There are no statues of the Madonna at the corners of the streets, as there are everywhere in the Belgian towns. We got back to dinner—table-d'hôte at five. It was a very good dinner. I sat next to the Russian consul, a nice quiet old man, who looked like a Lutheran minister, and spoke pretty good English. We lionised again to-day till three o'clock. Our landlady charged us very moderately—only about ten shillings per diem each. I believe we shall be ready for sea by Friday. The sailors won't like to sail again on that day. As for me, I have no such feeling.

Wednesday, Jan. 16.—This morning Emmie, Dr. Kay, and I got a shore-boat, and landed about eleven o'clock. We then took an omnibus for Belem, or Bethlehem Monastery, about three miles from Lisbon. Monasteries have all been suppressed in Portugal; convents are still allowed. The monks have, of course, been turned out from the Belem. Instead of them, 800 orphan children are fed, clothed, and educated. There is a grand church, the only one, I believe, which the earthquake did not throw down. It is the only gothic church in Lisbon. It was built in 1499, and its architecture is a mixture of Moresque and Norman. It is a very broad church, and its groined roof is supported by slender columns, richly sculptured. When we entered, these columns were bathed in the most beautiful colours, which streamed on them from the stained glass windows. It was the finest effect of the sort I ever saw. There are splendid cloisters attached to the church: I never saw any to equal them. We went into the old refectory of the monastery, where we saw 350 boys at dinner, with their hair clipped in the former Christ's Hospital fashion. . . . After seeing the Belem we took an omnibus part of the way back, and then went to see a church, and the English cemetery. It abounds in the usual heathen monuments, broken columns, extinguished torches, &c. One cross alone is visible there. The only tomb of any man of note which I saw there, is that of Fielding, the novelist. . . .

Our manner of life on board is as follows:—

At half-past eight the bugle sounds for preparation for breakfast; at nine, for breakfast; at twelve, for lunch; at half-past three, preparation for dinner; at four, for dinner, when the bugler performs. "The roast beef of Old England." At seven he plays "Polly, put the kettle on," when we "all have tea."

Friday, Jan. 18.—To-day we have been in the Tagus a week. Our repaired machinery has just come on board, but I much doubt whether we shall get away before Sunday, at the earliest. I should not be at all surprised if we have to remain a fortnight at Cairo. I don't care about this, if we are not put to expense, as I shall be able to see a good deal of Egypt, the Pyramids, &c. The *Tagus* has just come in on her way to England, and I shall send this by her....

Believe me ever your affectionate Son,

HENRY S. POLEHAMPTON.

Malta, January 23d, 1856.

MY DEAREST MOTHER,

We left the Tagus about twelve o'clock on Saturday. I did not in the least expect to be ill again, as I had so completely got over it in the first week. However, no sooner were we over the bar, than we found there was a worse sea than we had had at all. Very few ladies were to be seen after the first half-hour. I believe Emmie stood it till six P.M., in the saloon. As for me, I had determined to stay on deck as long as I could, but about three hours completely finished me. I was very ill, and obliged to go to my cabin, and there I stayed till one P.M. on Sunday. I tried to get up to service, but it was quite impossible. At one o'clock I got up, and determined to fight my way against the sea-sickness, if I could. I was fearfully ill four or five times while I was dressing, but I managed to finish in about an hour and a half, and got on deck, with one shoe and one slipper on, and in the last stage of exhaustion; so that I was not only angry with people for talking to me, but for walking about before me. I felt as if I hated all the world, and that if it had been attempted to throw me overboard, I should not offer any resistance. However, I soon came to a better state of mind and body, although there was still a heavy sea. It was some consolation to be told by the chief officer, that during the night we had had the heaviest sea since we left England, and that he was feeling ill himself.

About half-past seven P.M. we got into smooth water in Gibraltar Bay. It was a fine moonlight night, and the rock stood out in grand relief. The bay was crowded with shipping. At eight P.M. we had Evening Service; Mr. Stewart read prayers, I the lessons, and Dr. Kay preached. Here the Governor of the Philippines came on board. I stayed on deck till about two A.M., for it was a beautiful moonlight night, and I was anxious to see the first of the Mediterranean. To-day we have passed many small rocky islands; among others, though from being under water they are not visible, the Gallinas rocks, where the steam-frigate *Avenger* was wrecked in 1848, in which poor young Napier went down. On Monday we were about twenty miles from the Spanish coast, and had a splendid view of the Sierra Nevada—a beautiful range— the top covered with eternal snows.

The band is playing Scotch quadrilles; some of the passengers are playing at whist; some writing; some reading; some walking on deck. We have one hundred and five passengers, and are about two hundred and fifty altogether, including officers, crew, firemen and stewards. We all sit in the saloon. It is impossible almost to sit in the sleeping-cabins, as they keep the ports down for fear of shipping seas. Emmie would have the bull's-eye in her cabin open yesterday. One of the officers told her he thought she could do so with impunity. I told her I thought not, and I proved right; for, about six in the evening, while she was combing her hair, a sea came in and wet her through and through, and left about three inches of water in her bed! However, it was all soon put to rights; but it shows how dangerous it is to keep the sleeping-cabin ports open even in calm weather.

We expect to be in Malta to-morrow morning about four o'clock. We are quite uncertain whether we shall have to stop a fortnight in Cairo, or whether we shall be able to get on at once. This is owing to our detention at Lisbon.

It is great fun, when one has got over the sickness, dining on board when the ship is rolling. Then mahogany frames are placed on the table, which stand up about two inches from the cloth. These frames are divided into little squares, in each of which there is room for a plate, tumbler, and wine-glass. Between the two rows of frames, in the middle of the table, the dishes and bottles are placed. Presently the ship gives a roll, and a heavy piece of beef charges you furiously. You have to receive him on the point of the bayonet or fork, and then away he goes to try and break the square opposite. Then comes a fire of artillery which there is no resisting, in the shape of a bottle of wine. You may imagine, too, what a noise is created by fifty plates and knives and forks suddenly rushing across the table, and back again; and then comes a peal of laughter at the capsize or other mishap of some unfortunate individual.

I am very fortunate in my brother clergy on board. Dr. Kay was a double-first at Oxford; is a very learned, but a very humble-minded and most agreeable man. He is Principal of Bishop's College, Calcutta. Then comes Mr. Stewart, whose brother is Vicar of Maidstone. He has just had a living given him by the Bishop of Winchester, near Southampton; he, too, is a most agreeable man, full of fun, and yet thoroughly earnestly-minded and good. He and my two ladies have struck up a great friendship, and we shall all be very sorry when he leaves us at Alexandria for the Holy Land.

I think I told you that we have two full services every Sunday; and now we have a chapter in the Bible read and prayers in the saloon every morning.

You must use your judgment about letting my friends see my letters; they are quite unworthy of much attention, but they are, so far as I am concerned, quite at the service of any one who cares to know how I am getting on.

I need not say how constantly you, my dearest Mother, Emily, and my brothers, are in my thoughts! You are all ever present to me, and I would I were going to meet you at the end of my voyage. But it may not be so; and you know we are all voyaging to a harbour where, if it is not our own fault, we shall meet to part no more for ever;—and, humanly speaking, we have a good chance of meeting again in England in seven years.

I imitate you in writing long letters. If I write half as good ones, I need not be ashamed.

Remember me to Mr. Yardley and all my friends in the parish.

Peninsular and Oriental steam-ship Pera,
70 miles east of Malta,
January 24th, 1856.

My dearest Mother,

This morning at about four o'clock "our shipmen," like St. Paul's, "deemed that they drew near to some country," and about 6 A.M. we came to moorings in the Quarantine harbour. On going into the saloon I found that Ellen had received letters from Henry Salt, telling her by any means to meet him at Calcutta and not at Bombay; so she is going on with us.* I shall be very glad indeed to see him again. We found that the people at Malta had for some days been

* Mrs. H. Salt is Mrs. Polehampton's sister. She and her husband, Lieut. T. H. Salt, Bengal Artillery, were stationed at Meerut at the time of the mutiny there, in May, 1857.

very anxious about the *Pera*. One gentleman, an Indian officer, who has now come on board, and whose wife came out with us, told us he had been nearly distracted; for it was generally supposed that we were lost. Directly after breakfast we went on shore, and landed just under the new English church; it is a handsome building, though neither Greek nor Gothic. They might have done much better with the 13,000*l.* it cost—the late Queen Adelaide subscribing 10,000*l.*; but I congratulated myself that it was no worse. It is not very unlike in tower and spire to All Saints, Oxford. Malta is all white stone; narrow streets, with heavy stone balconies and oriel windows to the houses. The streets remind me a good deal of pictures of Jerusalem which I have seen. It has not the light and airy look of Lisbon, but there is much more real architecture. Lisbon would be nothing without the iron balconies and green paint. It looked very strange to see English soldiers on guard, and everywhere about, in such a strange outlandish-looking place. There is a delicious smell of orange-blossom and violets mixed close to me: it comes from a bouquet which we got in Valetta to-day. We were asking our way to St. John's cathedral, when I suddenly heard some one say, "Why, that must be Polehampton!" and, looking up, there was Meredith. We were very glad to meet. He is chaplain in the *Algiers*, 90. He was full of wonderment to know where we were going. He went with us everywhere, and saved us an infinity of trouble and cheating. Nothing could exceed his kindness or the heartiness of his manner.

While we were waiting for the moorings to be loosed, a number of Maltese came alongside, dressed only in drawers, and called out for "money for dive." Some of the passengers threw sixpences into the sea, which they dived for and caught before they had sunk many feet. One fellow actually dived right under the ship and came up the other side, for which feat he got two shillings; he must have gone down twenty feet at least; and then he had to dive about forty feet in breadth to clear her. I have dived twenty-five feet, but I should not like to go under a ship of the size of the *Pera*.

This is Friday morning, January 25. We have had, since leaving Malta, the same beautiful calm weather which has attended us from Gibraltar. As we have sailed over this sea I have been tracing out St. Paul's voyage, with Emmie. Fancy what he must have suffered, a prisoner, in a ship of that period, with 276 people on board! We have not more than 250 in this great ship, 300 feet long and more, and we do not find that we have any too much room.

Peninsular and Oriental ship *Hindostan*.
Thursday, January 31st.
Red Sea, off Suez.

We got all right into Alexandria. It is a wretched place, but has much to interest in it. The bazaars are filthily dirty; Eastern bazaars are, I should think, the original of our colonnades. See any of Bartlett's pictures, illustrating the East, which represent Eastern bazaars; they are very faithful. The hotel at Alexandria in which we were is far better than that at Lisbon. The Eastern dresses are most beautiful and interesting, and make me feel half sorry that we Europeans, men at least, have so completely given up all decoration in dress. There are three races in Egypt:—the Arabs, who govern; the native Egyptians, who are governed and bullied to the last degree; and the Nubians, who are the servants, but who are far better off than the native Egyptians. The Nubians are almost black, but they are a fine race of men; with beautiful expressive eyes and teeth, though they are rather flat-nosed. They are mostly over five feet ten inches in height. There is a grace and dignity in the way in which all the male inhabitants of Egypt walk, and generally deport themselves, for which one looks in vain in Europe.

We left Alexandria for Cairo by railway, on

Tuesday morning at ten o'clock, and got into Cairo about six in the evening. The railway is as good as any in England excepting the Great Western. In two years it will cross the Desert to Suez. You would never be tired of looking at the costumes and manners of the Egyptians; the faces of most of the men, and their stature, are remarkably fine, and they all look like a people capable of taking a first class among the nations of the world, if they were only properly governed.

Cairo is a beautiful place. The English and French quarter is a fine square, or three sides of a square, with large gardens in the middle and rows of trees. The hotels are very fair indeed. Both here and at Alexandria they have an odd custom about hotel-servants. There are four or five waiters, no chambermaids; and the only way one can get waited on is by engaging a dragoman, a man who is a kind of hanger-on of one of the hotels. He brings them customers, and the master of the hotel allows him to come in and do everything for the lady or gentleman who engages him.

At Cairo we had a very nice fellow as our dragoman, a Syrian, from Jerusalem, a Christian. He was baptized in the Church of Rome, at Jerusalem, but he had come to Cairo as servant to Mr. Leader, the English clergyman, who had given him a Bible, and a great deal of good instruction, which he has certainly profited by to the extent of being perfectly honest. I had a great deal of interesting talk with him, both on religious and other matters.

I had no time to see any of the lions of Cairo, much less to go to the Pyramids. I could only go into the bazaar, which is very beautiful, and tolerably clean. The picturesqueness of the whole scene it is perfectly useless for me to attempt to describe. It brought the Arabian Nights' tales vividly to my mind, as it must do to the minds of all those who have read them. I bought an amber mouth-piece for Fenton in the bazaar, which I am told by judges is a good one. The climate in Egypt now is English June, but a fiercer sun. The nights are delightful, neither too hot nor too cold, excepting quite towards morning.

Yesterday at two P.M. we started from Cairo; one detachment of our party had gone overnight, one at nine in the morning. Each detachment consisted of five vans, with six passengers in each, drawn by two mules and two horses. At starting there was a thunder-storm, a thing which they say has been unknown in Egypt for years and years. It laid the sand of the desert completely, so that we had not a particle of dust day or night. Before we had got a mile out of

Cairo our leaders began to fight most furiously. They dashed all across the road; the poor mules had to follow; now they came round fighting, and looked us in the face; then they got right round a tree, and I thought we should have been over; and finally one of them bit the conductor's arm, who went to separate them, till the blood came. The driver called the one who was in fault an "evil spirit," in Arabic, lashed him furiously, and at last got him to go. The ladies behaved very well; Emmie, Ellen, Mrs. Costello, Miss Dickson, Dr. Kay, and I, were in one van. The people told us that these little rows were more the rule than the exception, and that an overland van had never been known to overturn. We were seventeen hours going from Cairo to Suez; we changed horses every six miles. Three times we stopped to eat—dinner at four, supper at eight, breakfast at two in the morning. We had plenty to eat, but not of the best kind. Chickens, tough as crows, and brown as Nubians; bread, hard as bricks; no milk, excepting at one station; very queer butter, made, I should think, of camel's milk. The vans are more comfortable by far than our coaches; there are supports for the arms, and plenty of room to stretch one's legs. We were very merry; every now and then a great jolt started us from our seats on some uneven part of the road. There is the skeleton of a camel by the side of the road at intervals of about a mile throughout the whole journey. We passed about four hundred camels travelling in single file, laden with our luggage, the mails, and other goods. The ladies were of course tired when we arrived at the very indifferent hotel at Suez, but not at all more, I think, than if they had travelled from Aberystwith to Shrewsbury. It was rather cold at six in the morning, and I got out and had a good run for a mile or so by the side of the van. Suez is much worse than Alexandria in every respect. Emmie and some of the ladies went to bed for an hour; we breakfasted at ten, and at twelve took an Arab boat, and came down the Red Sea about four miles to this ship. It is a much more airy ship than the *Pera*, but not nearly so long. You may imagine that the journey across the Desert, under favourable circumstances, cannot be anything so very awful, when I tell you that I have not been in bed at all after being seventeen hours in the van, and that the ladies all seem at least as fresh as the morning after a ball. But the rain had laid the sand. Clouds were before the sun most of the day, and the greater part of our journey was in the night. When it is hot, dry, and windy, the dust must be almost insupportable. The diorama of the overland route is a most faithful representation of all that takes place. Dr. Kay sang the Psalm, "When Israel came out of Egypt," last night, to a Gregorian chant, as we drove through the desert, and I joined him.

It is almost needless for me to mention how impressed I was, even in the railway, with the recollection that I was travelling through one of the first civilised countries in the world; that it was the scene of Israel's bondage, and of God's fiercest wrath upon their oppressors; of our blessed Saviour's refuge from Herod; and, in later days, of Napoleon's, Abercrombie's, and Nelson's victories; of the massacre of the Mamelukes. The whole land teems with story, and there is hardly a pebble or square inch of ground but has its own peculiar interest. I first saw the Pyramids from the railway-carriage window! it did not diminish, however, the impressiveness of the sight.

This is the last letter you will have from me until we reach Calcutta.

Ever your most affectionate Son.

Peninsular and Oriental steam-ship *Hindostan*,
Ceylon Harbour.
Monday, February 18th, 1856.

MY DEAREST MOTHER,

I WROTE last from Suez, which place we left January 31st. We had a delightful voyage down the Red Sea. The heat was not at all oppressive, neither have we felt it so up to the present time. I can sit on deck till twelve at night, and not feel in the least chilly. My dress consists of a thin alpaca coat, and the thinnest kind of flannel trousers, and in bed I have had no covering over me excepting a sheet since we left Suez, and the port and door of our cabin have been always open. This is the cool weather in these latitudes; what it must be in the summer is a thing more easily imagined than described. From Suez I have had plenty of room in my cabin, my only companion being General Armstrong; a most agreeable gentlemanly man he is. His daughter married a Shropshire man, and on the strength of Shropshire we have all become quite intimate. Our chief friends are the two Generals, Colonel and Mrs. Haldane, Dr. Kay, Mr. Balmain, an old brother officer of Henry Salt's, Mr. Jenkinson and Mr. Outram, who are young men going out in the Civil Service. Mr. Outram's father is Governor of Oudh in the

Bengal Presidency. Dr. Kay manages to talk to people of all nations, from the French to the Arabs, so that the drivers across the Desert understood him. He has had several long Latin conversations with some Roman Catholic missionaries to China, of whom we have five on board. He is in great request to settle all kinds of arguments, in which people always appeal to him. He and I preach alternately morning and evening.

The coast of the Red Sea is very fine—lofty, rugged rocks, the outline of which is picturesque in the extreme. I wish you could sit by me as I write in the stern cabin window, looking out upon the shore of Ceylon, about a quarter of a mile distant. I have not yet smelt any of those spicy breezes about which I used to say a hymn to Miss Ansell when I was a good little boy. It looks very lovely, this island of Ceylon; the day is bright, like a warm July day in England. I hear there are all sorts of pretty things to be bought here. Boats are coming off manned with Cingalese—nice mild-looking men of a fine chocolate colour, with merely a cloth round their waist, reaching to their knees. I shall never cease to regret that I did not bring out with me an apparatus for daguerreotyping. There's a native boat just come under our stern, rowed by three men; it's not a foot broad, narrower than our outrigger eight-oars at Oxford. They go at a great pace. "Baba, ain't you going on shore? eh, Baba!" is being at this moment incessantly reiterated close under me. Palms and cocoa-nut trees extend all along the banks of the island, and make up a lovely sea-view. It looks so beautifully dark and shady between their stems, and such fresh sunny green above. Many of our passengers leave us here for China; one of them I shall part from with real regret to-day. He is an American, a captain in their merchant-service, a very good-looking gentlemanly fellow. I was the first to see his merits, and now he is a great favourite. He is a Socinian; but I hope that I have taught him to believe in Christ as God, though he cannot yet quite take in the doctrine of the Trinity. He is an earnest inquirer after truth. We have always, since leaving Suez, walked two hours on deck, from ten to twelve, talking chiefly on religious matters. God bless you!

Bishop's College, Calcutta,
March 8th, 1856.

My dear Tom,

It is your turn to hear from me, for I have not sent you a line since we parted. Last Sunday week we anchored at six o'clock P.M. at the mouth of the Hooghly. The name of the river recalled to my mind that other very different "river Hooghly," as we used to call it, near Datchet Weir, because of its resembling the real Hooghly in the difficulty of its navigation— its only resemblance to the original. At the mouth of the river we took a pilot on board. They are stationed there a few miles out to sea in brigs, in which they are always obliged to be cruising on the look-out for vessels bound up the river. An East India pilot is a very different being from any of that profession in England. A full pilot gets 1,000*l.* per annum. They enter the service at about fourteen, as leadsmen, and then rise gradually through all the branches. Besides their pay they always get a present, generally about 20*l.*, from the owners of the ships they take up. The navigation of the Hooghly is most difficult and dangerous. It is from two miles to half a mile wide from the mouth to Calcutta, full of shifting sands, many of them quicksands. A vessel striking on one of these disappears in the course of a few hours.

No pilot dares to take up a ship at night, so we lay at anchor till Monday morning, when we sailed, and arrived at Calcutta about 4 P.M. As we went up, the leadsman was taking soundings nearly all the way, heaving the lead from the paddle-box. One moment he sang out "By the mark 6!" the next, "A quarter less 3!" the second cry meaning that we had not more than six inches of water under our keel. However, we got up all right. The last mile of the voyage was up Garden Reach. Here there are the houses of Calcutta merchants on the right bank, each standing in its garden, having quite a Richmond-villa appearance. On the other side are the Botanical Gardens, and Bishop's College, which is the only dwelling of any importance on that side of the river.

You don't come upon Calcutta all at once. Your first sight of it begins by the houses which I have mentioned, widely detached from each other—large, white, flat-roofed buildings. This is the Calcutta domestic style of architecture. At the top is a balustrade, like that at the top of Christ Church, Oxford; then two stories of rooms, outside each of which is a verandah supported on pillars, the space between the pillars being filled up with thin blinds, called "Chicks," which light, or rather shade, the verandah, into which the rooms open.

When we came to anchor, which we did just opposite Bishop's College, at the Peninsular and Oriental Company's wharf, we were surrounded by boats, and Mrs. H. Salt was on the *qui vive* for her husband. However, he didn't appear for a long time. At last he came, looking very well and handsome, having on his head a black wide-awake, with a red gauze handkerchief wound round it to keep off the sun. Soldiers wear red ones in undress. Your brother wears commonly a black wide-awake, with a white handkerchief wound so many times round it that it is thicker than a towel twisted. The part to protect is the temples and the back of the head. It is no matter about the crown. Well, we landed and went to Spence's Hotel, which is close to Government House. The sitting-room opens into two bed-rooms, one on each side; there are no windows to the sitting-room, which is lighted from the bed-rooms. This is a common arrangement in India. I don't like it; it makes the sitting-room so dark. We had one little dinner-party, consisting of ourselves, two brother officers of Salt's, and George Moultrie, who is in the Bank of Calcutta, and is a very nice fellow. Aitken, an old Etonian, a great friend of Cheales', and Colvin, also an Eton man, whose father is Governor of the North-West provinces, are clerks in merchants' houses here. Aitken took his degree at Exeter College, Oxford. One of the first things you notice in India is the excessive hardness of the beds, which I like, and also of the pillows, which I don't, and have rebelled against so far, as to order soft ones for my own house. Salt is a very good fellow, and is very much liked in his regiment.

On Friday, after seeing the Governor-General arrive at Government House, we set off for Bishop's College, whither Dr. Kay (for whose acquaintance I have to thank you very much) had invited us. It was dark before we could get to the river. We were in a carriage with Emmie's ayah, whom we picked up at the hotel. She is a very good one; but, being a Mussul*man* (or woman), there are many things which she won't do, and so we are going to get one of lower caste to take up the country. I had, in the dark, to find a boat, to get the luggage and ladies on board, &c. My Hindostanee is very limited, and none of the common people can speak a word of English, except some who serve in shops. Emmie went into fits of laughter at hearing me give directions in Hindostanee, such as mine is; not that she can do any better. After a long pull down the river we got to Bishop's College about nine o'clock, and were most kindly received by the Principal.

Now I must go to morning-chapel, for which

the bell has just begun to ring. No! I must "*cut*" this morning, or I shall not finish this, as letters must be ready by ten o'clock. Won't Edward say, "Ah! that's just like Ben!"—I went to chapel after all, for I thought it would be a bad example to the students, especially the natives, if I stayed away. I am very glad I went. It is a lovely morning, like May in England: and it is a privilege which I shall not long enjoy, to join in the daily services of the Church.

Our manner of life at Bishop's College has been thus: We get up at six and take a walk, and then come back by 7.15, and bathe and dress; chapel at 8; breakfast at 9. Then I have most days had to go into Calcutta on business, getting licensed, settling about payment to Widows' Fund, choosing furniture, crockery-ware, &c., and arranging about our journey up country. You may think that all this could be done in a morning; but Bishop's College is on the "Westminster" side of the Hooghly, which is half a mile broad: then, on landing, we have to send a boatman for a "gharree," or cab, which generally takes half an hour in coming. Then there is a three-mile drive into the business part of Calcutta. Directly after landing, one drives through a native street for half a mile; then comes a bridge over a branch of the Ganges. A church for a suburban district is just by the bridge. A son of Mr. Yate, of Wrockwardine, Salop, is the incumbent, a chaplain in Honourable East India Company's Service. He is a very nice fellow, two years my junior in England; four years my senior out here. I am going to preach for him to-morrow evening. Then, after crossing the bridge, one is on the Course, the Regent's Park of Calcutta; and a beautiful drive it is. It is nearly a square: on three sides are the houses and gardens of rich Calcutta people, English and Native, on the fourth side runs the Hooghly, covered with fine ships of all nations. It is a splendid and novel sight to see ships of 2,000 tons anchored, not, as in London, alongside of muddy, smoky warehouses, but along the bank, in many places green, and covered with trees. In this Course the Calcutta people take their morning and evening drives. I should think it must be five miles round at least. On one side, farthest from Calcutta, is the Cathedral. You know the model at Oxford, in the Bodleian Library. That gives you far too good an idea of the Cathedral. The model is alabaster; the original is brick, covered with white plaster, as is every building in Calcutta. There is no stone within many hundred miles.—We drive across the Course, and then are in the business part of Calcutta. First come the English quarters, several very fine streets and squares. The shops are splendid; no shop-windows, but everything inside. They are much larger than in London, and more showy, I think, and everything almost is nearly double the price of London goods. Then come the native quarters, narrow streets, &c. However, there are capital shops here, and here every knowing person will come to buy furniture, earthenware, &c.; for they are to be got at half the price one pays at English shops. The natives attend sales, and pick up things cheap. They always ask a very high price, but no one thinks of giving it. Here is an instance, which holds good in everything. I wanted a small mahogany box for Emmie; a man ran after my gharree in the street with two. I selected one, and asked, "How much?" "Four rupees." "I'll give you *one*." A look of disgust, and the man disappeared for three or four minutes; but presently ran after the carriage, put the box down on the seat, and said, "Take it, Sahib!" so I gave my rupee and got my box. I believe, as a general rule, that if one buys of native tradesmen, and has one's clothes made by native tailors, one may live much more cheaply than in England. I see I have indulged in a Herodotean parenthesis. After shopping in Calcutta, we came back to dinner at 6.30. Dr. Kay has several times asked people to meet us. Nothing could have exceeded his kindness to us. He is an excellent man, and as learned as he is good. I wish they would make him Bishop, when Dr. Wilson dies.

Last Thursday I found out from Mr. Fisher, the Bishop's *locum tenens*, that I am to be stationed at Lucknow, in Oudh; at least he gave me my choice of four stations, and I, on Henry Salt's advice, selected this. Many people have congratulated me on my good luck. They say the climate is very good, quite cold in winter. It will now be one of the most important stations in India. We came out with the son of General Outram, the Company's head man at Lucknow, and a very nice fellow we found him. We are to start for my "Living" on Monday. We go about seventy miles by rail, and six hundred or so by carriages. These carriages are very comfortable, but I hear the horses are rather wild, and that there are occasional capsizes. We shall be a week getting to Lucknow. We shall drop in upon Henry Möller at Allahabad; and we have plenty of introductions.

On Sunday last I had to preach in the Cathedral at the evening service. There was a very fair congregation. I preached on 1 Philipp. ix. 10: "And this I pray, that your love may abound," &c. (see extracts in Appendix). I wrote an exposition of the two verses, and brought in an exhortation to the people to teach the natives by example, to be gentle and forbearing to them, and not to relax, but to let their love abound more and more in spreading the Gospel. . . . The interior of the Cathedral is better than the exterior. There is a good deal of violet-coloured glass, which produces a very good effect; and the open seats and stalls are wonderfully good, considering that the architect was an engineer officer, who knew nothing about ecclesiastical architecture. The roof is the worst part; it is like a railway-station roof. The effect of the punkahs is not so bad as you would have expected. Bishop's College is built in pseudo-Gothic style; but the chapel is very pretty in spite of its irregularities. It is a little larger than that of Pembroke College, Oxford. The view from the college, of the river and shipping, is as pretty as you can imagine, and we got delightfully cool breezes from the river. Neither of us have suffered at all from the heat yet. The hot season has set in, but has not nearly attained its height. Cricket had been left off the week before we came. It is nonsense to say that the heat here is not greater than in England. It would be madness to play at cricket now, and it never was too hot to do so at home : one is so much more immediately under the sun here, and one gets its rays on one's head. Mr. Allen, to whom Edward gave me an introduction (a brother of the Archdeacon's), has been very civil; as also Mr. Bayley, a son of Mr. Butterworth Bayley, to whom his father gave me a letter. Steel, an old schoolfellow, and chaplain at Dumdum, ten miles from Calcutta, gave me an invitation, but I have been unable to go. Colvin and Aitken have both called, and were very pleasant. Colvin brought with him a card-case, which I gave him nine years ago, which was very gratifying, as showing he had not forgotten me.

Get, if you can, a little book, called "The Eastern Lily gathered." I will vouch for the truth of it. I have met, at Dr. Kay's, the girl's husband. He now lives at Bishop's College, having married, as his second wife, a daughter of the native professor, Mr. Bannerjea, who became a convert about twenty years since. I am writing this in a confectioner's shop in Calcutta; so I cannot tell you the publisher. . . . I am anxious to be at my work. My intention is to learn Hindostanee perfectly, and then to do all I can in missionary work. I hope to write by next mail from Lucknow. I preach at Bishop's College to-morrow morning.

Ever your affectionate Brother, &c.

Lucknow, April 7, 1856.

My dearest Mother,

You are one of the very best letter-writers I ever knew: you give all those little details which are so valuable far from home. I told you of our staying at Bishop's College with Dr. Kay, whose kindness exceeded my most sanguine expectations of Indian hospitality. He is one of the best and most learned men I ever met with. I often thought of the Holmeses, while we were there. The College is in a delightful situation, though too low for the rains. The fire-flies were so splendid, the trees used to look almost as if on fire. As soon as the sun goes down, about six (and there is no twilight), the air is full of " the fire-fly's gleam," as Heber calls it, and the voice of the cicala; it goes on all night incessantly, and is very delightful. There is a nice garden at Bishop's College. English flowers do well here. There are few Indian flowers, but flowering shrubs are in abundance. What you miss in Indian gardens, and in all India, is the fresh green turf. They say it is very good in the rains; but I have never seen any grass in India in which there was not half an inch between every two blades. It would not do to lie down on. The Cathedral is quite full in the morning, and pretty well filled in the evening: it is the most "fashionable" congregation in Calcutta. The choir consists of men and women in the gallery; they sing very fairly; but it is not what we in England call Cathedral Service. I did not like Calcutta; it is neither an Indian nor an European town. I used to enjoy my trips by water from Bishop's College to Calcutta and back more than anything.

Well, on the Monday in Passion-week we left Calcutta. We went by rail about 130 miles to Ranegunge—a capital railway. We got there about six o'clock. We passed in the train a French settlement, Chandernagore. There are two in British India, this and Pondicherry. They had them, I believe, before we conquered India. We took them from them during the last war, but gave them back, foolishly, for they are in the heart of India. They can do little harm, being so small, otherwise than by serving as observatories of all we do.

At Ranegunge we took, at the Inland Transit Company's office, a carriage called a "gharree." It is a kind of van on four wheels, drawn by one horse. In this we came to Lucknow, 600 miles. The gharree is about six feet long, and three feet six broad. Horses are changed every five or six miles, and, excepting when they jib, go about seven miles an hour. We started at seven o'clock: we had with us a bottle of water filled fresh every day, a bottle of brandy, ditto of cholera-mixture, ditto castor-oil, a lamp, candles, some fruit, bread, biscuits, a ham, and knives, forks, and plates. There is plenty of stowage room. Our bearer, who is an up-country man, *i.e.* not a Bengalee, or we should not have hired him, slept on the roof. At starting we used to sit, as you do in a coach; but about nine o'clock we used to put up a board, which connects the seats together, and make ourselves comfortable for the night. I felt responsible for a good deal, and therefore slept more lightly than I am wont. We used to travel till about nine in the morning, when the sun gets hot, and then stopped at one of the Dâk-bungalows or inns, provided by Government; of which there is one about every ten miles. There are two sets of rooms in each; a sitting-room with a bed in it, a dressing and bath-room; there are three servants; plenty of water; and they are tolerably furnished. You can get fowls, which they call *murghis*, and eggs, at all of them; but seldom bread, and nothing to drink but water; so it was well we supplied ourselves. The Dâk-bungalows stand a little way back from the roadside. It is a splendid road, as good as any in England—as straight as a line everywhere. It was generally almost dusk when we started. At about six A.M. I used to go and sit on the box with the coachman, and thus saw the country pretty well. For the first day the country was beautiful—fine hills, mountains almost, along the base of which we went. The sacred hill, Parisnath, was one of them. After this it was a level plain nearly all the way to Lucknow; not such a thing as a slope even. The country looked, for the most part, sandy and barren, but there is much cultivation, I am told, away from the road. I was astonished at the numbers of people whom we met walking along every morning, and at the traffic by bullock-cars, which is immense. Most of them seemed laden with bales of cotton. It was quite cool at night—cold sometimes. We had a thing called a "rezai," a native counterpane, with which we covered ourselves. Emmie made up, before we started, some curtains of muslin, doubled, with which we covered the door and windows (they are sliding doors), so that we could have air without dust.

About nine, as I said, we used to come to a Dâk-bungalow. Then Emmie went to her toilet, while the bearer and I got out the bottles, tins of provisions, &c., and the Kitmutgar belonging to the house killed a fowl, or murghi. We used to see them running after these unfortunates, as soon as we came in sight, which were either made into curry, or served up *au naturel;—unnaturally* tough they were. We seldom had done breakfast before half-past eleven. Then we used to read, at least I did, while Emmie worked; and so the day passed pleasantly enough.

On Friday morning I was sitting on the box, when we suddenly came to the top of a slope, and there was *Benares* before us, an immense Hindoo city, the chief residence of the Brahmins. It lay stretched out for four or five miles, I should think, on the top of a high bank on the other side of the Ganges. We crossed over in the gharree, on a kind of boat, a quarter of a mile, and then, leaving Benares on our left, drove to cantonments, about three miles on. The English never live in the Indian towns, but in these cantonments; which consist of a collection of bungalows, each in its compound, or field, part of it laid out as a garden, with fine wide roads between. We were just too late for morning church. We went to the Dâk-bungalow as usual. I called on the chaplain, Mr. Verrett. He was very kind, and sent me in his carriage to see the Company's College, about a mile from Benares. Here about six hundred Hindoo youths are educated in everything, which will make them useful members of society, Christianity excepted. They learn to despise idolatry, however: and as they would not be sent at all if Christianity were taught, the existence of these colleges is, of course, a good thing. The building would do credit to

Oxford or Cambridge. It is the finest European building I have seen in India. The style is perdicular Gothic. There is a fine central tower, and the whole thing, though not strictly correct, reflects great credit on the architect, a major in the Company's service. I forget his name. He is dead; worn out with hard work in superintending, and even carving ornamental stone-work with his own hands. The Principal was away, but I was very civilly received by the Vice-Principal, Mr. Griffith, of Queen's College, Oxford. We started later than usual that we might be able to go to church: an ugly building, no particular shape, flat roof, Doric columns.

On Saturday morning we got to Allahabad, which is situated on the opposite bank of the river, like Benares. We sent to tell Henry Möller, who is in the 11th Native Infantry, of our arrival. He first sent a regular Oriental present—a brace of quail, cold meat, bread, three bottles of beer, two of claret and two of sherry—and then came himself. He stayed with us till evening; when we went to the house of Mr. Spry, the chaplain, to whom we had an introduction. He and his wife are very nice people. We slept at their house on Saturday night, and on Sunday morning, at seven o'clock, I assisted Mr. S. in administering the Holy Communion, and read prayers for him at night. We spent Monday at

Arrahpore, a village, and reached Cawnpore, a large town, Henry Martyn's cure, on Tuesday. Called on the chaplain, Mr. Moncrieff, a very good man and popular. He is an extempore preacher. I met at his house, making a morning call, Mrs. Colvin, wife of the Judge of Cawnpore. She took me in her carriage to the only furniture-dealer in Cawnpore, and there Emmie and I chose necessary furniture for our house. Went on in the evening. At daylight I took to the box, as usual, anxious to get the first peep of my new charge.

Lucknow is situated on a great plain, richly cultivated, with fine barley-crops, &c. A river, nearly as broad as the Thames at Windsor, runs through the city. The first thing I saw rising above the trees, in which Lucknow is plentifully shrouded, was the minaret of a mosque. Every mosque has two of these, high, slender towers. There were nice green hedges of some shrub growing on each side of the road for some miles before we entered Lucknow. Plenty of my "parishioners" were walking along the road —tall, good-looking natives; very superior to the Calcutta people. All the natives of India are a sort of chocolate colour. Among them was a sprinkling of Sepoys, who all gave me the military salute. Lucknow is a very large city, with more than 100,000 inhabitants, mostly Mahommedans. There are mosques every hundred yards almost, of various sizes, with their domes and minarets, richly painted with various patterns, as are the houses. The architecture is almost Moorish; streets rather narrow, not *very* dirty. At one end of the city, near the bridge,—an English iron bridge,—is the Residency, where Sir James Outram lives, a large English-built house; and close by is the house where we are staying, Mr. Gubbins's. He was expecting us, and received us most kindly, and has entertained us ever since. Lady Outram wrote to ask us to come and stay at the Residency, as soon as she heard of our arrival. Her son was a fellow-passenger of mine in the *Pera* and *Hindostan*, and I got very friendly with him. I think Lady Outram one of the best specimens of an English lady that I ever met; so unaffected and natural; so glad to have a clergyman once more, that it is quite delightful to have anything to do with her. She takes the greatest interest in everything for the good of the people—natives and Christians.

We should have been in our house before this, but it is not ready for us; all the furniture has to come from Cawnpore, fifty miles. It is a very fair house, with the best garden in Cantonments. There are plenty of strawberries; we have had them sent up here for breakfast every morning, and there are orange- and lemon-trees, and quantities of other fruit-trees, vegetables, and flowers. There is a nice verandah all round. I have got nearly all my servants; they live here at present and wait on us. I like my bearer—my valet he would be in England—very much. Our *khansamah*, or butler, is a venerable old fellow with a white beard, like the picture of Abraham in Mant's Bible! We have a man called a *chokedar*, who guards the premises; he carries a sword, spear, and shield! Just now Lucknow is full. At Cantonments there are three native regiments. The English officers of these regiments, with their wives and children, form my congregation there. There is a little church holding a hundred people. In the city my congregation is about two hundred, chiefly civilians. There is a really very pretty Gothic church, considering its date, 1810. At the other end of the city is my largest congregation, the 52nd regiment, all English, 1000 strong. We have service in the open air; chanting beautiful, by the band. My predecessor was Kirwan, whose fag I was at Eton. He is on furlough in England. The hot winds have just set in; the heat out of doors from nine to five is insupportable almost, and the glare is dreadful.

With all that I have had to do, you may imagine I have not had much dulness, nor have I yet felt more than a slight touch of home-sickness. I try to think how I may do most real good before I return. I have a noble and most interesting field for exertion. My English congregations are nearly 2000 in all; then there are some, I do not yet know how many, native Christians. We shall apply for, but I doubt if we shall get, another chaplain. Don't think I shall over-work myself. I shall do, I hope, as many hours a day as it is prudent; but I will do no more, as I should only incapacitate myself for work altogether. I like what I have seen of Indian society much. There is a girl's school for native Christians, which Lady Outram visits a great deal. The 52nd has a school, and there is a college called the Martinière, a very fine building. This I visit too, so you may fancy I have enough to do. The third Sunday service I volunteered. I cut the morning service in two, giving Morning Prayers to the 52nd, and Litany and Communion at the city church, alternately.

The people are as civil as possible. I walked the other morning through the city about three miles. I was alone among thousands. If the English had been unpopular, should I not have been insulted? Nothing could exceed the well-mannered behaviour of the natives.

There are, I am glad to find, many really

religious men among the 52nd; there are forty communicants in the regiment.

Ever your affectionate, &c.

Cantonments, Lucknow, May 2, 1856.

My dearest Mother,

On Sunday morning my elephant did not come in time; that is, he came at five, instead of 4.30 A.M., and as he only goes six miles an hour at the fastest, I should have been late for my service at the 52nd barracks, if I had not put my horse into the breaker's buggy, and driven him to Lucknow. It is three miles from this to the bridge over the river, on which Lucknow is built, and nearly two miles, all through the city, to the 52nd barracks. So you may imagine what a large place Lucknow is. The river is about as wide as the Severn at the Shrewsbury railway bridge. Now come with me in my buggy to Lucknow. Just as I start, the elephant walks into my compound. I abuse the mahout and syce, in a curious mixture of Hindostanee and English, and drive off. A good road, perfectly level, with tall hedges on either side of some shrub like willow. Here and there is a clump of mango-trees, which look very much like oaks, good sized ones too, and pepul-trees, not unlike poplars, which are very fine and shady. The bheesties are just beginning to water the road, that the riders and drivers to and from Lucknow may not be annoyed by the dust. The horse trots capitally, almost too fast for the unfortunate syce or groom, who runs by his side; they all do this here. Now I overtake a lot of bullock-vans carrying all sorts of things; now I meet a fellow on a camel. Half-way we pass a rich nawaub's (native gentleman) house. On each side of his gate are two cages with bars open to the road, in one of which is a splendid tiger, in the other three or four small leopards. On my left, a little farther on, is the Dâk-bungalow for travellers. And now Lucknow begins. First, there is another nawaub's house, with a horrid old Mussulmaun fakeer, stark naked, excepting a cloth round his loins—nasty old brute—sitting at the gate begging. He looks such an old villain, that I have never been able to make up my mind to give him anything. Next comes a mosque, and a rather handsome one too, with Mussulmauns at prayers. I can see into this mosque as I go by. There is nothing in it but a very small altar. Well, now we are in the suburb of Lucknow; low small houses, flat roofs, shops below, greengrocers chiefly, built of brick, all covered with plaster; many of them painted beautifully with all sorts of patterns. Now we come to the bridge, a very handsome one on brick piers, plastered and coloured yellow. On the right you see many tall minarets and gilded domes; on the left one or two Hindoo temples; plenty more minarets and domes, and the Residency on the highest spot in Lucknow. It is a very large house, coloured yellow, not very unlike Dotesio's hotel at Slough. By the bye, General Outram has gone to England for his health, and Lady Outram and her son, much to my regret, to the hills. Lucknow stretches away as far on either side the river, and is a very imposing looking place. I walk the horse over the bridge, and turn sharp to the left, in which direction I drive, through streets all the way, quite straight for two miles. The streets are full of people, all in the finest white muslin, except the coolies, the universal fags of India, who do all the carrying, and are a separate caste, and the bheesties, who are watering the road out of skins, which they carry on their backs.—I must go and wake Emmie, who has been asleep for an hour, to come and take a walk before it gets dark. It is now six o'clock in the evening, and it is always dark in India about 7 P.M., and light about 4.30 A.M. There is little difference, I believe, all the year round. We cannot walk out of our grounds, at least it would not do, no one ever does, and there is plenty of space in our own garden and compound, which is nearly half a mile round. Before I go, I will tell you about the heat. This has been one of the hottest days; go out after 10 A.M., and you feel as if you were standing before a large kitchen-fire; there is nothing like it in England. But the air is quite clear, and though hot it is not stifling. In-doors, if your tatties (grass blinds) are kept wet, it is nice and cool, as long as the west wind blows; with the east wind they don't answer; and then there is nothing for it but to keep every breath of hot air out of the house, and to sit under a punkah kept constantly moving. There are our goats waiting to be milked, with five kids; they give us plenty of nice milk morning and evening.—But you will think we are a long time getting to Lucknow! Well, we go on through the streets, no grand houses, mosques every hundred yards or so, now and then a splendid one; at least, in form they are, the material is only brick covered with plaster. Now we come to the barracks; two immense squares with low buildings all round them; formerly the King of Oudh's stables, now the barracks for the private soldiers of the 52nd Queen's, and not bad ones either. The men are just being formed into ten companies of one hundred each; about

From a Sketch by Sir MOUNTSTUART JACKSON, Bart.

LUCKNOW.—The City Church previous to the Siege.

three hundred march off to the Roman Catholic chapel, the rest are marched up to a number of forms put ready for them, just outside the hospital, in the open air. I exchange a few words with the Colonel and other officers whom I know, (there are nine Eton men in the regiment, two Peels of my time,) and then go into the hospital and put on my surplice and hood. I then come out and stand at a desk put on a rising ground, so that I am about four feet above all their heads, and begin the service. Opposite me stand the officers; to my left and right are drawn up the men. This is at a quarter before 6 A.M. It is quite cool—I give them, on one Sunday morning, prayers and sermon, and on the next, Litany, Communion-service, and sermon. The service takes just an hour. The band sing very well; they chant all the responses, Jubilate, Te Deum, so that we have almost cathedral service, and very good too; no instrument except a clarionet to pitch the note. Before I leave the barracks, I must tell you what I do with this regiment. I go every Wednesday night to the hospital, and have a service in the ward, and, if there are any bad cases of sickness, see them privately. I start soon after five, and get there by 6.30. I also go on Thursday night at the same time, to the same place, and preside at a prayer-meeting, which about fifty men attend.

They hold it every night; one of them reads the Bible and expounds it, and one night they have extempore prayer, and on the other the prayers of the Church of England. The meeting is composed of Churchmen and Dissenters; there is only one officer who comes, the quartermaster. It is very gratifying, and very surprising, considering what one's impression is of soldiers in general, to find so much genuine piety, as there undoubtedly is, among them. Last Thursday was my first night of going to them; it reminded me so much of my Copthorn lecture! There were quite fifty men. In the General Thanksgiving they took me by surprise, by all joining aloud; it had a very beautiful effect, and it seemed as if they were all truly grateful to God for His mercies to them in this strange country. I preached extempore, sitting down, just as I used to do at Copthorn. It was Ascension Day, and I took for my text a verse from Psalm lxviii. "Thou art gone up on high." Well, it is time we should leave the barrack-yard. We now get into the buggy again, and drive back on the same road, till we come near the Residency, when we turn off, and find ourselves clear of native and among European houses, with gardens and trees—really fine houses too. Close to the Residency is the church, covered in with trees, standing in a large walled-

in space, not a churchyard; we don't bury in or
near churches in India. As I have already said,
it is by no means an ugly, though not a correct
church. I regret to say that the east window
is a sham; perhaps I shall have it opened some
day; and what look like aisles on each side are
used as verandahs, in which stand the natives
who pull the punkahs. It is now 7.15 A.M.,
and my congregation is all assembled. Last
Sunday I gave them Litany, Communion-service,
a short extempore sermon, and the Holy Communion. The church holds about one hundred
and thirty, and it was quite full. I had twenty-
eight communicants, and thirty-eight rupees
offertory; people give more here than at home.
A rupee is the same as a florin. After service I
washed and packed up the communion-plate, of
which there is only one set for the two churches,
and drove home. I found Emmie just ready for
breakfast. After breakfast I had an hour's
sleep, and till six P.M. read and wrote. At 6.30
I have service in the Cantonment church; it
holds one hundred, and is just like the other,
without the aisles; there were eighty-two people
at church. On Ascension Day I had about twenty
congregation, and fifteen communicants at this
church, and it was muster morning too, so that
many could not come. I keep saints' days.

This is my regular Sunday's work. I need

not have taken all three services; but, if I had not, a layman would have done one of them, which I wish to avoid, if possible.

This is the first time a Queen's regiment has been quartered here. It was sent in anticipation of a row on account of the annexation of Oudh. I do not think it will remain more than six months. Indeed, if the people remain as quiet as they have been hitherto, it is not improbable that the Company's regiments will be taken away, and the protection of the country entrusted to two or three regiments which are now being formed out of the late king's army, in each of which regiments there will be only three English officers. But there will still be a chaplain here, because the English civil population will increase. This uncertainty prevents my doing anything at present about a new church. If the English regiment were to stay here as a permanent thing, we should want a very large one. In the Company's regiments there are about twenty-eight officers (English); the drummers are Christians also; the rest are Mahommedans and Hindoos.

I believe that there is no doubt that the people are only too glad to be under English rule. The country has been miserably governed; there were always civil wars going on; the king paid his enormous army very irregularly, and when they got much in arrears, I am told he would give them a village to sack.

I was called away to hunt a bat, which had got into our bed-room; we caught him at last, and really his head is as big as a large rat's. He looks like a vampire, and has no end of teeth. Vampires are popular fallacies, I know, but to look at this fellow you would almost believe in them. Fancy, the late king had four hundred wives! They cost an immense sum monthly. I was told this by one of the Assistant-Commissioners, who had lived here eight years, and has seen a great deal of the court. He also told me the king had a regiment of women.

I think I have told you all about my work. I have not thoroughly got into it yet. There is a hospital here for the troop of artillery, who are English; and I must visit them one night in the week. I am trying to establish a day-school in Cantonments for the children of these men, and of the drummers in the Company's regiments. The 52nd, of course, have a school, but all their children are at Meerut, their last station. There is a Christian girls'-school in Lucknow. It is attended by the children of the clerks in the Commissioners' offices, who are nearly all half-castes—half English, half native, and by those of some few native Christians. It works very well; and the first-class girls are

in reading and religious knowledge equal to our
first-class girls at St. Chad's. Then there is in
Lucknow a college, called "La Martinière."
It was founded by General Martin. He was a
private soldier in the King of Oudh's army, but
rose to be a general. He was a Frenchman.
He amassed a great fortune, and built a grand,
fantastic house, just out of Lucknow, which he
at first intended for a palace for himself. He
was a Mussulman in practice, and had a great
many wives. Towards his death his conscience
pricked him; he sent for the Roman Catholic
priest, and made over his palace to trustees to
be turned into a college for the education, with
board and clothes gratis, of seventy boys of any
religion or country. He also founded a similar
institution in Calcutta. The late King of Oudh's
father wanted him to sell him the Martinière;
but he asked a ridiculously high price for it,
which, of course, the king would not give; he
said, however, "It does not signify; I shall get
it at his death." But the old general was too
'cute for him. Knowing that a Mussulman will
not live where any one is buried, he left orders
in his will that he should be buried in the
Martinière; and there he is. I have seen his
tomb—marble, guarded by the figures of four
Sepoys. It is under the great hall, with an
inscription describing him, and the words, "May

he rest in peace." I have not properly anything to do with the Martinière, but Mr. Schilling, the new Principal, whom I know, and who is a very good fellow, is particularly anxious that I should go and examine the boys as often as possible. I have now a native, who says he wishes to become a Christian; he was a pupil at the Martinière, where he learned English, and comes to me every day for instruction. We are getting on very well, and I think he is in earnest. You will understand that there are pure English, half-castes, and natives, educated at the Martinière; and an English boy seems to have first given this young man a desire to become a Christian. He is an orphan; but is maintained here, since he left the Martinière, by a friend, formerly an inhabitant of the same village as himself.

May 8th.—Breakfasted with Captain Corbett at the 52nd mess. At breakfast were two or three of the Eton men, who are in the regiment. One of them, Mr. Crosse, told me that he had just seen my name in *Bell's Life*. It was in *Bell's* account of the late match with Cambridge, in which he has given lists of all the former crews. I told him I was not ashamed, as I had two bishops to keep me in countenance, whose names appear in the same paper. I then read the account of the race, which greatly interested me. I know Roche of Christ Church, No. 4 in the Oxford boat.

I should doubt his constitution being up to the work; but he is a fine-looking fellow—six feet three inches, I should think. I knew him when he was a boy at Shrewsbury. The race does equal credit to the crews. It is the best on record. Oxford cannot be said to have been beaten; the crew showed itself quite as good as Cambridge, for even a wave or two striking the boat would have made the difference of half a length, by which only Cambridge won. I expected that Oxford would have been disheartened by their beating at Henley last year, and would have been beaten hollow in the long race. It is time Cambridge should win a race or two. The officers of the 52nd are very gentlemanly nice fellows. This evening I have to go in again on the elephant to give the men prayers and a sermon, as my custom is on Thursdays.

You write, my dear mother, most capital letters; invaluable in a foreign country, they are so circumstantial. I am very happy here, and I think I am useful; so you must not make yourself unhappy about me. Of course, I often long to be in England, but this is not a bad country to be in. There is plenty of good society; a chaplain is looked up to and respected, if he does his duty, full as much as in England.

I will give you a list of our servants and their wages:—

	Rupees per month.
Khansamah, or house-steward	10
Khitmutgar, or table-attendant	7
Dhobee, or washerman	8
Ayah, or lady's-maid	8
Bawarchie, or cook	8
Sirdar-bearer, or valet	8
Bheestie, or water-carrier	4
Mehter, or sweeper	4
Chokeedar, or watchman	4
Four Punkah coolies—two for day, two for night	3 each.
First mallee, or gardener	3
Second ditto	3
Third ditto	3
First mate-bearer	4
Second ditto	4
Two Syces, or grooms	5 each.
Grass-cutter	3
Bukhari-wallah, or goat-boy	1
Dhurzhee, or tailor	7

The rent of our house is £60. So that I suppose we shall get our board and lodging and servants for about £280 per annum, certainly under £300. And now what did —— mean by saying that living in India cost twice as much as in England? Fancy our servants coming to us yesterday, and wanting three more to help them! Didn't I send them to the right-about pretty quickly!

Ever your affectionate Son.

Lucknow, June 17, 1856.

MY DEAR EDWARD,

PRAY do send me a diary. Every scrap from England is interesting, and your letters are feasted on as they arrive. I thank you for your fresh assurances of affection to me, but you must not let thinking of me make you low-spirited. We shall meet again in this world, please God, when we have grown a little older and wiser, and we shall feel all the more pleasure in each other's company from having been separated so long. What is that Burns sings?

> "We twa hae paidl't in the burn,
> Frae morning sun till dine,
> But seas between us braid hae roar'd,
> Sin' auld lang syne!"

I had in my mind's eye at the moment our paddling up that brook at Pontesbury together last summer. What a pleasant day that was, and what a nice lot of trout we killed!

I have, until my boxes arrive, hardly any books except a few I borrow from the 52nd Library. By the bye, we kept the 4th of June at the mess; there were six or seven Eton fellows present,—among them Bayley and Crosse, of the 52nd, of Cheales' standing, and Capper, of about the same standing in the Civil Service. Flamstead, who was at Eton with me, and is in

the 52nd, was asked, but could not come. By
the last mail I wrote to the Provost of King's a
long letter. I am going to have a party here
if Emmie is well enough on Election Saturday,
and we shall, weather permitting, "go up;"
there are two four-oars here. I wish you had
seen me pulling stroke to four naked Cingalese
at Galle, in Ceylon, also to four more respectable
Portuguese. These next few lines are for
John :—" I have found my two grey alpaca
"jackets, two pair of very thin grey flannel
" trowsers, thirty-six shirts and socks, and
" pocket-handkerchiefs in proportion, ample for
" the voyage. Have a cap for the first part of
" the voyage, if you come, like those you and I
" used to row in; for the second, a black wide-
" awake covered with white muslin (they will do
" this on board) is the thing for a parson.
" Don't have your coats made like Rochforts;
" have them made as long as your usual clerical
" frock-coats, they look better, and the skirts are
" not in the way. I have a black alpaca coat
" for Sundays. You will want, if you start for
" India when I did (January), a great coat only
" as far as the Bay of Biscay; thence to Alex-
" andria, English summer-clothes; thence to
" India, India summer-clothes."

The rains have set in now, and last till the
end of September. Mr. Gubbins told me

yesterday, and he has been twenty-five years in India, that he considers Lucknow the pleasantest and coolest place in the plains.

My horse came down the other day, and broke his knees, and so I was obliged to get another, —a handsome, strong, black horse, for 120 rupees—£12. Almost every horse here has been down. The roads are good, but the natives shoe the horses infamously. I cannot do my work without two horses. Colonel Campbell, 52nd Queen's, told me last Sunday that he should apply for extra pay for me, as I was doing so much work; I hope I shall get it, but I doubt. Tell John, if he comes out, to bring a large piece of thin grey flannel for trousers, it is splendid wear for India,—invaluable for parsons.

Ever your affectionate Brother.

Cantonments, Lucknow, June 30, 1856.

My dearest Mother,

Tuesday. — Lieuts. Stopford and Henley's quarters, near the Hospital of the 52nd.—I have just buried a man who died of fever yesterday; I left Father Bernard, the Roman Catholic priest, on the ground waiting for another; he is a fine-looking man, wearing a long beard and moustache. He wears at funerals a long cassock, over which he puts a transparent surplice reaching not much below the middle, a stole of black and red with a yellow cross at each end, and a long hood. I have been very particular always to have clean surplice, hood, and stole, at funerals, as the Roman Catholics are very sharp observers, and I do not wish our Church to suffer in any way in the eyes of the men. We know that there is a better garment in which we must be clad, and that surplices and hoods form no part of our religion; still these things should not be neglected. The Roman Catholic priest speaks scarcely a word of English; he can only make himself understood with a smattering of Hindostanee, English, and Italian, and this, as you may imagine, very imperfectly. Many of the Roman Catholic soldiers in hospital have asked me to advise them, and to pray for them.

I have two or three very agreeable friends here, the chief of whom are Crosse, Stopford, and Henley, all Lieutenants of Her Majesty's 52nd. Henley is one of the old Oxfordshire Henleys. Poor Stopford had a very bad fall last night, and hurt his leg. These Indian horses, though good and fast, are constantly coming down. At this moment this room, which is Stopford's bed and sitting room, is full of officers come to condole.

It has been melancholy work for the last fortnight. The 52nd have lost on an average three men a day from cholera. I have buried two, three, and four a day, and have been here by half-past five in the morning for nine consecutive days. Yesterday, after I had finished here, I spent the day at the Gubbins', and from thence made a great many calls on the clerks in the Government offices here. I am happy to say that the men in hospital seem very grateful to me, and that my ministrations seem to have the effect of soothing them. Many of them, poor fellows, are very much frightened at the prospect of death. I saw a man brought in with cholera yesterday; four men immediately took charge of his hands and legs, and began rubbing them. His legs were violently cramped; I could see the cramp seize his toes, and gradually run up. Then it would cease for a while, and then come on again. It must be great pain; for the men shout out lustily. When the cramps reach the stomach it is generally all over. Most of the men have died in ten or twelve hours; one was only three hours.

There is a very nice person staying at Mr. Gubbins', a Mrs. Block. She was born near our old home at Greenford. She knew the Haffendens well, and seems never to tire of talking about Greenford and Cuckoo Lane. She is very pretty, and sings like an angel.

Ever your affectionate Son.

Lucknow, July 18, 1856.

My dearest Mother,

. . . . I told you in my last how bad the cholera was in the 52nd. It is now, I am most thankful to say, better. There has not been a fatal case for four days; but there were two new cases yesterday. I saw both the men; one of them was one of the finest men in the regiment. He had been ill four days, and would not report himself. (He afterwards died.) The other had been on duty with the sick, and was taken suddenly. A man came in the day before, who told me he had had no premonitory symptoms, but was seized with cramp in the toes and feet, which gradually extended upwards. He, however, is now doing well. The men seem much more cramped here by cholera than I remember to have seen them in Shrewsbury; there they seemed to suffer more from purging.

The cholera at Lucknow seems to have presented a different feature from what it usually does. Men *generally* get well after the cramps leave them; but *here* they have got weaker and weaker, and have died of exhaustion after seven or eight days. Between June 16 and July 16, the 52nd have lost, as nearly as I can tell, forty-seven men by cholera, and several by apoplexy and dysentery. The average number of deaths was two per diem, till about three days ago. At Agra the Queen's 2nd regiment has lost a hundred men; fifteen died in one day! There, also, several civilians and officers died; here the disease has been wholly confined to the privates and non-commissioned officers. One very sad case took place at Agra, of which I shall tell you, as I knew something of the poor fellow, who died.

About three weeks ago I had a call from a Mr. Augustus Chauncey, of the Madras army, who said that he was passing through Lucknow, on a tour of inspection for the Government Electric Telegraph-office, and was staying at the Dâk-bungalow. There he found a poor Englishwoman in great distress; he described her case, and begged me to see if something could not be done for her. It so happened that I knew all about the case. The poor woman had been governess in a civilian's family—had been seduced —and had afterwards lived with one or two

officers, one of whom still allows her enough to
live upon. She professed to me great remorse,
and determination to leave her former way of
life. All she wanted was a home, where she
could have a chance of reformation. I made
every inquiry for her, and could hear of nothing;
and, having been much occupied with the cholera
at the 52nd, had done nothing about her case for
some days. Mr. Chauncey found her at the
Dâk-bungalow; heard her groaning, I believe;
went to see her; heard something of her case;
and came to me, three miles in the heat of the
sun, to try what could be done. He begged me
to do all I could, and left with me fifty rupees,
i. e. £5, for her assistance; or, if she did not
want it, for any other distressed person. I was
a good deal struck by the man, and asked for his
address that I might write to him. To-day I
I heard of his death at Agra of cholera. He
seemed a really religious man; and it is pleasing
to know what was one of the last actions of his
life. I wish I knew who his relations were, that
I might tell them of this. I am happy to say
that I have, after much difficulty, found the poor
woman a home. I hope I may be able to re-
claim her, but I have some fears, especially as
she had taken to drinking, as she says, " to
drown sorrow," while at the Dâk-bungalow. But
I will do all I can.

There is no cholera, or scarcely any, among the natives of Lucknow. We have had one case in cantonments, a private in the Artillery, who died after three days. I am certain cholera is not catching, or I should have caught it long ago. Many a dying man's hand has been in mine; and the men who attend on the cholera patients run far greater risk; but I don't think one of them has died. Four men are told off to attend on each cholera case for twelve hours. They do everything for the sick men, including almost incessant rubbing of their legs.

It has gratified me much to find the men in several cases, when I have been talking to them on their sick, and sometimes dying, beds, reminding me of things which I had said in sermons; in one case, several weeks before. Two of the little band of fifty, who have a nightly prayer-meeting, have died; and the contrast between the manner in which these and some of the other men have met death, has been very striking. In the latter case, sometimes great fear has been shown; sometimes indifference to all but their pains; sometimes trembling hope. In the former, the men have been so calm and resigned, and expressed themselves so much in accordance with the teaching of Scripture, that it has been quite a comfort to hear them. Several of the men, who attend the prayer-meeting, have been very useful to me in reading to and praying for their comrades, when I could not go. I see in the men, who strive to serve God, in the 52nd regiment, the truth fully exemplified, " Thou wilt keep him in perfect peace, whose mind is stayed on Thee." With a private soldier it is almost as it was with the primitive Christians—a man who professes religion, is sure to practise it too.

It is really the fact, that, speak to whom you will here, man or woman, you can scarcely get any one to say a good word for India. There is hardly any visiting during hot weather, *i.e.* from March to the middle of July. By that time the rains, which set in at the beginning of the month, have cooled the air a little ; and people begin to think of their neighbours, and not so exclusively of keeping themselves cool in their own houses. Emmie has been quite well hitherto; she has felt the heat very much, but it has not made her ill. I have been as well, through all this trying time, and in as good spirits as ever I was in England.

However, all that goes on around me teaches me forcibly the most needful, solemn, lesson, " Be ye also ready;" and I hope I shall so be found, if cholera or anything else comes and hurries me into my grave, literally in eight or ten hours. But don't be frightened, my dearest mother; I never felt less "like dying" than at present. I take great care of myself, and keep out of the sun. I think people abuse India much more than it deserves. I can be very happy here, for one; and I am not at all sure that I do not prefer the heat of six months in India to the cold and dirt of the same space of time in England. But there are few who have so much to do, or such absorbing work, as I have; and I embrace unlimited parochial work as a blessed alternative to pupilising, even though it has to be done in hospitals, where the thermometer has never been seen by me below 84.

August 1st.—I was unable to get this ready to go by the last mail. I was writing it in a great hurry, when I was called off to bury a man of the 52nd.

Just after I wrote, the 52nd shifted their camp; the place they went to was exposed; there were two or three hot days, and several men died of apoplexy in consequence. There have been also a good many deaths of diarrhœa and dysentery. Altogether the Roman Catholic priest and I have buried about seventy men, women, and children of the 52nd since June 16th. I have used no precautions, except never going to see the sick fasting. I think I told you that, at Colonel Campbell's suggestion, I had sent in an application for horse-allowance for journeys to the 52nd.

He sent me a form—so many journeys, so many miles at eight annas, or one shilling, per mile. My little bill for April, May, and June amounted to 20*l.* and they granted it. A day or two ago I had a nice letter from Lionel Barton, brother of Barton of Pembroke. He is stationed at Mooltan, a most awful place by his account. The Indians even say that there is only one hotter place in the universe, and that *not in this sublunary part of it.*

Our boxes arrived about a month since. The books all came well, though some showed damp. Not so the pictures, some of which were broken, or injured by damp, though packed in zinc and tin. The other day I was lucky enough to get a very nice dog for Emmie. Henley of the 52nd had a number. He had given a very handsome liver-coloured spaniel to his Khitmutgar, because she was *gun-shy,* and I bought her for eight rupees. She is one of the nicest dogs I ever saw. She sleeps in our room at night, which in this country is no bad thing, as both French doors are open, and there is nothing to prevent any one from walking in, except a reed-screen, called a " chick," which hangs before each door, and acts as a wire-blind. If the chokedar turned rascal, as one of mine did, any one might come in.

On Saturday last, on returning from Lucknow, I found all the servants in a great state of excitement. A stag had come into my compound, and they had had a grand hunt, but could not catch it. On Sunday, on coming back from church, I found they had been after it again, with the same result. I made a lasso and suggested the use of it. On Monday evening, on my return home, they had caught it. The chokedar had lassoed it, throwing the slip-knot very cleverly over the antlers, as the stag rushed by him. It is rather smaller than one of our English stags, but is very pretty; has a fine pair of antlers and a beautiful spotted coat. I think it must have escaped from one of the King's parks. However, I shall annex it to my establishment—evidently the correct thing to do in Oudh! It was very wild, when caught, but, by kind treatment and feeding (the Hindoos are the best people in the world for this sort of thing), it has become so tame that to-day it would let me stroke it. It is tied by a very long rope to one of the trees in the compound. It has taken kindly to the goats, and we hope soon it will go about with them and feed. I have a boy to take care of my goats. There are six or seven, and every evening and morning, before tea and breakfast, they are milked just outside the verandah, and the milk comes in foaming. Goat's milk is nearly as good as cow's. It is a pretty sight to see the milking going on. The goats are black and brown.

There are three fine trees just before our verandah, and the chequered sunshine and shade, and the goats, and the squirrels running about and sitting up and eating, and Chloe, our new dog, stealing after them like a setter, and always being "sold," just as she gets within an inch of them, by their running up a tree—altogether form a very pretty picture. It has just begun to rain tremendously, and there goes the boy to "call the cattle home." Do you remember the lady at Mr. Clement's, who sang that?

The rains here are not what I expected. They are much heavier than in England, but we have often two or three days without any, and then it rains, but not so unceasingly as in England, for two or three.

I have not seen a snake yet; but one day we killed a nice little animal, called a Bis Cobra, in my school-room. A native, who is going to become a Christian, and who now lives in my compound, and of whom more anon, came to me, crying out, "Oh! Sir, there is a 'junwar' (which means a beast) that long in the eschool," by which he meant school. All Hindoos put an *e* before the *s* at the beginning of most words. So I thought it was a tiger at least, and sallied forth with my revolver. When I got there, I saw a thing about eighteen inches long, just like a lizard, so I thought it was a pity to waste powder and shot on him; and said to the bearer, "Maro," which means "kill." So the bearer said, "Bahoot atcha," *i.e.* "very good," and he made a cut at the *junwar* and missed him; upon which the junwar made at his naked legs, and very nearly bit him, which it was providential he didn't. The bearer skipped nimbly on one side, and hit at him again; nor did he miss him, but smote him, that he died. And, when he had taken him up by the tail, he exclaimed, that it was no lizard, but a bis cobra, and that, if he bit any one, it was certain death in five minutes; and Mr. Gubbins tells me he is right. So much for the bis cobra. Nothing of the sort can very well get into our house; for there is a sort of low embankment all round the verandah, made of sharp stones, which reptiles don't like crawling over, as it hurts their bodies.

Yesterday morning I drove Emmie in the buggy to the city church. There were two grand christenings at nine o'clock. Mrs. Block, a very nice young married woman, of whom I told you before, who has been staying at Mr. Gubbins' for her confinement, brought a very fine boy to be christened; and Dr. Fayrer, the Residency surgeon, brought another. Mr. Block is a young civilian, about five years my junior at Oxford. As we drove out of the churchyard, Emmie called out, "Oh! there are two *lovely* monkeys: I wish you would get them for our compound." Nasty brutes! I thought they sat there looking like the evil spirits, who might have been driven out of the babies! Mrs. Gubbins told her it would never do to have them. Indeed, who would have caught them?

Our fruits have all come to an end some weeks since. All we get now from the garden is Indian corn, which we roast and eat for dessert, some greens, and young lemons, which are coming in, and of which we make lemonade every evening. We have now, too, a share in the ice-club, so that we can have it iced, if we like.

You would laugh to see me now. I am sitting in my shirt sleeves, my nether limbs clad in white *pyjamahs*, very wide trousers, made of jaconet; and very cool and comfortable I am, thank you. The Baboo is sitting with me, copying out my registers of births, &c. to send in to the Registrar at Calcutta. This Baboo, which means *gentleman*, and is generally applied to the second caste of Hindoos, next the Brahmins, was educated at the Martinière, where he learnt English. A friend of his there, an English boy, used to talk to him about Christianity, and made a great impression on him. A half-caste lady, who is living here, got hold of him, and talked to him more about it, and, when I came here, sent him to me. For some weeks he used to come every day to read the Bible with me, and went to the school to learn arithmetic and writing more perfectly. At last, his friend who had adopted him (he is an orphan), found out that he was a believer in Christianity, and so they began to plague him dreadfully. Then the mistress of the house would not let him eat with them, so he came and begged me to let him live anywhere in my compound. I happen to have rather a nice little room attached to the school, so I have given him this, and he lives there. He does a good deal of writing for me, and I give him from the offertory about ten rupees per month. He is very useful as interpreter. He knows the doctrines of Christianity well now, and I shall hope to baptize him in about a fortnight.* I shall make him, I hope, competent to take a tolerably high clerk's appointment, and then he will be independent of everybody. If my old clerk in the cantonment church were to die, I would make him clerk. The natives call the clerk the *Chota padré,* or little Padré. Every one calls me the Padré Sahib. Last week I had the happiness of baptizing a Mussulmaun. He came to me, when I first arrived here, saying he wished to become a Christian. He could not speak a word of English. He said Dr. Carshore, a chaplain here

---

* For the end of his history, see Mr. Polehampton's Diary and that of Mrs. Polehampton.

some ten years ago, had talked to him a good deal about Christianity, and that he was convinced of the truth of it, and wished to be baptized. Of course I would not baptize him till I was satisfied of his knowledge, and, as far as I could be, of his sincerity. So I got Dr. Naismith, the doctor of the 17th Native Infantry, a very good man, to have him at his house every Sunday morning to instruct him. Dr. Naismith reads the Bible and explains it every day to his servants. Most of them come, Hindoos and Mahommedans. They don't mind hearing about Christ; some of them believe, I really think, but they are afraid of professing Him, like the Jews of old, "lest they should be put out of the synagogue." Well, in four months' time Dr. Naismith said he considered him thoroughly well instructed in the Christian faith. He examined him for more than an hour before me and interpreted all his answers, and I was quite satisfied. I should have liked to baptize him during Divine Service; but, as it was necessary that Dr. Naismith should do all but the act of Baptism, as I cannot read Hindostanee well enough, and as there were many explanations to be made, and Dr. Naismith could not come to church next day, having to march with his regiment at 4 A.M. on Monday, the baptism was necessarily on a week-day. The poor fellow was very devout, and Dr. Naismith says he verily believes he is in earnest. He has tried to imagine every possible motive for his becoming a Christian, but can find no reason but the right one. After he had been baptized a week, he, too, came to me and said, that he had had such fearful persecution to undergo that he would be much obliged if I would give him a place in my compound. So I am having part of a cart-shed converted into a house for him. It will be about three times as big as one of St. Chad's almshouses, and much nicer in all respects. He is the son of a shawl-merchant, and is a widower with one child. He purposes to teach Hindostanee and Persian, and perhaps I may get him some pupils. I *will not* keep him in idleness: this of itself would be a sufficient motive for many natives to become Christians.

It is impossible for me to be a missionary to any extent, especially if there is to be always an English regiment here. I have more, much more, than I can do properly among my own countrymen; who do indeed want keeping in the right way, and whose vicious lives are the main hindrance to the conversion of India: and they are, I believe, not one quarter so bad in this as in many stations. But here are two converts, one Mahommedan and one Hindoo. They have come to me without my seeking. They tell me of many, who believe, but are afraid to profess openly.

Looking at this, I do say, that if a decided and well-sustained effort were made, India might, without the *special* and *extraordinary* interposition of Providence, become in great part Christian before many years. We are to have a mission here; but I have heard nothing of it lately. I must see about that and many things, now that the cessation of the cholera gives me breathing time.

The beginning of your letter, dated June 8th, made me melancholy, and yet happy. It is a great pleasure to feel that one is so loved, but sad to know how you feel my loss. But you comfort yourself with the best of all consolations, the hope of a blessed hereafter. What would life be without this? God grant we may all meet in heaven, my dearest mother! It will be no fault of yours, if I miss my eternal inheritance, for you never failed to guide me both by precept and example. We have both lived a considerable part of our allotted time: let us take care to spend all that remains (and God only knows which of us has most left!) to His glory, and in furthering His cause in the world.

Ever your affectionate Son, &c.

Lucknow, August 2, 1856.

My dear Edward,

I THINK there are a few passages, which have occurred since I came to India, of which I have not informed you. One was a tremendous pull, which I had in Calcutta. We stayed at Bishop's College till we left. We had to go by train on Monday morning, and our way to the station was by the river Hooghly, which runs past Bishop's College. Dr. Kay had allowed us ample time to get there *with* the tide; but, just as we started it turned, and it *does* run on the Hooghly! We were in a sort of house-boat, like the Lord Mayor's barge on a very small scale, rowed by eight men—Hindoos. Well, they made very little way, and I saw we must be late, unless I worked also. So I took stroke, and pulled nearly the whole way to the station—four miles: tremendous work it was, and such oars! All our luggage was in the boat, so you may imagine what work it was. We got to the station to the moment; but they would not wait for us to have our luggage put in, and we had to stay in Calcutta for another week. It was a great bore after my tremendous pull, and coaching the crew up to the work as I did.

Another little passage of arms took place about

a month ago. It was a Sunday morning, and I had finished my first two services, and was coming home. From the city church into the main road leading to Cantonments, there is a short, sharp descent. The horse I was driving, an old discharged cavalry horse—a very good one but for a spavin on the near hind leg—would not walk down the hill, so I let him have his own way, and he went down at a very fair pace; when we got to the level, we were going, I dare say, twelve miles an hour. Immediately after the bottom of the hill there is a pretty sharp turn to the left, round a mosque. I was keeping pretty close round, it being my proper side, and was just round the corner, when I was "awar," as they say in Shropshire, of a break, with two natives driving a horse at a furious gallop within eight yards of me. He was closer to his wrong side than I was to my right side. There was nothing to be done; no avoiding him; nothing to do but to let the old charger go, lest we should be run down, which I did, and we met in full career. The shaft of the break took the old charger full in the chest. If it had been a sharp shaft, it must have spitted him. As it was, it had a broad end, and only cut away the skin and hair, and did not make a bad wound. But my shaft, which was a sharp one, and very straight, took the break horse on the head; at all events he went down as if he had been shot, and he never rose any more, but died then and there, as —— used to say. I jumped out and told the natives who I was, and where they might find me; but they knew they were in the wrong, made no remonstrance, and I heard no more about it to this day.

On Monday I am going to have my first pull here, with two of the Lucknow civilians, Couper and Simson, and Captain Hayes, who also has a civil appointment here, and is very kind to me. When on furlough, six years ago, he went to Magdalen Hall and took his degree. I always make a point of addressing him Captain Hayes, M. A.

Ever your affectionate Brother.

From Mrs. Polehampton.

Lucknow, September 3, 1856.

My dear Mrs. Wood,

I am sorry to tell you that my reason for writing by this mail in dearest Henry's stead is a very sad one. He has been for the last fortnight ill with fever. There seemed to be nothing serious at its commencement, and Dr. Hutchinson,

View of Mr. Gubbins's House.

who attended him, appeared not at all uneasy. After the first few days, however, as I did not think him gaining ground, I begged Dr. H. to call in Dr. Fayrer, the civil surgeon, who is considered very eminent. We all thought him going on well after this, and they began to give him quinine, thinking the fever had left; when one day it suddenly increased very much, and for one whole night he was delirious. I sent for the doctors at daybreak, who, when they came, immediately made me cut off all his hair, and applied a blister to the back of his head. They then advised me to take him instantly somewhere for change, and, as one of them was on his way to make arrangements for our going to the Chief Commissioner's cantonment Residency, he met Mr. Gubbins, who would not hear of such a plan, but said, "Why not bring him to my house?" There we have been ever since. On his arrival here, a great number of leeches were instantly applied to the head and spine, and other strong measures adopted. Thank God, they shortly had effect, and by the next day the fever was almost wholly reduced. He is now going on well, but his weakness is extreme. I can give you no idea of the Gubbins' kindness. They are not, of course, allowed to be with him at all, as I am ordered to keep him perfectly quiet. We have here about ten of our own servants with us, so that I have everything done for him, exactly as I should at home.

Ever yours very affectionately,

EMILY A. POLEHAMPTON.

Mr. Gubbins';
Lucknow, September 20, 1856.

MY DEAREST MOTHER,

It is now a month and three days since I was taken ill, and it will be a fortnight at least before I am allowed to do any duty in Church. To relate the beginning of my illness. In consequence of my having to go so often to the 52nd, during the five weeks through which the cholera prevailed, I was wholly unable to take exercise. I used to start nearly every morning from home at 4.30 A.M. so as to be at the 52nd burial-ground by 5.30. Then after the funerals I used to breakfast with Stopford and Henley of the 52nd, and then go to the hospital, where I used to remain from one to two hours, and then drove home. Of course I could take no exercise all day, and in the evening I felt bound to drive Emmie out, otherwise she could have got no air. This state of things went on for a fortnight, and then the 52nd moved into one of the king's parks, a mile from the barracks and hospital; and there, in a couple of days, was another hospital formed. So that now I had two hospitals to visit, the farther of the two seven miles from my house. After I had visited the hospital in the park, I used to drive to the Martinière College, and there breakfast with my friend Schilling, the Principal. I generally used to stay with him till 9 or 10 o'clock, and then drove home when the sun had become hot; but this I thought would do me no harm, as I had a thick muslin cover on my hat and the head of the buggy up. With all this want of exercise, by the time the cholera was over, I should think I must have weighed twelve stone and a half. My weight in England never exceeded 11.8 for the last eight years. So I set to work to reduce myself. Though the cholera was over, there was still much sickness, so that I had to go to the 52nd most mornings.' In the evening I drove Emmie out. We used to wait till every one had gone, and then I used to give her the reins, while I got out and ran by the buggy. I did this seven or eight times, and, as I always ran more than a mile fast, I was coming down very satisfactorily. About this time, *i. e.* about six weeks ago, I was asked to row in a four-oar, which there is on this river. I complied, and had six or seven rows before I was taken ill. There is a regular boat-club here, supported both by military and civilians. There are two four-oared boats; one built in England, very like the four-oared gigs which London rowing men use for going down to London-bridge, &c., a very good boat of her kind, and the other built out here on her model. The men who asked me to go were civilians of my own age. The stroke is Mr. Couper, Secretary to the Chief Commissioner; I was No. 3; No. 2 is Mr. Simson, the Deputy Commissioner; No. 1 is Sir Mountstuart Jackson, Bart. the Chief Commissioner's nephew. He is fresh out from Eton, and is only nineteen. Our steerer was generally Dr. Partridge, of whom more anon. We used to start from about the centre of Lucknow, and row down stream to the Martinière, about four miles. My crew was a very fair one; Couper and Jackson decidedly good. When we got to the Martinière, at least as near as the river runs, we got out and mounted our elephants—a necessary thing, as two hundred yards of marsh lay between us and the Martinière; and then we went back to dinner with Couper and Simson. Well, I soon found that *evening* rows interfered with my work; so I asked them to come in the morning, and they agreed. The first morning Couper met us at the river side, looking (as he was) half asleep; and, as he shook hands with me, he looked very solemn and said, " There's no fool like an old fool," alluding,

I suppose, to our being all, save the Baronet, old enough to know better than to row at such a wild time in the morning as 5.30.

We had our row that morning and got a little wet from a shower, but nothing to signify. I then went to the town hospital, and so home to breakfast at nine. The next morning I went again, but Couper could not get himself up, and sent a note to say it was blowing a gale of wind. So Jackson and I, who had come together, went to Couper's to breakfast, and then I drove to the park hospital and remained there two hours. I saw several fever cases, &c., and felt rather unwell, which I put down to my not having gone to bed till nearly twelve the night before. I sat up to write to you. After breakfast I felt very unwell, and lay on the sofa all day, and ate no dinner. In the evening Emmie persuaded me to send for Dr. Hutchinson, my next door neighbour, the surgeon of the 71st Regiment, Native Infantry. He didn't tell me anything; but he told Emmie, judging by the rash I had, that he thought I had small-pox, but that he couldn't tell till the eighth day. From the Thursday I was taken ill till the following Thursday (between which days Dr. Hutchinson had called in Dr. Fayrer), I was miserably uncomfortable. I could neither sit nor lie with comfort, and could get no sleep, nor could I read or be read to. On Wednesday night, six days after I was taken ill, they gave me a sleeping draught. In the course of the night I became delirious. About three A.M. I fancied I was ordered to get up, shave and dress; so up I got, summoned the bearer, to his intense astonishment, made him get the things, and then (it was a wonder I didn't cut myself), in a second or two, by most desperate slashes, took off my moustache of a week's growth. Then I went back to bed and slept. . . At one time I felt some one bathing my head; it was Emmie, and strangely those lines of Marmion came into my head—

> "Is it the hand of Clare, he said,
> Or injured Constance bathes my head?"

And I suppose, in the connexion with these, the following lines from the same poem,—

> "Above his head
> He shook the fragment of his blade,
> And shouted, 'Victory.'"

And I did shout "Victory," so loud as to make the house ring again. By and by I got very faint, and thought I was dying. I was perfectly happy. I heard their voices faintly about me, but I could not speak, and did not wish to do so. And then I fainted, or fell asleep. Presently I awoke again, and found myself in the same room with the same persons round me.

I thought I was dead; that it was the judgment-day, and that I was only waiting for the angels to carry me away to judgment. I felt perfectly safe and secure, "my iniquities blotted out, and my sins covered." I prayed for all of you, and inquired if you were safe; and I thought a voice told me to wait God's pleasure and I should know all. Then Hutchinson and Fayrer every now and then would come suddenly to me and try to rouse me. I sang, I fancy to myself, for Emmie says she did not hear me, " Lend, lend your wings," but I stopped at " I mount, I fly." Emmie says, however, that I chanted part of a chant quite correctly, which I don't remember doing. I don't know how long all this took, but I fancy about two hours. In the meanwhile the doctors had come to the conclusion that I ought to be taken to some other house; and Mr. Gubbins begged that they would take me to his, and he came with Dr. Fayrer to mine. Presently I was seized upon by four men, and carried into Dr. Fayrer's close carriage, which was at the door. I had an idea that they would take me to the church, and that then I should go to heaven, and I was disappointed when they passed it and drove to Mr. Gubbins' house. There they took me out and carried me up-stairs, and put me on the bed in the same room, in which we slept for three weeks, when we first came to Lucknow. I slowly came partially to myself, but I was not quite right for any length of time for nearly a fortnight. What between leeches and blisters, I had pain enough; for Bengal leeches are not like English; they are as bad as Bengal tigers.

The worst night I had was that in which I dictated a letter to you (which was never sent). I lay, I do not know how long, in fearful agony. I saw nothing, but felt bound down "in adamantine chains." "Slowly my sense undazzled;" I felt at first like nothing but a mass of pain. I had no consciousness of being. At last I found I had an arm, then a leg, and gradually came to life. I would not undergo again the fearful suffering of that night; no, not, I think, to return to England with an ample fortune, though I could be assured that it would last but a short time, and pass away, as that did.

God has been very merciful to me, and has taught me lessons during this my first sickness, which, I trust, no amount of health or prosperity will ever make me forget.

I forgot to say that on the morning succeeding that awful night, Dr. Fayrer called in Dr. Partridge, our steerer, who is considered very clever in all diseases of the brain. I recognised him directly. They decided on giving me ether, which, Emmie tells me, they seemed to consider a kill or cure sort of remedy. It did me great good; and once since, when I woke up in confusion in the night, Emmie gave it me and set me right. I cannot tell you how well and tenderly she has nursed me. Poor little thing! I wonder I did not frighten her out of her senses.

By the bye, my dear mother, I wish you would write to Mr. or Mrs. Gubbins; the latter would be best, perhaps, and thank her for her very great kindness to me. Here I have occupied, with Emmie, her only two spare rooms for a second month, when she has friends waiting to come; and she has been like a mother to me.

There is a suspicion here that at the Mahommedan festival of the Mohurrum, which took place last week, there was to have been an insurrection. Five hundred men of a Native Infantry regiment were marched into Lucknow, and the 52nd had orders to hold themselves in readiness at a moment's notice. And since the festival, which passed off very quietly, Asuph ud Dowlah, a great Rajah, who lives half-way between this and cantonments, and has, as I think I told you, a brace of tigers at his gate, has been put under arrest, and has a cordon of Sepoys all round his house. We are delighted to hear that Sir James Outram is to start for India in November, and is coming back to Lucknow.

Sunday, Sept. 21st.—The Rajah, whose name

I have not given correctly above, was yesterday evening acquitted and put out of arrest. He drives about in an English carriage and pair, and is a very gentlemanly-looking man; and his son, a boy of sixteen, is extremely handsome. He is very intimate with many of the English, who are glad to borrow his elephants, go out shooting with him, &c.

Dr. Fayrer says nothing would do me more good than a shooting expedition; and he wants me, when I am strong enough, to come out for a day or two after snipe and deer. When I left off shooting, years ago, I had just accomplished the feat of occasionally knocking over a single lark flying: so my shooting would not be much. But I am sorely tempted to go and see what life in the woods is like. We should go to the woods which skirt the Nepaul hills. There are lots of tigers there, and I *should* like to be able to send you a skin from one of my own killing. However, there's a good deal to be done between this and March. Fayrer says there is never any danger, excepting when a howdah gives way; and this is a thing which seldom occurs.

(For Edward).—Tell Trefusis, if he is coming to see me, he had better come by March; and at all events I'll insure him some tiger-shooting, which is what he will get in very few parts of India now.

Last night I was introduced to a brother-in-law of Watson's, Mr. Dashwood, 48th Native Infantry, a fine-looking fellow. This morning I was not allowed to go to church. I think I could stand it pretty well; but I look very like a lunatic with my cropped hair; and I dare say I should have frightened Schilling, who, in my absence, does the duty.

Mrs. H. Salt has been very ill. I trust we shall neither of us forget the lessons which God has taught us in sickness; and that we shall " pay our vows, which we made and promised with our lips, when we were in trouble."

I do so hope Chesterton will never be sold till I am dead. I do so long to spend some of my last days among the sweet solitude of the " Walls," and of that lovely little valley, where the trout-brook runs. I fear I shall again be unable to write to my Aunt Bache, and that is why I wish she should see my letter; for she is to me almost what you are, and my cousins I love as if they were my sisters.

This letter has reached an inordinate length: but you must remember that my letters to you are the only journal I keep: and surely this contains the journal of one of the most important events of my life; I may say, *the most important*, and the most blessed; for in this, my first real illness, now that delirium has all long passed away, and I am " sitting and clothed and in my right mind," the conviction, which first came in delirium, still cleaves to me, and is the greatest comfort I have, that all my old "iniquities," committed before my sickness, "are blotted out and my sins covered." Yes! when I lay delirious on my bed that first morning that I lost my reason, a voice surely spoke to me, telling me that it was so, not for anything that I had done, but for my dear Redeemer's sake. I do *not* believe this was delirium, delusion, or fancy.* I have always, for years past, been in the habit of confessing to God and praying for forgiveness of certain particular sins, which I thought the worst. And I never could feel, till I heard that voice, that I was forgiven; but now I feel it surely. I know I have committed many, even in the short space since my recovery. "I count not myself to have attained: but this one thing," by God's grace, " I will do: forgetting the things that are behind," I will " reach forward to those which are before; for the prize of my high calling in God through Christ Jesus." I did not mean to have told you this; but I am not willing that it should be unrecorded.

I believe there is to be an expedition to Persia from this place, to bring the Shah to reason. The express from England, *viá* Bombay, not a month out, has just come in: so that we know

* See note to Memoir, page 35.

that the Russians have given up the Isle of Serpents and Kars: that the Queen Dowager of Oudh has arrived in England, and that Captain Bird, who was an officer here, and has undertaken, for a very large consideration, to plead her cause, has been exciting the mob at Southampton. Now that I am let behind the scenes a little, I am convinced of the justice and the necessity of the annexation. There is a blue-book about Oudh coming out soon, which will tell a great deal, of which people have no idea.

During my illness Mr. Gubbins showed a great deal of feeling. I saw the tears drop from his eyes several times, when he was trying to persuade me, in my lucid intervals, to be quiet. My bearer also, Nazir, showed much feeling, which I believe to be genuine. As for old Abraham, the Khansamah, he is an old humbug! He used to come and tell Emmie he had been crying all night. But I *saw* Nazir crying very quietly, when he didn't think I saw him, or had sense to observe. Well! I think my yarn is nearly spun. I forgot to say what a pleasure Mrs. Block's songs (the remembrance of them) were to me, when I was ill. She was here, you know, when I first came to Lucknow. All my old poetry, hymns, and everything I ever learnt came into my head. The Bible was my greatest comfort; but I had much pleasure in remembering old hymns and songs.

Ever your affectionate Son, &c.

Cantonments, Lucknow,
October 4, 1856.

My dearest Mother,

The mail leaves this on October 8th, so it is time to begin something for you. We came home last Tuesday week, and I have been slowly gaining strength ever since. To-morrow I am to begin duty by taking the evening service at cantonments. It is a little church, not requiring more voice than the remnant of old St. Chad's. I have already taken several christenings. Every morning since my return, I have been out by half-past five (it is not light till five now), and have ridden or walked for an hour. I could not ride, being too weak, till four or five days since. I generally meet Mr. Gubbins or Dr. Fayrer half-way between this and Lucknow, and ride back with them. Mr. Gubbins is always "chaffing" me about my horse; he is only a large pony, but he carries me capitally, and moreover goes very well in the buggy. I have another, a white horse, a "caster," as they call it, from the Cavalry. He is a good horse, barring a spavined leg, which, however, only makes him go a little lame for a hundred yards, and then he is tolerably fast, and very strong and steady. Apropos of my spavined horse, which I drove this morning, I remember a poem in an old keepsake, called, I think, the

"Wedding Ring." The gentleman took the lady, in the poem, to a jeweller's shop; and there was a picture of him fitting on the ring. The poem began—

> "Nay, Annie, turn not so away,
> And look not to the door,
> When we have ta'en a twelve-mile ride,
> To view the goldsmith's store;"

and, after a good deal more, there was this verse:—

> "And look, where comes on *spavined* steed
> Our vicar pale and wan;
> Full soon may we his Reverence need!
> Heaven bless the holy man."

So it's quite orthodox that I should have a "spavined steed," and he *just is* spavined!

What babies we are when we are recovering from sickness! I used to delight so in flowers. Dear Emmie used to bring two beautiful passion flowers, all wet with dew, and put them on a pillow for me to look at every morning, when I was so weak that I could scarcely lift my head. She used to send me passion flowers from the Crescent, before we were married; so her doing so here had the charm of bringing back old memories, and so added beauty to the flowers. Passion flowers are almost the same here as in England. I used to like to get all the jewellery I could on the bed, and Emmie's gold bracelet.

Anything with colour in it I delighted in. I fancy it is so with all sick people.

It is well to see as much as we can of each other's "inner life." We ought not to be ashamed of it, for, as Longfellow says,—

> "Yet what binds us friend to friend,
> But that soul with soul can blend?
> Soul-like were those hours of yore;
> Let us walk in soul once more."
>
> *Hyperion*, chap. iv.

. . . . The dried flowers [some which were inclosed] I gathered on Thursday morning last. I drove very early into Lucknow, to see a native called a "Darogha," a steward, I fancy it means, who takes daguerreotypes, to get some for you. He is generally to be found in the Imaum Barrah, the tomb of the late king's grandfather. I drove there, but the Darogha was absent. The Imaum Barrah is a large quadrangle, about the same size as "Tom Quad." at Christ Church, surrounded by very beautiful buildings. At the farther end is the King's tomb. It is contained in a large hall, full of all sorts of curiosities. There are many immense chandeliers from England, remarkable only for size; and a wooden horse, from a saddler's shop in Calcutta, is highly prized! With all this, there are some beautiful shrines of silver. The King's tomb is one. It is about eight feet long, and four broad, all silver, as also is his mother's. In the court are tanks of water, something like those at the Crystal Palace; and by the side are creepers trained, and the prettiest creeper is a little red flower, two of which I picked and dried for you, and there they are, not very pretty now. I thought Lucknow, as I drove through it the other morning, one of the most beautiful cities I ever saw. The mosques are kept beautifully white, the domes and minarets often gilded. The material is contemptible; only brick, covered with plaster; but the forms of the buildings are good, and they are kept clean outside. At the Imaum Barrah end of the city, the streets are very wide, and, thanks to the English, perfectly clean and hard.

Monday, Oct. 6th.—I got through the service very well last night, without any fatigue. There was a very full church; about ninety people, as many as it will hold. This morning I thought I would have one more try for your daguerreotypes; so at a quarter-past five, I started in the buggy for the Imaum Barrah, taking with me the Baboo, as interpreter. The Darogha was not up, and kept me waiting so long, that it would have been derogatory to my dignity (a matter to which one has to attend carefully in India) to stay any longer. So I came away unsuccessful once more. The Darogha is getting bumptious through having so much notice taken of him. He is the only man in the station who does daguerreotypes, and everybody wants them; so he is becoming an important person, and it does not take an Oriental long to find that out. He is a gentleman, and does not take pay; so one has no hold on him. But to-day, a half-caste man, who knows him, came here to ask me to get him a situation, which I promised to try to do; and charged him at the same time with a letter to the Darogha, which I hope will prove successful before the mails go out. To-day Emmie and I bought some seven or eight very nice pieces of agate, which a man brought here, for three rupees, just half what he asked for them.

The Bishop of Madras comes here, November 20th, on visitation for the Bishop of Calcutta. I shall have, I dare say, fifty candidates for confirmation.

Affectionately yours, &c.

Cantonments, Lucknow,
October 16, 1856.

My dearest Mother,

I want to try and send you a bit of a journal, so here goes for to-day.

Oct. 16th.—Up at six, later than usual, but

the sun does not rise now till six. Cantered my black pony into Lucknow to Dr. Fayrer. He was not in when I arrived, but Mrs. Fayrer was just going to " Chota haziri," or little breakfast in the verandah, so I sat with her. She is a charming and excellent woman. They were married just four days before us, and are about our ages. She showed me her little boy, whom I christened three months ago, a very nice little fellow. Medical men here are treated —if they are gentlemen—as such, which is by no means the case always in England. They occupy in the regiment just as good a position as any officer of their standing. Dr. Fayrer is now civil surgeon, having got that appointment for distinguished service with his regiment in Burmah. Drove back to breakfast at nine. Employed with Jadub Chunder, the Baboo, and in overlooking the gardeners, who are laying down turf in the court at the back of our house, till eleven, when I went by appointment to visit the wife of Captain W——, who has just lost a little girl. At her request I read and expounded a chapter in the Bible (1 Thess. v.) to her, her husband, and two sisters. I trust I gave her some solid comfort. Home at half-past one. Variously employed till three, when we went to dine with Captain Macpherson. N.B. Dinner at three is "tiffin" to fashionable Anglo-Indians, who dine at eight. But the Macphersons and ourselves are very quiet people. Very pleasant three hours till six, when we all went out in Captain Macpherson's carriage. Drove round cantonments about three miles, and to the band. A band of one of the regiments plays every evening from sunset for about an hour, and there is always a crowd of carriages and buggies there. Gentlemen get out of their carriages, and go about talking to ladies at their carriage-doors. At about seven they all go home, most to dinner, we to tea. We were put down at our gate, and then found your letters. Found a note from Dr. Anderson, who is the doctor of one of the newly-raised Oudh regiments, asking me to meet him in the city to-morrow at seven, to be taken by him to a place called "Moosa Bagh," or Moses's Garden, to see a sick, and, he fears, dying officer of his corps. Now I must go to bed. But first I will tell you two things or three. First, I saw, in Lieutenant Stopford's rooms (52nd Regiment), the other day, for the first time, a flying fox, stuffed. The wings measured four feet from tip to tip. They are like those of a bat. (There goes "God save the Queen," from the band; so we shall sleep.) The head is exactly like a fox, with such teeth! but they only prey on the fruit-trees. Secondly, I am afraid that the fever and crunching ice have materially damaged my teeth. Thirdly, I bought Emmie a beautiful edition of the "Pilgrim's Progress," for a wedding day's gift. She had long been wishing for one, and I picked this up at our bookseller's, by great good luck, beautifully bound and illustrated : a small book: price, six rupees. I have been reading it with the greatest delight, never having done so since I went to Eton, in 1832. I miss the ugly figure of Apollyon, which used to be in our book, and which I dreamt of for years. Our Satan is an elegant, nude figure, with wings like a flying fox. But what a wonderful book it is! Second only, I think, to the Bible and Prayer-book. That man had the Spirit of God, if any ever had. I am glad to be approved of by the Bishop.[*] I will try to deserve his praise better yet. I have really only done my bare duty. So now, good night.

Moosa Bagh, Oct. 17*th.*—I arrived here at half-past seven this morning. After driving past the Imaum Barrah, in Lucknow, I had to turn into a suburb, and drove through streets where there was barely room for the buggy. But none of these streets were dirty, though the hovels on each side were wretched. The Indians are particularly clean, modest, and

[*] Bishop Wilson, of Calcutta. See Memoir.

decent about their sewerage arrangements; and there are fewer smells in Lucknow, a city of 100,000 inhabitants, aye, *far* fewer than in Shrewsbury, a town of 25,000. Indeed, I have hardly ever been offended in this way since I came here.

As I drove down this labyrinth of streets, teeming with people (all so quiet and orderly), I thought how easily they might *burke* me, syce, buggy, horse and all, and no one would ever be the wiser. Perhaps the length of time, during which the Indians have been civilised, will account for their lower orders being, in some respects, ahead of ours. They were quite as civilised as they now are, when our ancestors were painted savages. Their native carriages are exactly like those represented in Layard's Nineveh, copied from sculpture in that city; and they never would have improved, probably, had not we come among them.

Well, on emerging from this suburb, after about twenty minutes, I found myself on an open plain; and soon I perceived, far away, about two miles off, a palatial-looking building, to which I came in due course. Behind is the Moosa Bagh, an inclosure about three-quarters of a mile square. The garden seems to have been neglected for years; but the English have cleared away all the jungle, so that it is healthy enough. At one corner of the square, inside the wall, lives Dr. Anderson, the surgeon of the 7th Oudh Irregulars. He has built himself a small bungalow, where he and his wife live. They are very nice Scotch people. After a cup of tea, I walked with him to the large building, a palace built by a eunuch of the late king, and left to his majesty. It is really a very fine house. All the officers of the two Irregular regiments quartered here live in the palace. There is an extensive view from the windows over a vast plain; but it is bounded, at no great distance, by trees, so that one cannot see very many miles. The river Goomtee winds along about half a mile from the palace, and I could see cantonments about four miles off, as the crow flies. Plenty of fine green wheat crops were visible.

I found poor Lieutenant Petrie, whom I had come to see, dying of dysentery. A very good man—Captain Babington, of the 4th Irregulars—who lives in the palace, had talked to him a good deal on religious matters; and, I trust, had done all that I could have done. Lieutenant Petrie was very anxious to receive the Holy Communion, and, as Anderson did not think he would live out the day, I administered it to him, Dr. Anderson, Captain Babington, another officer, and the doctor of the 4th. The poor fellow's state of mind seems, so far as I can judge, satisfactory. Just before I left, to come back to Dr. Anderson's, I was introduced to Colonel Gray, the commander of the Irregular Brigade. He had been forty years in India without going home. Came back to breakfast at ten, and here I must remain till five o'clock, as it will not do for me to go back till the sun begins to go down. It is as hot often in Australia as here, Dr. Fayrer's brother tells me; but the sun's rays have not that deadly power that they have in India. At one time during this summer, your degree of heat in England was as great as ours; but there you can go out and lie in the shade, which would be death to us. By the bye, Mrs. Anderson told me that, the other day, as she was lying down on the sofa asleep, she was awoke by a hissing, and, on starting up, there was a cobra di capello on the ground, within three feet of the sofa. She jumped over the snake, and ran out, and the servants killed it. I saw its corpse to-day. It is quite five feet long. Its bite is death in twenty minutes: no remedy. It is the first snake I have seen in India. Just as I was going to see poor Petrie once more, Captain Babington came in to say that he had departed without a struggle. He was not quite himself, but enough so to know those about him till the moment of his death. The road hence to the city is so bad, that I could not venture to drive it at night, especially as neither I nor the syce knew it, so Dr. Anderson drove me in. It was quite dark, and there was no moon. The road was full of deep ruts, but the mare went the whole way at twelve miles an hour, and never made a false step. I never had such a night drive before, and I do not particularly want such an one again; for at the rate at which we were going, had the mare come down, we must have flown out over the splashboard. Got home at eight.

Saturday, Oct. 18*th.*—Sermon-writing nearly all day. Lieutenant Petrie was to have been buried this evening at half-past five; but, owing to delay in making the coffin, the funeral did not begin till half-past six. All the officers in cantonments, as well as those at Moosa Bagh, attended. The body was carried by the men of the Company's Artillery, English; and a firing party of Sepoys and the band of the 13th Native Infantry preceded the coffin. There are three burial-grounds here; one close to the 52d Regiment, one in the middle of the city, one here about a quarter of a mile from this house. Lieutenant Petrie was buried in the last. The officers met at the 71st Regiment Hospital, about two hundred yards from the ground. I waited at the burial-ground gate; and the sight and sound of the advancing funeral train, lighted by torches, and playing the Dead March in Saul, was very impressive. After the service the Sepoys fired three volleys, and all was over with poor Petrie for this world.

Sunday, Oct. 19th.—Started at half-past five for the 52nd Regiment. Got there at a quarter-past six, and began service immediately. Only gave them the Litany and a sermon. Preached on "When he slew them, they sought him: and turned them early, and inquired after God." Psalm lxxviii. 34. It was very solemn to remember that, since we last met, our numbers as worshippers had been thinned by fifty at least (I don't count the Roman Catholics), and that I too had been nearly joining the departed. I began with an extempore address of about five minutes, in which I called attention to the circumstances under which we met. Colonel Campbell has been very kind and attentive to me; and his hearty greeting, when he first met me after my illness, was something to remember.

I had just time, between seven and a quarter-past, to drive to the city church. It was quite full. The Martinière boys sing capitally. We never had a choir in St. Chad's, which could compare with it. We have no instrumental music. The bandmaster of the 52nd and one of their band sing with the boys; and the ladies are beginning to join well. This week I hope to do something towards establishing a choir in cantonments. It will have to consist of the congregation, ladies and gentlemen. Got home by half-past nine to breakfast, having to pay a visit by the way to a woman at the Dâk bungalow. She is, or pretends to be, in distress for money. She is a half-caste. Chaplains in India are a good deal troubled by half-caste clerks out of employ, travelling through their stations to others.

I have been delighted to find so much real religion in India. Captain Babington at the Moosa Bagh is an excellent man, and seems quite the evangelizer of the place. There is, however, much scepticism.

Employed during most part of the day in preparing my third sermon, for this evening. I have got through my three duties, thank God, without the slightest fatigue. I saw Mr. Schilling to-day, who is just returned from Landowr in the Himalayas. He says the scenery is grander than anything he saw in Italy or Switzerland, though not so beautiful. I hope to get some hill station for six weeks or so next March or April. The hills are six days from here for married people, four for bachelors.

Monday, Oct. 20th.—Walked from six to seven on the parade-ground. Three bands combined were practising for the review, which

General Anson will hold here in November. It is very pleasant having so much music here; the bands play four times a week in the evening, and are constantly practising in the morning. At seven A.M. drove into Lucknow to a confirmation class of females, which I had appointed to meet me at the school. Home to breakfast. At eleven a class of twelve musicians from the 48th Regiment Native Infantry. The musicians in these regiments are nearly always Christians, of English and Portuguese descent. The Portuguese had once very large settlements on the coast in the Bombay Presidency. Ten out of twelve of these men could read well. Their ages vary from fourteen to forty. At twelve I had three other candidates from the 13th Regiment Native Infantry. I am very much pleased with the demeanour and state of knowledge of my candidates, both male and female. The poor drummers don't know much, but are very anxious.

Wednesday, Oct. 22d.—Yesterday I kept no journal; I'll tell you why. At six o'clock I went out for a ride. I hadn't gone a hundred yards before I heard horses behind me, and Mr. Gubbins' voice saying, "Ah! that's what he calls getting up early." I turned round, and there were Miss Ommanney, Mr. Gubbins, and Dr. Fayrer. Dr. Fayrer turned off to make

a visit; the two others came on with me.
We walked our horses through the station,
and then, coming to a sandy road, where
I had never been before, Mr. Gubbins proposed
a gallop; so off we went. We had ridden about
three-quarters of a mile, when a native ran right
across Miss Ommanney's horse, and got knocked
down, but was not hurt, as it was sandy. I
remember riding on about a quarter of a mile
farther, and becoming from some cause or other
rather unsteady in my saddle; and then I don't
remember anything else, till I found myself on the
ground asking for my spectacles. Then I don't
remember anything else, till I found myself at
my own door, and my horse trying to kick Miss
Ommanney's. I was supported up the steps,
and deposited on the sofa. I was conscious that
I had had a fall, but I could not remember anything for a long time; couldn't think why my
hair was so short, &c. Mr. Gubbins wrote a
note for a doctor, and got home as fast as he
could with Miss Ommanney. Emmie came in
just after he was gone; no one had told her I
had had a fall, so you may imagine she was rather
frightened to see me lying on the sofa looking
somewhat pale. However, she is not given to
hysterics, and so she did what was needful very
quietly, and I got quite right in about an hour.
It seems that Mr. Gubbins heard some natives

shouting, "He has fallen," and, looking round, saw my horse running away, and me in the arms of two friendly natives. He caught my horse, and somehow or other got me on him, and I rode home; all the way making profuse apologies to Miss Ommanney, of all which I can remember nothing. The back of my head was cut and bleeding, but not badly. Mr. Gubbins says, the horse must have kicked me as I fell, as there were no stones and I fell on the sand. I suppose my head is too weak after the fever to stand violent exercise, and that I became suddenly giddy and fell off. I ought to be very thankful that my fall was not on the hard road. "So no more at present" from your affectionate son, "which" I hope this will find you as it leaves me; not with a sore head though.

The elephants are withdrawn at last. I am not sorry, for I had no work for mine. They are not to be compared as a means of transit to a riding-horse or buggy, except in going down narrow passages, or in tiger-shooting, or over swampy ground.

Your affectionate, &c.

Lucknow, November 6, 1856.

My dearest Mother,

. . . . You say you should like to be at my first dinner party! I don't know when that will be, for my time is and has been completely taken up with my work, and I see scarcely anyone but those, with whom it throws me into contact. . . . . . I am obliged to be very careful about horses. Yesterday morning I drove to the city church, and baptized two children of the head clerk in the chief commissioner's office. After the baptism we were driving away side by side, when suddenly his horse, a fine powerful mare, reared up and stood with her fore feet raised over my horse's back. I thought she would come down on him, but Mr. Kavanagh pulled her round, and down she came on her side, and smashed the shafts of the phaeton he was driving. These Indian horses are very vicious brutes—I mean those of the native breed; the Arabs are perfect in temper. . . . . I cannot write to-night; I suppose the pain I went through this morning upset me. Am I not like a young bear, with all my sorrows to come! I never had a pain, until I came here, worse than a flogging at Eton, or a blow on the shin from a cricket-ball. However, I don't put down these to India; they have been such as might have happened anywhere else.

I am glad you do not frighten yourself about me, and that you put your trust where alone it avails to place it. You in England, and we in India, must leave all, as far as meeting again in this life is concerned, entirely in God's hands; always be prepared for the worst, while we hope the best. And yet how terrible it would be to me to hear of the death of any of you!

But God will give us strength to bear whatever He sends us, if only we draw near to Him, and treat Him with the love which we owe to Him as His children. I am most grateful to Him for sparing me to Emmie and to all of you, and for His mercy in taking care of me the other day when I fell from my horse. Suppose I had been alone among the natives! Mr. Worsley, of the 13th Native Infantry, had a fall from his horse while riding a good way in the rear of his regiment, on the march to Cawnpore. He broke his leg and collar bone; he called some natives to his assistance, but they would not go near him; said they were not his servants, &c., and he actually managed to crawl to his horse, and he got on it, and rode to his regiment without any assistance.

. . . . I *wish* they would send another clergyman here. I have so much to do; so *many* things, that I can do nothing well. Why, I have what would be called a large parish in England—seven miles from end to end, and at least four miles in breadth; and two districts, each of them thirty or forty miles off, that must be visited at least once a year each. . . . . My heart sometimes sinks within me, when I think of all the time that must elapse before I can *see* England again, and of the far greater time before I can permanently settle there. If I have a family, I shall probably have to end my days here working for their support. But all this I desire to leave to God. If only He will order for me, I am content.

God bless you, my dearest Mother.

From Mrs. Henry Polehampton to Miss Polehampton.

Lucknow, November 7, 1856.

My dear Emily,

The idea of your sending me a lock of your dog Dandie's hair! Chloe happened to be sitting by me when I opened the little packet, and took the greatest interest in its contents. She is one of the very nicest dogs I ever saw, and is very handsome, and universally admired. I should like you to see her in the buggy, taking her evening drive with Henry and me. She accompanies us regularly, and sits on the other side of Henry, as upright as possible, in order to raise herself to his height, and rests her head against his shoulder in the most affected manner. She is just the sort of dog in which you would delight; a large, handsome, silky-haired English spaniel. I must not forget to inclose some of her hair for you, and I wish I could send her likeness. How much I should like you to see our house and garden! We have been making improvements in both, and I think they are far preferable to any others in cantonments. We have been revelling in custard apples lately, which are perhaps the best of the Indian fruits. These are now nearly over, and the oranges, with which our trees are covered, are fast ripening. I fancy we shall have to put up with these for the cold weather, as there is not much else to be had now, till the strawberry season commences, about the end of February. As to the roses, red, white, and deep crimson, and other flowers, they are still blossoming as profusely as when we arrived here in March, and promise to do so all the year round; neither is there any variation as to their quality or abundance. I miss the English flowers, though, inexpressibly; especially wild ones, and would gladly give all our Indian flowers in exchange for violets and primroses. These are sometimes to be had here in pots, and are looked upon by their possessors much as hot-house plants are at home, and treated with the greatest care and attention. I should be so much obliged if you will send me out next summer, if all is well, some daisy seeds, as I am particularly anxious to cultivate them here, if they will be induced to thrive in this climate. We hope to have all sorts of English annuals in our garden for the next cold weather, and shall be able to get them direct from home, as we mean to have a box sent out some time next year. The English flower-seeds that you buy in India are not to be depended on, and in many cases they fail altogether; whereas really good annuals, sent out from England, flourish here beautifully in the cold weather.

. . . . I wish I could send you some of the native costumes, which are very pretty, especially the caps and other head-dresses. I am so sorry that the servants are all beginning to wear warm clothes for the cold weather. The dark colours look so bad after the pure white, which they wear throughout the rest of the year. An ayah's dress is very pretty, composed of a sort of figured white muslin, in three or four parts; the skirt, body, scarf, and head-dress all of the same material, bordered with a scarlet stuff called saloo. Mr. Nazir, our head bearer, you would, I am sure, admire exceedingly. He is really very handsome, and by no means unconscious of the fact. I am sure he considers himself, next to his master, the most important person in cantonments. He reigns supremely over the other servants, who evidently think him a very great man. . . . . .

Your affectionate Sister,
E. A. POLEHAMPTON.

Lucknow, December 7, 1856.

MY DEAREST MOTHER,

On Monday last we received your letters, dated October 22, written just after your hearing of my illness. You seem to have been in a state of great anxiety, which is not to be wondered at. I should be in the same state if I heard of the illness of any of you. I suffered most after Emmie wrote to you, though the chief danger was over then.

Oh, no; one's blood is not in a constant "state of boiling" in India. We have, here at least, nearly six months of very agreeable weather. From the 15th of October until the beginning of March, men who can stand the sun upon their heads during the day can play at cricket. It is

now like the end of September in England,
except that the sun in the middle of the day is
fiercer, from being almost immediately over one's
head. We have a fire lighted about seven o'clock
every evening now; we burn wood, for there is
no such thing as coal here. I would not change
Decembers with you. They say it will be much
colder yet; and that in January, and part of
February, we shall want fires all the day. The
days are all just like each other; bright, clear,
and cloudless. It really is a splendid climate
now, though we shall have to pay for it after
March! In our house, and generally in cantonments, there are no mosquitos. We have
had curtains made, but never use them; but in
the city they swarm; at the Gubbins' they
almost pull you out of bed!

. . . . Fenton's letter about my illness was
very kind, and just like him; but he and all rate
me too highly. "Absence makes the heart grow
fonder."

. . . . It will be a fortnight to-morrow since the
Bishop of Madras left us for Cawnpore. On Sun-
day morning, at half-past six, Mr. Cuthbert, the
Bishop's chaplain, and secretary to the Church
Missionary Society in Bengal, preached to the
soldiers at the barracks, in behalf of the Oudh
Mission; a first-rate (extempore) sermon, more
addressed to the men's hearts than their pockets,

M

and I know that it had a good effect. I think the collection was £30. At the city church, at eleven A.M., I first said the Litany; then the Bishop and Mr. Cuthbert read the Communion Service, after which we sang "Come, Holy Ghost, our souls inspire," and then had the Confirmation Service. There were forty-nine candidates, and I trust they were well prepared; I had worked hard with them. The Bishop gave them a very good extempore address directly after the imposition of hands. They did not return to their places, but remained standing before the Communion-table till this was finished. Then the Bishop preached for the Oudh Mission; we collected more than £70. So now I hope we shall soon start the Mission. Some one, whose name has not transpired, has subscribed, I think, £500 for the same purpose. On Monday, the Bishop, Mr. Cuthbert, and myself, went to the Martinière, in Mr. Gubbins' carriage. After going over it, we stopped at the quarters of her Majesty's 52nd, and the Bishop consecrated the burial-ground of the regiment. The men were drawn up in a hollow square, about six hundred in number. I read a petition to the Bishop to consecrate; then we walked about the ground saying the Psalm; then he offered some prayers; after which a hymn was sung, and then he gave the men a capital extempore address. It was a most striking scene. The Bishop stood on a child's flat grave-stone, elevated by three steps; on it had been placed the large drum, to serve as a reading desk. An open grave was close at his feet, and all around us lay the poor fellows whom we had so lately buried there, the first tenants of the ground. In a row, in front of one side of the square, were the wives and children (a good many of them widows and orphans) of the soldiers. Mr. Cuthbert read St. John v. from verse 19 to the end of verse 29, and the Bishop founded his address upon it. He gives action, and his preaching is very effective. He drew a most thrilling picture of a death-bed scene, the death of a Christian; spoke of the delight with which we listen to the account of such an one, and then described the change. I cannot give you his words, but he did it *well*, and was equal to the occasion, which is saying a great deal. I like him much; he is very kind, and, I am sure, thoroughly good.

I met him at dinner, at Mr. Gubbins', in the evening, and a little before his departure (he travelled by night) he desired to have a few words with me, and we had a very long conversation. He said he had been very much pleased with all he saw and heard of me, and that he should certainly tell the Bishop of Calcutta how things were going on. If I had not been ill things would have been much better, and we should have had double the number, or nearly so, of confirmees. But I know how far to take to myself praises; I know I might have done much more in spite of my illness; I know I have my seasons of coldness and of indolence, which sadly interfere with my work. Of course it is pleasant to be praised; but if men could only see us as God sees! However, I will give you an extract from the account of his visitation here, which Mr. Cuthbert, by his order, wrote in the Record Book. I give you the extract because I know it will please you. "The Bishop would "express his warm sense of the correct and con- "scientious manner in which the Station Chap- "lain, the Reverend Henry S. Polehampton, is "performing his duties in this place, where he "has effected much already, though under several "disadvantages. It is only to be feared that "his strength will fail under his many duties, if "he do not receive assistance before the hot "weather."

. . . . The Commander-in-chief, General Anson, was here at the same time with the Bishop, and we had a grand review, to which I escorted the two Misses Ommanney. One of the Commander-in-chief's aides-de-camp came to me at the church on Sunday, and said, "How are you, Mr. Polehampton? The last time I saw you was at Eton, at Miss Middleton's." It was George Clive, a relation of Lord Powis's. He was at Miss Middleton's, when Edward was there with Amias Poulett, and I saw a good deal of him, both then and now. He is a very nice fellow, a thorough gentleman.

. . . . The 52nd, to my great sorrow, go, in three weeks, to a hill-station; and the 32nd succeed them.

. . . . You seem astonished at our taking ten servants to Mr. Gubbins'; and you ask where he put them all! They slept in the verandah. Indian servants all have their own houses in their master's compound, which, as you know, means the inclosure round his house. They are nearly always married. I dare say there are nearly fifty children in my compound. We see the little naked things running about, but they never come near our house. The servants' houses are built of earth, tiled. They are generally about twice as big as a St. Chad's almshouse; low and dark. I have been into one or two which were really very tidy. . . . .

Good bye, my dearest Mother.

Lucknow, January 7, 1857.

MY DEAREST MOTHER,

.... EDWARD's letter had just been put into my hands, in which he expressed a wish that there might by this time be three of us, instead of two; and his wish was soon gratified, for at half-past eight in the evening of December 30, my first-born was ushered into the world, and highly delighted I was to hear Mrs. Pender, the nurse, say, "It's a little boy." .... On Wednesday and Thursday both Emmie and the baby went on as well as possible. . . . . As I walked slowly home by moonlight, I was thinking how happy I was to have a son, and was saying to myself, "I have a son," in all the languages I know. On my arrival at home I found the nurse looking very blank; she told me the baby had just had a convulsion fit. . . . . Not liking the nurse's account, and fearing the result of another fit, if one came on, I baptized the child, calling him Henry Allnatt. We thought it better not to tell Emmie of his illness, until the doctor came again. When he did come, he told me for the first time that the child had been very delicate from his birth, and that, though he certainly might get well and live, he thought it very likely he would not. So, by his advice, I then told Emmie he was unwell. She took alarm at once, and was very much distressed, but soon recovered and became quite composed. . . . . He was in his mother's bed nearly all the time. I nursed him myself for about an hour by the fire. I went to sleep, and when I awoke I found our little darling much quieter, and I thought better; but Emmie did not think so. . . . . The nurse took him away from her, and held him near the fire, and then, after gasping for breath a little while, he died. Poor little boy! I prayed very earnestly that he might be spared, but it was not to be. Mrs. Pender carried our little dead lamb back to his mother, and it was piteous to see how she folded him to her arms and cried. After a while the nurse carried him away, and laid him out in his little basket cradle, just below Emmie's bed, where she could look into it. . . . . In the evening, Emmie, who had been very quiet up to this time, and had been intently watching baby's face as he lay beside her in the cradle, had an alarming hysterical fit. . . . . Dr. Partridge desired he might be buried next day, as he said it was of the greatest importance he should be taken away from Emmie, for that hanging over him and gazing intently on him, as she never ceased to do, was having a very bad effect upon her in her weak state. She did not make much objection when I told her. When I awoke in the morning, she was still gazing on her child. At ten o'clock Captain Hayes and Dr. Partridge came. I had asked the former to come, and had also asked for the use of a little close carriage of his, to carry the baby to the cemetery. He brought his brougham too, and he and Dr. Partridge went in it, and I with my dear little boy in the close carriage; the only ride we shall ever have together! But first, there was the cruel task of taking him away from his mother. She begged to have him a little while longer; she had him taken out of his cradle and put on a pillow by her, and then she folded him in her arms, and wept over him in a manner which made me feel more than I ever felt in my life. Then she had the coffin put where the cradle had been, and placed him in it herself, and put some little dark red roses, which grow in great luxuriance in our garden, and of which she is very fond, in his hands and on his breast; and then she bravely covered him up, and I carried him out and fastened down the coffin out of her hearing.

I cannot tell you how I suffered at seeing all this. I do not pretend to feel the child's death as I should have done, had he been able to recognise me even, much more had he been able to speak; the disappointment is what I chiefly feel. But Emmie's feeling is much more than this. No one can feel like a mother, especially for an infant.

Well, we drove down to the cemetery. Captain Hayes and Dr. Partridge took the coffin, carrying it slung at each end with a white cloth; and I read the service. I had had a brick grave made close by the side of a beautiful little tomb, under which Mrs. Forbes' little girl lies. She is Emmie's greatest friend out here. Captain Hayes, who has shown the greatest feeling throughout, threw a rose in upon the coffin. We stayed and saw the grave arched over;—and then I left my first-born son to lie there, till the sounding of the Archangel's trumpet, when he, at least, will rise sure and certain of the resurrection to eternal life! God grant that we also, my dearest mother, may become in heart and mind even as this little one, that so we may obtain the promises which are only to those of child-like soul.

When I came back, I found Emmie very calm and composed, and so she has continued ever since.

I forgot to tell you that what most deeply distressed me, after the baby's death, was to find that in my absence Emmie had had her own and my daguerreotype brought her, and had put one of his little hands on one, and one on the other, and the Bible, which her mother gave her, against his breast! It is very sad for her, poor dear little Emmie, to lose her first-born child. I had been looking forward to her having it as an object of absorbing interest when I was away from her "in the parish;" and how much more must she have looked forward? But God's holy will be done; and I feel it indeed a blessing to know that, if I have not a child on earth, I have one in the Paradise of God. "God hath not dealt with us after our sins, nor rewarded us according to our misdeeds." He might justly have punished me by taking away the mother as well as the child; but, thanks be to Him, she still is spared, and I may yet hope for another child.

I know how this will disappoint and grieve you all. I would not have written so fully every particular, but this is my journal; and the birth and death of my first child are not matters lightly to be passed over.

I remember I used to think sometimes, when I saw very little coffins being brought into St. Chad's, that it was superfluous to read the service over such young children; but I have since learnt to think more reverently of our Saviour's words, "Take heed that ye despise not one of these little ones; for I say unto you that in heaven their angels do always behold the face of my Father."

Edward told me to be sure to call our boy "Benjamin!" but, like Rachel, his mother will call him Benoni, child of my sorrow! Thank

God, our story has not more nearly resembled that.

:   Ever your loving Son.

Lucknow, January 10, 1857.

My dearest Mother,

I HAVE some better news for you in this letter. Last Saturday week, to my great regret, the 52nd marched out of Lucknow; and the 32nd marched in. The 52nd only went four miles out the first day. Colonel Campbell wrote and told me that I must now take service at the barracks for the 32nd; but I told him and Colonel Inglis of the 32nd, that with their leave I would finish the old year with the outgoing, and begin the new year with the incoming, regiment.

So on Sunday morning (very cold it was) I started from this at seven o'clock, and drove to the 52nd camp. I arrived there by eight, and found the camp composing a long and broad street of tents, at the top of which was the Colonel's. It was a picturesque scene. The men were just falling in for church parade—all in full uniform, with their muskets; and the officers, while I celebrated service, had their swords drawn, which I never saw before. There were many camels about, ready to take the baggage, and a few huge elephants. Altogether the scene had a sort of half-Indian, half-English look. Hollow square was formed, and I gave them part of Morning Service, for the sun was growing too hot to go through all. I preached on the end of the year;* the necessity of reviewing the past, and of making resolutions of amendment for the future; and concluded with a farewell address, recapitulating all that we had gone through together; praising the regiment generally for its good conduct, and exhorting the really Christian men in it to continue in their course, and laying before those, who would hinder others from joining them, our Saviour's fearful warning on that head. I never had a more attentive congregation, and I believe that I never had truer Christians among any of the congregations I have addressed than are to be found in that regiment.

After service I breakfasted with the Colonel, and he then said he had something to tell me; that the regiment desired to give me a remembrance or testimonial, and that they wished to know what I would like. This rather posed me, because I did not know the amount to which they intended to go; but he said presently, "You may say anything up to £50." I was *so* astonished! I had not expected anything, nor had I desired it; I had really never given it a thought.

* See "Extracts from Sermons."

"Well," he continued, "now say what you want most; I may just as well tell you we have collected over £80; and you had better think over it, and write to me at Cawnpore." . . . . I think it will be a silver inkstand, but I have left it as much as possible to them. It is indeed most liberal of the regiment.

. . . . Don't be too much cast down about my last letter. I wish I could have sent you better news; but the great consolation is, that I might have sent you worse. If we take this light visitation as we ought, "who knows but that the Lord may turn and repent, and leave a blessing behind him!" At all events, dearest mother, in all the changes and chances of this mortal life, let us keep our hearts fixed on the "better land."

Lucknow, January 23, 1857.

My dearest Mother,

. . . . Emmie's spirits are better; but the loss of her baby has sunk very deeply into her heart. She does not seem to find pleasure in anything but in thinking of him. I feel the disappointment very much; especially when I see how nicely some of the "baby boys" of my friends here are getting on. But God's will must be done; and I trust, if we take this chastisement as we ought, He will yet make us happy, by giving us another son.

* * * * *

Next week I am going to visit one of my out-stations, Sultanpore. It is ninety miles away from this. It is off the grand trunk road, and is to be reached only by " sandy lanes." I shall have to go in a palki; what is generally called in England a " palanquin." I expect to dislike it extremely. One can sit up or lie at full length. Besides the four bearers, I shall have a man to carry my baggage, which will be in two tin boxes, one slung at each end of a bamboo pole; and a torch bearer. The rate of travelling is about four miles an hour. The bearers are changed, I think, every six miles. I shall start on Thursday about two o'clock, and get in, if all be well, about six P.M. on Friday. There is only one *inn* (as you would call it; " dâk bungalow," *we* call it) on the way, a half-way house. I am going to stay with the Blocks. Mr. Block is Commissioner there. There are two weddings awaiting me, a Captain B——, and the assistant Commissioner..... I shall take my revolver; for only the other day a chaplain and his wife, travelling up the grand trunk road to their station, were made to get out of their carriage, and were robbed openly of all they had; the coachman assisting the thieves. However, such things are very rare, and I know a lady who went by herself the other day, by palki, to Sultanpore. . . . . Colvin was here the other day. He told me a story of a lady who was travelling by palki alone. Every now and then, when they got tired, the bearers put her down, sat on the top of the palki and smoked; and, when she remonstrated, they kicked at the sides of the palki, and said, " Chupro, Bebee, chupro !" (" Hold your tongue, ma'am, hold your tongue !") I wonder what Miss —— would have done under the circumstances !

January 24*th.*—I was going to tear this letter up, because the transition from grave to gay in it seems so sudden, that it almost appears as if I did not feel my child's loss. But you know that it is not so; and now I have so little time left, that, if I do not send you this letter, you will not get one at all. I am going to drive Emmie out for the first time to-day. She wishes to go first to our baby's grave. This evening I have to bury an officer of her Majesty's 32nd, who died rather suddenly yesterday from the effects of a sunstroke last hot weather. The 32nd have succeeded the 52nd here. Colonel Inglis and his wife are very nice people. She is a daughter of Sir Frederic Thesiger. I have one old schoolfellow in the regiment, Captain Yarde.

He was an oppidan at George Dupuis'; and, I think, was in Edward's remove. The officer whom I am going to bury to-day is only the second who has died since I came here, nearly a year ago. Indeed, barring the outbreak of cholera in the 52nd, the station has been very healthy. When I return from Sultanpore I intend going to Seetapore, my other out-station. It is fifty miles from this. I hope to march there; taking Emmie with me. She seems to like the idea. This is the only other way of travelling in this country, excepting on the grand trunk road. We shall ride not more than about twelve miles a day; and our tents will be carried on camels. I suppose our servants will have to walk, but I don't quite know. Captain Simons of the Artillery, a friend of Henry Salt's and mine, has just come in from a tour of a month in this way, and has offered to lend me his tents. The change will, I am sure, do Emmie good. . . . .

Your letters will probably arrive just after I have sent this. We have fires all day now: thermometer about 60. I found so much old wood lying about my garden and compound, that I have not had to buy a bit. It costs in the bazaar a rupee for three maunds, and we burn about a maund a day. It has only cost me the cutting up. I pay a man for a day's work two annas, about threepence. This is the general rate at which labour here is paid. The food which the poor people eat, rice and dahl, is very cheap. The Irregular Cavalry are paid 20 rupees a month (£2); out of this, they find themselves *everything* — buy their horses, clothe and feed themselves and their horses. How they do it is wonderful. They are a very fine-looking body of men, and not badly mounted. Their dress is a thick quilted buff-coloured coat, long boots, and a red turban. Dr. Partridge is their doctor, and he told me the above. They even pay for their arms—swords, lances, and carbines. Well, I must close this rambling epistle. Send it round to my brothers.

Good bye, my dearest mother. With best love to Emily and all the rest,

Believe me, your affectionate Son,

HENRY S. POLEHAMPTON.

P. S. I inclose for your perusal a copy of my letter to Colonel Campbell.

" MY DEAR COLONEL CAMPBELL,

"PRAY accept yourself, and kindly convey to
" the officers of the regiment under your com-
" mand, the expression of my most sincere thanks
" for the kind and liberal manner, in which you
" and they have shown your appreciation of my

"services among you, as a Minister of the
"Gospel.

"You will, I am sure, believe me, when I say
"that I neither expected nor desired such a
"reward, for simply (and, as I cannot but feel,
"very imperfectly) discharging my bounden
"duty. But, since it has seemed good to you to
"present me with a substantial mark of your
"esteem and approbation, you may rest assured
"that your gift will be most proudly received and
"carefully treasured by me; and handed down
"to those who may come after me, as an encou-
"ragement to exertion, and as a proof of the high
"esteem in which those are held by British
"soldiers, who endeavour to carry out that, for
"the performance of which they (and among the
"foremost the 52nd Regiment) have ever been
"renowned, namely, their duty in that state of
"life in which it has pleased God to place them.

"I humbly trust that my ministrations among
"you have not been in vain. But whether in
"this respect you owe anything to me or not, I
"know that I am most deeply indebted to the
"52nd Regiment for *teaching*, which is pro-
"verbially better than precept; for *example*,
"bright example, not only of conduct becoming
"to the soldier and the gentleman; but also of
"that which graces the true consistent Christian.

"That the blessing of God may rest upon

"all and each of you, wherever you may be;
"that He may preserve you from disease and
"pestilence; 'cover your heads in the day of
"battle;' bring you safely again to our own
"loved country, and, at last, to that better land
"where 'they shall not learn war any more;' is,
"my dear Colonel,
"The earnest prayer of
"Yours sincerely,
"HENRY S. POLEHAMPTON."

* * * * *

The 52nd were all through the Peninsula and Waterloo, where they helped to repulse the last charge of the French, together with the Guards. It is a great source of mortification to them that they were not in the Crimea.

Seetapore, Oudh, February 16, 1857.

MY DEAREST MOTHER,

IN the last letter I wrote you I promised that I would give you a full account of my two journeys to my out-stations, Seetapore and Sultanpore. I will now try to perform my promise, though I don't know that I have anything to tell which can interest you much.

On Friday, then, January 30, at three in the

afternoon, I started for Sultanpore. I went in a palki, carried by four men; four others run by the side of those who carry, in order to relieve them, which they do about every three minutes; and another man carries over his shoulder, slung at each end of a bamboo, tin boxes, which contain all that one cannot carry in the palki. At night there is also a man to carry a torch, that the bearers may see where they are treading; so that by day there are nine, by night ten men running with you. Each set of men carries you about ten miles. They go at the rate of about five miles an hour. The motion is not particularly disagreeable; one soon becomes accustomed to it. The palki, which I had, was about six feet long, three feet wide, and four high. A mattress fitted into it, on which my bearer made up a regular bed for the night, with sheets, blanket, and counterpane, all correct. During the day I lay on the outside of this. At the end of the palki, over my feet, was a shelf and drawers, in and upon which I carried my larder, cellar and pantry; two loaves of bread, salt, one chicken, one duck, four hard-boiled eggs, one bottle of water, one of wine, one of beer, knife, fork, tumbler, plate, &c.

Well, at three o'clock off we started—I did not like leaving Emmie alone, but she would not have anyone to stay with her, nor go to stay with anyone, though she had offers of both. So I was obliged to content myself by making a speech to the head servants, telling them that I confided their mistress to their care; and by putting on another "chokeedar" or watchman.

When the bearers take one up, they give a groan; as much as to say, "What a heavy wretch this is!" then after one or two steps they begin a monotonous sort of song, the words of which sounded to me like "rats in a hay-field, rats in a hay-field," over and over again. The first four men run about one hundred yards with you, then change shoulders, and run another hundred yards; then the other set of bearers come on and do likewise, and so on throughout.

My first stage was from cantonments to Lucknow, right through the city, and about four miles beyond it. By the time we had come to the end of this stage, the sun was beginning to set; so I got out and walked, and found it so pleasant that I walked about fourteen miles before I thought of turning in. It was then nine o'clock, and I sat down by the roadside and had my supper, the bearers squatting round in a ring, looking on; one holding a torch for me to see to eat by. After supper I went to bed, and slept well, until I was aroused by the bearers at the end of the stage, asking for "bucksheesh." As I had been told by the postmaster not to give them any, I refused; the consequence was, that the new set of bearers, finding that they were unlikely to get any "bucksheesh" either, got lazy and impudent, and I was awoke about the middle of the night by their putting me down. I got up and exhorted them to proceed; they said "Very good," but went so slowly, and laughed and made such a row, that I was obliged to get out again; and, this time, finding that they were disposed to be impudent, I was obliged to use a weightier argument, giving the most offensive of them divers pokes in the ribs with a stick which I carried, and which, by the bye, Sturman Latimer gave me years ago. As soon as they saw I was not to be trifled with, they went very well, and I had no more trouble. But I found out afterwards that it is always usual to give "bucksheesh," four annas, about fivepence, to each set of bearers. Soon after daybreak I found myself at a well, close to a fine tope of mango trees. Thinking it a good opportunity for a wash, I got out. I saw two tents pitched under a tree; but learning from the servants that the Sahib, who inhabited them, had not arrived, I proceeded with my toilet. I had scarcely finished, when I saw two ladies riding up; upon which I dived into my palki. When I had made myself respectable, I came out again, and presently a servant came to inquire who I was; upon which

I desired him to say I was the "Padré Sahib;" whereupon there came an invitation to breakfast with Mr. Ommanney, the Judicial Commissioner in Lucknow, to whom the tents belonged, and who was out on a judicial tour in the district. His wife and daughters were with him, and I had a very pleasant breakfast; getting good tea and all manner of delicacies, instead of cold water and ditto duck, on which I had intended to breakfast. About half-past ten I took to my palki again; about two P.M. the bearers put me down close in front of some Englishman's tent by the roadside. I was very much disgusted, as I had not the least intention of introducing myself to a stranger, and wanted, besides, to get to the end of my journey. So I was strenuously exhorting them to go on, when the Sahib himself appeared from the tent in the shape of Mr. Block, with whom I was going to stay at Sultanpore. He is assistant Commissioner there; and you will remember my having often spoken of his wife, who was staying at the Gubbins' when we first came to Lucknow. He was out on a business tour, and his tent was surrounded by natives with petitions, &c. We had a glass of beer together, and then he ordered his palki, and we went on towards Sultanpore. We did not arrive until eight P.M.; the last seven miles we walked, and I had some very pleasant conversation with Mr. Block, who is a good specimen of an Oxford man. He is about four years my junior. I found Mrs. Block as agreeable as ever. .... On Sunday morning at eleven we had service in a large room at Mr. Block's house. Nearly all the English in the station, about thirty, were there. I preached from Acts i. 8; generally on the duty of bearing witness for Christ, and particularly for the Oudh Mission. The collection amounted to about £8, and I am in hopes I shall receive more yet, and that a good many of my congregation will become monthly subscribers. I also administered the Holy Communion to about eighteen people. There was no evening service, owing to the distance which most of the people had to come.

On Monday morning I married Captain Bunbury to Miss MacAndrew; the bride was very lady-like and good-looking. The wedding took place in the drawing-room of the bride's brother, and we adjourned to breakfast in a large tent. On Tuesday I married Mr. Stroyan, the second assistant Commissioner, to a lady, whose name I forget. This wedding took place at Mr. Stroyan's house, and the breakfast was at Mr. Block's. Mrs. Block made the wedding-cake herself; and very good it was. The bride was a very pretty girl of seventeen. The reason why the wedding took place at the bridegroom's house was, that the day before he was taken ill of scarlatina; so he just got out of bed to be married, and went back again directly afterwards. He could not stand during the service. His wife wanted to go and nurse him; but the doctor would not let her, and she was to see no more of him for a fortnight. However, she and her brother came to the wedding breakfast, which in spite of all was a very merry one.

Now a word about the country, through which I travelled to Sultanpore. It is a dead level all the way; but everywhere the ground is covered, as far as the eye can reach, with crops of wheat and barley, now about a foot high, and a lovely green. The country grain was also in flower, one sort a pretty light blue, the other yellow. Almost every two thousand yards there are topes, or copses, of mango trees. The mango is not a very pretty tree; it is too round and wig-like, as Miss Ansell used to say of my attempts at trees when she was teaching me to draw; but still it gives the country a well-wooded appearance. There were other trees occasionally, like fine elms, of which I don't know the name. It is impossible to conceive a more dead level than all this part of India. Since two hundred miles from Calcutta, I have not seen a hill! But one does not miss them so much, when, as here, the landscape is everywhere bounded by trees. Most people tell me that this is the prettiest part of the plains of India. It is not, as you may imagine, to compare with English scenery. The want of fresh green grass is quite distressing to an Englishman, excepting just at this season, when all the country is covered with fresh green crops. There is an immense quantity of corn grown in Oudh, but the straw of the corn is very short, and the ear small. The reason is, I am told, that the land is never allowed to lie fallow, and that the farmers put no chalk or lime on the land. The chief Commissioner here told me that he believes many large tracts of land in India have had crops of wheat raised from them year after year for two thousand years! The land has never been allowed to lie fallow, except occasionally, when a change of government, and consequent anarchy, drove the people from their homes.

On Tuesday evening at six o'clock I started from Sultanpore on my way home. I had not gone a mile before a storm of thunder and lightning came on, and I was obliged to take refuge for an hour in the last house in the station. As soon as the storm abated I set out again, and was soon asleep. When I awoke at the end of the first stage, I found that the rain was coming down in torrents, and in consequence the bearers, who should have relieved the others, were not there. There was not a house nor even a native's hut near; so I had to wait in the middle of the road, while my bearers went to look for the others. After an hour they came back, saying they could not be found. At last I prevailed on the set of bearers who had brought me from Sultanpore, by offers of double "bucksheesh," to go on another stage. They did it very unwillingly, and no wonder, for they had come very fast over the last stage of ten miles, and the next was more than twelve. However, they started at last, and I went to sleep again; but I was awoke once or twice by their putting me down, and refusing to go on. I had to use every argument, save that of blows, to get them to the end of the stage, which they reached at one P.M., the rain still pouring down heavily. When we reached the next halting-place, there was *again* no relief of bearers! I could not make the poor creatures, who had already carried me twenty-two miles, go on any farther. (I should have said that they did not carry me all the way, for I walked six miles during lulls in the storm.) Well, there was nothing for it but to spend the remainder of the night in the palki, in the middle of the road. Happily it was water-tight, so that I was comfortable enough. A native came and asked me to his house, but I declined, not being able to make out how far off it was, and not feeling perfectly sure that I might not get mobbed and robbed. The man was very civil, went off, and got the "chokeedar" of a village, and put my boxes, which were standing in the road by the palki, under his protection. When I awoke in the morning, it was still raining hard. The man who had come the night before, and who turned out to be a kind of horse patrol, came again and offered me shelter; and as I could now see where I was going, I sung out for the bearers, whose presence I had secured by taking the simple precaution of not paying them, and made them carry me and the palki there. It was not one hundred yards from where I slept. I found a cottage made of bamboo and straw, very neatly made too: no furniture in it except the patrol's bed, and brass pots for cooking. Altogether, about eighteen of us were packed into it. I kept close to the door for air. Not until half-past seven A.M. did the new set of bearers make their appearance! It was of no use losing my temper; I was only too glad to get them at all. I gave my old bearers a good "bucksheesh," which they really deserved, and offered a rupee to the patrol. (Suwār, or rider, is the Hindostanee name of his office.) But he drew himself up, and said "he was a Suwār, and could not take 'bucksheesh;' but if the Sahib would write a line for him, to say he had behaved properly, he would very gladly take such a testimonial." I very willingly did, and he made me a great many salaams, and off we set. I had promised Emmie to be at home by eight on Wednesday night. This was now impossible; but, wishing to keep my time as nearly as possible, I promised the bearers double " bucksheesh" all the way; and the rate at which they travelled was really something surprising, considering that a palki with an Englishman of nearly twelve stone, and divers of his belongings, is no slight weight. Throughout the whole day until one o'clock on Thursday morning, I hardly got out once. I walked about ten miles in the evening, but I ate and drank in the palki as I went along. It is scarcely possible to read in a palki, and yet the time did not pass heavily. The country was refreshing to the eye, and my thoughts were with all of you at home, and busy in recalling divers passages in my past life. I found Emmie a good deal alarmed at my non-appearance, but of course anxiety was all stopped by my coming.

I remained at home until the following Tuesday morning, when we started for my other outstation, Seetapore. I forget whether I told you that two of the Artillery officers here, Major Kaye and Captain Simons, each lent me a tent. This journey I had determined to march; chiefly for Emmie's benefit, to whom such a change was strongly recommended by Dr. Fayrer. A perfidious native promised to bring me eight camels, which would have carried all my property; but only five arrived. However, he declared the others should be up by Tuesday morning; so I allowed him and his five to go on, and with them went my butler, table-attendant, water-carrier, my *Swain* or dish-washer (N.B. this *alias* will only be understood by old collegers), washer-man, and two men to pitch tents. These started at nine P.M., and had orders to pitch the tents, and have all things ready for breakfast next morning at nine o'clock, at a place called Mu-hona, twelve miles from Lucknow. Right early in the morning I got up; but the other camels did not appear. I sent to the bazaar for a bullock-cart and two bullocks; but could get none for a long time. I forgot to tell you that, having applied to the Commandant in cantonments for a guard, he sent me four Sepoys and a naick, or corporal. The naick managed to get one bullock-cart and bullocks, and I bethought me of my two bullocks, who draw water from the well and work in the garden, and also of a very tidy cart, which belongs to the house. The gardener made as many objections as " old Hundred," in " Dred," but to no purpose. So at last off we started. It was now too hot to ride, so I drove Emmie in the buggy; one syce, or groom, went with us, and one other, with a grass-cutter, led our two riding-horses. I had had a very nice little horse lent me for Emmie by Mr. Schilling. You may want to know why we needed such large means of conveyance. In the first place, there are two tents; the larger requires two camels to carry it, the smaller, one. Then there is a tent for the servants, and all their warm clothes for night, besides the cooking things and luggage. There is quite enough, I assure you, for five camels and two bullock-carts. People on a campaign can of course do with less; but yet this will give you some idea of what an immense " following" an army in this country must have.

Our road in this journey has been very much like that to Sultanpore, but not so pretty. To speak of it as a road to drive over, nothing can be much worse. It is nothing but a bullock-cart road, over very light soil, like sand. Most of the way are deep ruts, just like a farm cart-road in England; and the worst of it is, the axle of the buggy is longer than that of the bullock carts, so that the wheels don't fit. You may imagine what the road was, by my telling you that we were from one o'clock to half-past five doing the first march; just thirteen miles. We dined and had tea (our tent was pitched in a mango-tope, just outside the village of Mukona), and then we had to turn out into the night-tent, as the day-tent had to be packed up and sent on. We went to bed about eight, and slept as soundly as the chokeedar (who kept coughing all night to let the thieves know he was awake) would let us. I have already written you an unconscionably long letter, all about nothing; I will not therefore weary you with a journal of each day's march, but will merely tell you what our daily proceedings were.

I rose just before sunrise, at six; called the kitmutgar to bring " chota haziri," or little breakfast, and dressed. Served chota haziri myself to Emmie, in bed. She then rose, and I went to hurry the servants. Sent off the buggy with one syce, about three-quarters of an hour before our start, which was generally about seven. We rode until we overtook the buggy, which was usually about five miles, and drove the remaining five, the sun being pretty hot about eight o'clock. We rode very slowly, for Emmie is not up to much exertion yet. Our longest stage was fourteen miles. At the end of our ride or drive, we found our day-tent pitched, under a tope of mango trees, near some village, where water was to be got, and corn for the horses. Had bath and breakfast; by the end of which the servants, whom we left at our sleeping place, arrived with the night-tent, which they pitched. We then read or wrote till three, when we had dinner. By about half-past four, the sun was low enough to go out for a walk until six, when we had tea. Before we had well finished, the men, who had pitched the tents, began to untie the tent ropes, and take up the pegs, and we had to turn out into the night-tent, where I generally read to Emmie, "Dred" being the book, until nine o'clock; about which time, after much dismal groaning, as of one in the extremity of sickness, from the camels, who objected to being loaded with the proverbial "last ounce," the khansamah (or butler) and his party started to prepare for next morning, and we went to bed.

On Saturday morning we arrived at Seetapore, having started from Lucknow on the previous Tuesday—fifty miles in five days. I called, after breakfast, on Mr. Christian, the Chief Commissioner, and on Colonel Birch, commanding the troops of the station; two native infantry regiments. Then I went home and prepared my sermon. We were pitched in a mango tope covering an acre of ground, so that even in the heat of the day we could have a pleasant walk.

On Sunday morning Emmie and I breakfasted with Mr. and Mrs. Christian. They are very nice people, and paid us every attention. At eleven o'clock the congregation, just thirty people, arrived. Church is always held in Mr. Christian's "cutcherry," or law court. I administered the Holy Communion to eighteen persons. The afternoon service at four P.M. was well attended. The Christians pressed us to dine with them, but Emmie did not wish to dine out. We had on one of these days a call from Sir Mountstuart Jackson, who drew that sketch of Lucknow church, which I sent to Emily. Have you read the "Life of Hedley Vicars?" There is a portrait of Hedley Vicars prefixed to his "Life." Sir Mountstuart Jackson is like him in face, and I trust in character, though I don't know it. I like him, however, very much indeed. His uncle, by the bye, is to be no longer Chief Commissioner of Lucknow; we are to have Sir Henry Lawrence.

On Monday morning Mr. Christian, at my request, sent round a paper for donations and subscriptions to the Oudh Mission, for which I preached the day before. The donations amounted to £25; the monthly subscriptions to £4. Pretty well for a place, whose Christian inhabitants are not more than forty at the outside. Mr. Christian also promised to send papers to two or three other stations in his district, at which there are English residents. So I think the Oudh Mission is in a promising state, as far as funds go. And so it must be, if it is to do any good. It is no use sending one solitary missionary to a place like Lucknow, where there are, some say, 400,000 inhabitants; there ought to be at least five men there; more, if possible. I think that, to be successful, missionary enterprise ought, in India, to be conducted by a body of men stationed in one place, combining their exertions and helping one another. Then, when they have made some converts, they may leave them under the charge of one perhaps, and the main body can go to another place; but I believe that very little good can be done by isolated missionaries. The Oudh Mission, to do, humanly speaking, any good, ought to be supported with £1000 per annum at least. It is not established yet; as soon as it is, I will send you all particulars, and I shall be glad if you and my brothers can get subscribers to it. I am anxiously looking forward to the arrival of my brother-chaplain for help in organizing missionary, as well as other work. As I have, I think, told you before, chaplains, if they do their duty among their own flock, especially where there is an English regiment, can do little or no missionary work.

On Monday evening we rode to Mr. Christian's, to see his garden, which is the best I have seen in India. English flowers, which grow well enough in the cold weather, are its great charm. I took Emmie back to our tents, and went to dine with Mr. Christian. There was no party; and his baby, a little boy of four months, was taken ill, and frightened Mrs. Christian a good deal. Its crying, poor little thing, reminded me painfully of our loss. However, we heard next morning that it was much better.

On Tuesday morning we marched on our way back to Lucknow, taking different stations from those at which we pitched in coming. Our second station was a place called Peernuggur. Our tents were in a little valley, which reminded me of those about Chesterton; there was a winding river, and really green grassy banks; altogether it was a very pretty spot.

In the evening I borrowed a Sepoy's musket, made some small shot by cutting up bullets, and had three shots at herons; which were all signal failures. Emmie was with me, and did not forget to "chaff!" This was the only really pretty place on the march: the rest of the country is as flat as possible, but so covered with green crops that you cannot call it ugly. I was "raised" in flat country too, Middlesex and Buckinghamshire; so I don't so much object to it, if green and well wooded.

To-day we are at Baree; thirty miles from Seetapore, twenty from Lucknow. Our khansamah has chosen us a dreadfully ugly spot; but as he has done so well hitherto, both in catering for us and choosing stations, we don't grumble *much*.

The people, wherever we have been—natives I mean—are as civil as possible. I cannot say that they or the country *look* as if there had been much oppression, but those, who were best acquainted with Oudh before the annexation, say there was. At one village, the Zemindar, or largest landholder, came to make his salaam to me, as he said he always did to the "Sahib logues," or gentlemen, who pass through. He said he was very glad of the annexation, for that before it, a great Nawab had taken away his estate by force, and that he could get no redress; but that the Commissioner at Seetapore had examined his case, and had restored him his property. I have not a doubt that the annexation will be an immense benefit to the people, by enabling every man to be sure of his own, and by giving good laws. I trust also that a still greater benefit will follow by the successful preaching of Christianity, and by education generally. Excepting at certain seasons of the year, at stated festivals, you see hardly anything of idolatry in Oudh. Mahommedanism has prevailed so extensively here, at least among the higher classes and in the towns, that Hindooism seems to have become the "dissent," so to speak, of the country. Yet most of the lower orders, especially of the rural population, are Hindoos. I must tell you, what I dare say you know, but which I did not till I came here, that Mahommedans and Hindoos in India are all the same people by blood, only differing in religion. .... It is an interesting part of history, the Mahommedan conquest of India; and I intend to read it up well when I reach home.

I am told that all the prettiest part of Oudh is north of Seetapore. My tiger hunting has come to nothing, I suppose, for I shall not like to be absent any longer, as I am unable to leave a clergyman in charge. All the tigers in Oudh are confined to the other side of the river "Gogra," which you will see in the map. Captain Bunbury, whom I married at Sultanpore, told me that he had shot fifty.

Now, to pass from profane to sacred subjects. I suppose, to satisfy people's ideas of what a minister of the Gospel ought to be, I should finish this evening by going out and preaching in the village. The chief obstacle to my doing so is, that I only understand Hindostanee enough for housekeeping purposes; and if I did understand it sufficiently, I doubt if preaching, when one is on the wing like this, would do any good. I have as yet seen little or nothing of missionary work in India, but I know that in the Presidency of Bengal hitherto very little has been done; chiefly,

I firmly believe, because so few have set about it in earnest. The chaplains have had their hands full with their own work; the missionaries have been few, and the majority, I fear, not very able; the civilians and soldiers, up to a late date, for the most part, anything but what Christians ought to be. But a brighter day for India is, I am persuaded, now coming. With the help of God, if I cannot be a missionary myself, I will yet do all I can to stir up my countrymen to do what they can for the spread of the Gospel. But this great work must be set about in a very different way from what it has been yet, if ever India is to be Christianized by the English. We want some such men as Hedley Vicars, men of singleness of aim and purpose; many, very many such men. It is little wonder that hitherto so little has been done, when there has been but about one clergyman to some 200,000 people, and when the greater part of the laity have been Christians only in name. . . . .

. . . . I fear I have missed a post, but I hope you will always remember that no news is good. If any illness were to befal me, there would be plenty of people to tell you of it.

Are you curious to know what my "parish" does in my absence? Colonel Palmer, of the 48th Native Infantry, takes the evening service at cantonments; Mr. Schilling does the service in the city church; and Colonel Inglis, of her Majesty's 32nd, is chaplain to his own regiment. Would to Heaven that unordained men would not only consent to do the routine, but do *earnestly* the real duties of Christianity. It *must* be so here, if ever Christianity is to be spread. "Would that all the Lord's people were prophets," as Moses cried, when he was asked to forbid Eldad and Bildad from preaching in the camp.

Written at the Girls' School,
Lucknow, February 26, 1857.

WHEN I wrote the above, I was at Baree. About two A.M. I was awoke by a great noise in the camp, and on going out I found the servants assembled round the village chokeedar, whom they had taken and bound as a thief. This is what had happened. My tent was fifty yards from the servants' tents. At the door of my tent a sentry was marching up and down all night, and at one end of the servants' tent was the village chokeedar. A little before two A.M. the chokeedar called out to the sentry that he had caught a thief. The sentry told him to hold him, but he let him go. The servants awoke, and found that, from just where the chokeedar was stationed, all Emmie's and my clothes, which were in the washerman's possession, had been stolen; all the bearer's clothes, and all his and our other servants' brass cooking things. The servants declared that the chokeedar must be an accomplice, and so they had tied him up, and my bearer and the naick or corporal wanted me to let them beat him till he confessed where the property was. I would not allow this, but sent for the headman of the village, told him what had happened, and went to bed again. In the morning I sent for him, and found that he had searched everywhere, but with no results. Presently came in the chokeedar of a village two miles off. He said that he had heard from the headman of Baree of the robbery; and as soon as it was light, seeing four men with something under their arms, he seized one, who struggled with him and dropped what he was carrying, and then the other three men came up and rescued him. What he dropped proved to be one of my shirts and the bearer's things. I sent the chokeedar off under a guard to Mr. Christian's, and wrote to tell him what had taken place. I lost seven shirts. We reached Lucknow safely, and all the better for the march, on Saturday morning at half-past nine.

I found that during my absence there had been a row at Fyzabad, an English station, some sixty miles from Lucknow. A fakeer had been preaching a holy war against the English; ten men armed had joined him. The Commissioner went and reasoned with them kindly, but to no purpose, and at last one of them drew his sword on him. Upon this he sent for a company of Sepoys; there was a fight, and the Sepoys bayonetted eight of the ten men, killing three, I think, on the spot. The English officer commanding the Sepoys, and three Sepoys, were wounded.

. . . . Tell Edward I sent him my sleeve buttons by Mr. Henry Forester, whom I met the day before yesterday at the Gubbins'. He was on his way to England. You probably will never get such a long letter from me again.

Ever your affectionate Son.

Lucknow, March 9, 1857.

MY DEAREST MOTHER,

YOUR letter and Tom's likeness arrived the very day after the closing of the last mail for England. . . . . Mrs. Dashwood, who was so hopelessly ill, I am happy to say, has quite recovered. It has been almost a resurrection for her. . . . . On the 18th, Mr. Harris, my new brother-chaplain, will be here, if all be well. I shall be very glad of his arrival, for it is impossible for one man to do the work of this great station, as it ought to be done. He is a married man: I remember him at Brasenose College, Oxford.

* * * * * *

Yes, I remember singing the Evening Hymn that last night I was at home only too well. It is a great delight to feel how much you love me, my dearest Mother. I join you in praying that we may one day meet, where love will have no such rude shocks to bear as in this world of trial. You speak of Christmas decorations. Our servants know that Christmas is a " Burra din," that is, " great day," with us; and they decorate our gates with flowers, and bring all sorts of offerings of sweetmeats, &c. You speak of cold weather, and snow. Our cold weather, I am sorry to say, is all gone. In another three weeks we shall be unable to sit away from the punkah, and shall have tatties up. We have not put up our punkahs yet, but it is now too late to be out in the sun, except in a covered carriage, after nine A.M. The nights are just what one likes, delightfully cool. The days are yet perfectly bearable.

* * * * * *

I have no news to tell you. Everything *in statu quo*. My strawberries have just begun to come in. I had a nice basketful to send to a sick lady to-day. We ought to have an immense number...... Mr. Jackson goes, and Sir Henry

Lawrence comes, as Chief Commissioner, next week. Emmie's best love. She is very well.

Ever your most affectionate Son.

P.S.—Since I finished this letter, it has been all but lost. Our first dust-storm of the season broke upon us half an hour ago, and this sheet was carried out into the garden, and was going off to no one knows where. Emmie rescued it just in time!

I forgot to say that the blades and grains of wheat came all safe; and I will sow the grains at the proper time.* I have put into the envelope of this letter some leaves of the pomegranate flower, and an orange blossom or two. The pomegranate flower is the most beautiful red you can imagine. It is a heavy flower, or I would send it. The fruit is not worth eating, I think. Our orange flowers seem smaller than those I remember in England, though the fruit is not. We had an immense quantity of oranges. I sent away several hundreds as presents. They are nothing like so good as the Lisbon oranges. I fancy the orange was brought to India by the Portuguese, but I don't know. The scent of the orange and lime flowers in our garden now is delicious. Tell me if any scent remains when

---

* These grains of wheat had been brought to England by the writer from the field of Waterloo.

the flowers I send come to you. Your violets were quite sweet. I am tired and sleepy, so I cannot write you a good letter to-night. Thank you for planting the trees for Emmie and me and our darling. He has been transplanted to a better soil. I have just been out in the moonlight, and picked you some orange flowers. The pomegranate leaves I send come from a flower which has been all day in that little vase I gave Emmie!

Lucknow, March 9, 1857.

My dear Edward,

.... India agrees very well with every healthy man, who is sober and does not expose himself. I know Brigadier Gray, Commandant of the Oudh Irregular Brigade, who has been forty-five years in India, and has never been home. He never was an athletic man, but he is as brisk as possible. I have no fears for myself from anything in the ordinary way, so long as I am temperate, take regular exercise, and keep out of the sun. The 32nd (Queen's) have been remarkably healthy while they have been here, but they had the cholera on the march. It carried off fifty of them in a very few days, and the cases were wonderfully rapid; some only seven or eight hours. The Colonel is a very nice fellow, and Mrs. Inglis, a daughter of Sir Frederic Thesiger, a most agreeable, lady-like woman. Yarde, who was at G. Dupuis', is in the 32nd here. He is the only Eton fellow in it. A day or two ago, the Commandant of the station, the Chief Commissioner, and the Chaplain were all Eton men, and all living in three houses, all in a row! —Mr. Jackson, the Chief Commissioner; Colonel Halford, the Commandant; and myself. Now Colonel Halford is superseded, and Mr. Jackson is going away. Sir Henry Lawrence, who is very highly spoken of, is coming in his place.

Yes, I remember, and often think of that last pleasant day's fishing! This time six years I hope to be not very far from just such another. My poor little boy! he will never want that fishing-rod, which you saved in such a marvellous manner. I feel my child's death far more now than I did at first. We go to his grave every now and then. Emmie likes to take flowers there. Last Friday she took some and made them into a cross, and laid them on the flat stone which covers his grave. If we have twenty children, we shall never forget our first-born. But God's will be done; I don't deserve such a blessing.

On the 17th my brother-chaplain will be here, Harris of Brasenose. I am almost sure I remember his pulling 2 in Tuke's crew, when they bumped us! He will be here just in time to relieve me of some of the work before the hot weather sets in. . . . . Tell Brocklebank to write to me; I often think of him; we are old and fast friends. . . . . Thank you for keeping my birthday; I always keep yours.

Lucknow, March 9, 1857.

My dear Tom,

. . . . Your allusions to " little Benjamin " are, as you may imagine, somewhat saddening; but which of us may not be pained in the same way by allusions in a letter from abroad to some one, who is no more when it arrives?

. . . . Three sermons a week is a great demand upon me. I *cannot* write more than one a week. The Sunday before last I extemporized two, one to the 32nd in the city, the other at cantonments church. I have preached extempore a good deal to my English regiments. It tells more at all times to men of the common soldier class, especially in the open air, as nearly all my preaching to them is. When Harris comes, I hope we shall have two services in each church, and one at the English regiment.

Since I wrote the above we have been out riding, and were caught in the first dust-storm of the season. It was, however, not a regular dust-storm—one which begins perhaps hundreds of miles away, and envelopes you at midday in thick darkness,—but merely a local affair. We were obliged to ride home again, happily only half a mile distant, and very glad we were that the wind was at our backs. We met some miserable individuals beating up against it with great difficulty. The dust-storm, which we had last year, left a layer of sand everywhere of quite a different colour from ours here, so we judged it had come from a great distance.

. . . . . I don't want to say a word to induce you to come to India. *I* don't repent coming here. Emmie is very fond of it. I don't like it so well as I should a living of the same value in England, but I would not exchange my chaplaincy for a living of £300 a year in England. But the miseries of India have not begun with me yet. There may be, and probably will be, a time when I shall have to part with both wife and children, to send home ; and I dare say one gets more weary of the place every year. But at present I am very well content.

India is certainly a less healthy country than England. Here in Lucknow we have had on an average eight hundred Protestants residing during the past year, from February, 1856, to March, 1857; of these exactly one hundred have died. Thirty-eight were taken off by cholera; but, reckoning that as an occasional visitation only, yet sixty-two, a very large number out of the residents, are left, who died from natural causes. And of this number only nine were over forty years of age; of the rest, fourteen were children under nine years old, the rest were almost all under thirty. A good many Roman Catholics died besides the above; I think they have numbered about four hundred in population. I suppose it would only be fair to compare the above mortality with a population of the same number in England, including the same number of English soldiers, for I should think they are the most imprudent people in the world.

I am very glad to hear that Mr. Alford is made Dean of Canterbury. I don't agree with everything he says in his sermons or in his notes, but he is undoubtedly a very good man in every way. . . . .

    Your affectionate Brother.

Cantonments, Lucknow,
March 24, 1857.

MY DEAREST MOTHER,

I SUPPOSE we shall, by next mail or the one after, be getting letters from you, sympathising with us in the loss of our baby. How we are obliged, separated as we are, to rip up each other's wounds which are just beginning to heal! My poor little boy! I cannot help thinking, when mothers, on whom I am calling, bring in their babies, whom I have baptized, for me to see, how that my own little one would have been by this time as fine a little fellow as this, if it had pleased God to spare him. I believe I have said this to you before, and it is of no use indulging in these unavailing regrets. . . . .

. . . . One year has gone—six more to come—before I return to England. Don't think I am homesick; I am not a bit so yet. Excepting that I have a longing desire to see you all again, I would not leave India yet, if I could. I do not at all dislike the life I lead, and wish to see more of the country. The hot weather is coming on apace; we have not begun punkahs, and I intend to do without as long as possible, but I think another fortnight will see them in full swing. My strawberries have come in, and we get a beautiful basketful every morning, fine large ones, and well flavoured. We have been able to send a great many to people who have no gardens, and you may suppose that they are very welcome. We have another fruit ripe now, the "loquat." It is something like an egg-plum in appearance, acid, and very good with sugar. The English flowers, which flourish well in Indian gardens during the cold weather, are fast disappearing, but the roses bloom all the year round, and nearly all the trees continue in leaf in the same manner. They do shed their leaves, but not till the young ones push them off.

My brother-chaplain, Mr. Harris, has just arrived. He *is* the man I remember at Oxford, pulling in the Brasenose boat. I only remember seeing him once, and that was one night in the year 1845, when the B. N. C. bumped our boat in the races. After the bump, as the two boats lay together while the others passed, he was close by me for ten minutes. I have never seen him since. He is just my age, though two years my senior in the Company's service, and looks at least three years younger. He looks wonderfully well; but he had such a terrible low-fever at his last station, Peshawur, that he was obliged to leave it. He has now the promise of the next hill station, Dugshai, at Christmas next; and has come here merely to fill up the time. He has had a journey of more than six hundred miles. . . . .

Harris will take the pastoral superintendence of the Martinière, the Queen's regiment, and part of the civilians; while I shall have the remainder of these, the Artillery, the three Native Infantry regiments, and the Cavalry.

We have now three services on Sunday, and shall increase these to five; taking the "lion's share" of them in turn. It is not Sunday-work that tries me; I have always been, since taking orders, as fresh on Sunday night as on any other in the week. It is the Hospital-work in which I want help, and the responsibility of so many souls partly taken off my hands. (Chloe has just come in with a garland of white sweet-smelling flowers round her neck; some of the servants have put it on.) . . . . Harris has been telling me a great deal to-day about Peshawur; it is the frontier town of the Punjaub, the last piece of territory we have towards Affghanistan. Dost Mahomed, the King of Affghanistan, is our ally, but there are a number of border tribes whom we cannot control, and these give our people at Peshawur no end of trouble. If the English go a yard into the Affghan territory, they get shot at, and Harris says that his compound was constantly fired into at night, and shots exchanged between his chokeedars and the Affghans. . . . . There are two chaplains at Peshawur; but the station is so unhealthy in the hot weather, that, during that period, there is scarcely ever more than one Chaplain, as the other gets periodically knocked up. For six months in the year the climate is perfection, and the scenery beautiful; but for three months heat and malaria are very fatal. Harris tells me that, while he was there, twelve Englishmen died in one night, from apoplexy, brought on by the heat. They crowd our soldiers far too much in barracks. Officers and gentlemen don't die as they do.

Now I must tell you the chief event that has happened here since I last wrote; it is a sad one. I heard one day, about a fortnight since, that a Mr. Boileau, an assistant Commissioner at Gonda in Oudh, was killed in an attempt to capture a robber. Of course I was very sorry, but I did not think much more about it. Four or five days afterwards, on coming home with Emmie from our evening drive, you may imagine how we were shocked to find a man waiting for us with a letter from the Deputy Commissioner of Gonda, and a box containing poor Boileau's head. The letter was to request me to bury it, and to say that the body had not yet been found. The history of the affair was this. A notorious robber, named Fuzzl Ali, with his band of dacoits or highwaymen, has infested Oudh for several years past. A few years before the annexation, he, one day in broad daylight, stopped the King's prime minister in his carriage in the most public part of Lucknow. He had only three men with him, and the "premier" had a hundred at least, but they all bolted, and Fuzzl Ali dragged him out of his carriage, wounded him, and vowed he would kill him, unless he gave him a very large sum of money, and a free pardon. The minister promised to save his life, but Fuzzl Ali would not let him go till the then assistant Resident (an Englishman, of course) had given his pledge that the minister's promise should be fulfilled. The money was paid, but Fuzzl Ali was put into prison. I am told that the English considered that they were keeping their pledge by not killing him, but that Fuzzl Ali took a very different view of the case, considered that they had broken their pledge, and vowed vengeance; but I can't vouch for the truth of the last statement. Well, after a short time he escaped from prison, and I am told that at the annexation he offered his services to Sir James Outram, if he would grant him a small piece of land to live on; but Sir James, I suppose, had too high a sense of honour to employ a highwayman, and would have nothing to do with him. Fuzzl Ali has lately been very troublesome in the district, and parties have been sent out to take him. About three weeks ago, a Lieut. Clarke got intelligence of his being near Gonda, where poor Boileau lived. Boileau heard of this, and started one day for Clarke's camp, having only six mounted native police with him; but Clarke had left his camp, and had gone after Fuzzl Ali, so Boileau followed him; though it seems he and Clarke made for the same village by different roads; for Boileau arrived first, and posted five of his men at different outlets; he then went in himself with only one man, and found Fuzzl Ali and his men (who are said to be about twenty-five in number) cooking their dinner. They of course got to their arms, and then there was a parley between Boileau and Fuzzl Ali. The latter said that Boileau had no right to try to take him now that he was over our frontier, and in the Nepaul territory. Boileau, however, persisted in telling him to lay down his arms, and Fuzzl Ali and his men then fired on him, and he fell dead from his horse. They then gave chase to Boileau's six men, till presently pursuers and pursued came suddenly upon Lieut. Clarke's men, who were advancing to the village. These fired on Fuzzl Ali's men and killed four or five. The rest ran, and Clarke and his party took and destroyed all their property. Strange to say, Clarke did not find out that Boileau had been killed till next day.

The following day, Fuzzl Ali came back to look for his property, and found Boileau's corpse.

He cut off the head, and tied it up to a tree, where it was found; but the body could not be discovered. The head was sent to me for burial, as I have said.

I thought it my duty to inform the Chief Commissioner, and the Brigadier; and, as the head had been sent to me for Christian burial, I had a coffin made, so that the body might be inclosed in it, if it came; and I had the head put in it, box and all—for it was too much decomposed to be opened. The Chief Commissioner, and Brigadier, with the chief officers and civilians in the station, came and followed the poor fellow's remains to the grave. I had hardly concluded the service, when the body arrived, just in time to be put in the same brick grave with the head; but it was too much decomposed to be put into the coffin; and I was obliged to have it laid, in the case in which they had sent it, on the top of the coffin.

The affair has made quite a sensation here, where Boileau was well known to many. He was not more than twenty-seven. I have nothing more interesting to tell you, so I have given you all the particulars about this sad affair. I dare say you will see it mentioned in the papers. He is much blamed for his rashness, poor fellow! If he had waited a little, he and Clarke would in all probability have caught the whole band of robbers. Now they have got away farther into Nepaul. I had a letter yesterday from Captain Boileau, the cousin of the poor fellow who was killed, who commands all the parties which are now out in pursuit, and he seems to think that it will be a very difficult thing to catch Fuzzl Ali, as he is in the neighbourhood of thick forests, and of the Nepaul hills. He is a dangerous fellow to be at large, as he might at any time surprise some station in Oudh, and rob and murder half the people before the troops got the alarm. Gonda is fifty miles from this.

Mr. Gubbins and Dr. Fayrer are in the district, looking for tigers, but they had had no sport by the last accounts.

* * * * *

Your affectionate Son.

Lucknow, April 6, 1857.

My dearest Mother,

I don't know that anything has happened since I wrote last, worthy of record. Let's see. Mr. Jackson has gone, and Sir Henry Lawrence has come in his place. Sir Henry is a great favourite. He is the founder of the Lawrence Asylum (a college in the hills for the children of English soldiers), to which he subscribes £2,000 per annum. Emmie and I dined with him last week. He has been giving a series of dinner parties. Since that, Sir Henry gave the soldiers of the 32nd, and the Artillery, a *féte* in the Martinière park. Nearly all the station went. The soldiers had dinner at three, and afterwards races and "manly sports." It was too late in the year, and had better have been put off till the cold weather. Unlimited beer and the heat have in consequence increased my fever cases in hospital; but the men behaved remarkably well on the whole. There is no Lady Lawrence; she died a few years since; so Mrs. Gubbins is now the first lady here. Mr. Harris preached, for the first time, the Sunday before last. We have now five services in all: quarter past six A.M. at the 32nd; this lasts one hour, and allows a quarter of an hour to drive to the next service, at half-past seven, at the Residency Church; at half-past six there is also service at cantonments, and at the same hour in the evening at both churches. Harris and I shall take in turn by weeks the three services in the city. As concerns parochial work, I shall live here, and take these people and part of the city; and Harris for the present will live at the Martinière College, where Mr. Schilling has given him rooms, and will take the 32nd Regiment, and the other part of the city. There is no house for Mr. Harris fit to live in, to be had in the city; and what he will ultimately do, I cannot think. He will be seven miles distant from me, when he is at the Martinière. I continue to like him very much; he is active and energetic, and a thorough gentleman. We have not seen much of his wife yet, as she heard of her father's death just before coming here.

We are getting up subscriptions for harmoniums for both churches, and I shall order one for myself. A good harmonium is better in India than a piano. I cannot get a good piano under ninety pounds; a good harmonium will cost me twenty-five pounds. Pianos always get out of tune in the rains; and I don't think any piano would last, to be worth anything, ten years in India. On Sunday last, Major Edwardes was at church. He is on a visit to Sir H. Lawrence. He has been to Calcutta, to take his wife so far on her way to England. He is now Colonel, and Chief Commissioner at Peshawur; having thus, as you will see, a civil appointment. This is the case with three or four officers in every regiment. Sir Henry introduced me to Colonel Edwardes after church; when I told him that it was not the first time he had been one of my congregation. He was often at St. Chad's, when in England. He remembered me, and my grandfather's *name*, as Vicar of St. Chad's. Did I tell you that there are two Shrewsbury men in the 32nd, Jones and Evans? Jones used to carry chairs with old Yeomans, and had often heard me at St. Chad's. He is a particularly well-behaved man. We are all very well here, excepting Captain Wildig, who is in one of the Irregular regiments: he is in a very critical state. Three months ago, while I was in camp, his wife, who had just come out from England, died of liver complaint; two days afterwards he was taken with it, and has been very ill ever since, and I fear he is getting worse. He has two sons in England. He is a very nice man, and, I am happy to say, in a frame of mind which gives me great comfort. Last night, there was a fire in cantonments. Dr. Wells, of the 48th's, bungalow was burnt—not *down*, for the walls stand; but the roof was completely burnt off. It is supposed that some of the Sepoys of his regiment set it on fire, or else some old servant. I did not see the fire, but it must have burnt just like a haystack. No one was hurt, and he got nearly all his furniture out, one advantage of having no upper story. Our house is not so likely to catch fire as a bungalow, as it has a flat plaster roof, and very strong brick walls. We have not begun punkahs yet, though many of our neighbours have. We are holding off as long as possible. Some one the other day gave me as a receipt for keeping a house cool the following sage piece of advice: "Don't keep a thermometer." As I was going out of the room to fetch your last letter to look at, some clay figures which we have just bought caught my eye. You can't think how well the natives here make them. There are two men in particular in Lucknow, who, if you give them a drawing of a statuette, will model it exactly in red clay, like terra cotta; and though you only give them the drawing of the front, or one side of a figure, they will do the back, or the other side capitally. We have a pair of boys, about eight inches high, carrying baskets for flowers on their heads; standing on pedestals ornamented with fruit and flowers. They were copied from the "Art Union Journal." When General Martin built the Martinière, he had out some Italian artists, and the natives seem to have learnt to model from them. Really our statuettes are nearly as good as any you could buy in England, and make me the less regret the loss of those terra-cotta things which Edward got for me at Naples, and lost at Baden Baden. Now for your letter; two came the same day, one envelope contained one from you, and another from Emily, dated February 18th. Remember me most kindly to Major Hamilton; I always liked him extremely, and hope to see him again some day. People should never indulge in golden dreams of India. England is the most golden place in the world. Emmie and I do get well supplied with books now. We subscribe to a book club, which is supplied by Thacker of Calcutta, who has an agent here. It is rather a large subscription—everything English is very expensive here: but books we must have. I have read lately Boswell's letters; very interesting to lovers of his life of Johnson. I think there can be no doubt about the authenticity of the letters. It is a melancholy book; melancholy as showing how Boswell's evil nature was never conquered, in spite of knowledge of, and wishes for, better things. I have also read some sermons by Monod, a French Protestant divine. This book was not in the club: I picked it up at a sale. The title is "Sermons by A. Monod, translated by Rev. William Hickey. J. Nisbet and Co." I have only read the first and part of the second sermon; but the first, on the evidences of the inspiration of Scripture, I most strongly recommend. I get the "Evening Mail" now. I take it with Schilling. It is ten o'clock, and I must go to bed: for I have to be in Lucknow, for early service, at half-past six to-morrow. We have service in both churches every day this week. We had a congregation of sixteen each, this morning.

God bless you both, my dearest mother and Emily.

Ever your affectionate Son and Brother.

Lucknow, April 17, 1857.

My dear Edward,

You are the only one of the family to whom there is the least chance of my writing by this mail.

*　　*　　*　　*

By the bye, *our* burglar, Fuzzl Ali, was killed just after I sent off my last. You read in it, or in the one before, about his killing poor Boileau. He got away into Nepaul, which (as I dare say you don't know, you English are so ignorant about India) does not belong to us. He was followed by (at least) two parties; one commanded by Lieutenant Clarke, of the Oudh Irregulars, the other by Captain Boileau, the murdered man's cousin. We haven't very correct particulars yet; but from what I have been told, and read in the papers, Clarke came upon Fuzzl Ali and his men (about one hundred), in a pass of the Nepaul hills. Most of them bolted, but about a dozen stood, and fired on Clarke's party. He was wounded; one Sepoy killed, and six wounded; but they went in, and in three minutes Fuzzl Ali's party were shot or bayonetted to a man; that is, those who didn't run away, and who may yet live to trouble the Company. It is said that Fuzzl and his two brothers were both killed. I think it most likely, as I don't believe he would run, but I don't think it has been proved to a demonstration. The heads were sent to Gonda in Oudh, to be identified by a follower of Fuzzl's who has turned king's evidence. I was asking Captain Hardinge (a nephew of Lord Hardinge), who commands a regiment of Oudh Irregular Cavalry, about it the other day; and from what he said, I think it is doubtful whether they have got Fuzzl Ali yet. The Mahommedans here (the lower ones at least) rejoice in him. They say he was born under a star which won't allow of his being shot, and that he is more like a god than a man, &c. He is, or was, a brave rascal.

* * * *

This morning, at six o'clock, I drove Emmie into Lucknow, to be daguerreotyped. I sent my mother a daguerreotype of the Imaum Barrah, where they are done. The Imaum Barrah is a building in which are the tombs of one or two Kings of Oudh. The man who takes the likenesses is steward of the place, which is richly endowed. He is a very gentlemanly man, a Mahommedan, and most liberal. He won't take anything for his likenesses. He gives you freely as many as you want, and takes no end of trouble. I have no doubt his chemicals, &c. must cost him more than £100 per annum, at the least. This morning I was done with our dog, Chloe, at Emmie's special desire. The likeness of me is a profile, the best-tempered looking one I ever saw of myself, and the dog came out very fairly. I will send you a paper impression next mail. I was also done with Emmie. She's the worst sitter in the world, but the Darogha succeeded pretty well. I send you a paper likeness of us, done by him one day last week. They're bad; but perhaps you'd like to see how your brother and sister were looking lately. We look like " niggers," don't we? That book my hand is on in the picture is full of portraits of every one in the station. . . .

We are both very well, thank God! Emmie has at last consented to my sending two paper daguerreotypes of our poor little boy. They were taken about seven hours after death. He is lying, you will see, on the sofa, which I had had carried out into the court behind our house. The next time I send you a likeness of us both in miniature, I trust it may be a living one; but God knows what is best. Poor Captain Wildig, whom I mentioned in my last as very ill with liver complaint, died a few days after I wrote. I saw him almost daily for nearly three months.

He was a very nice fellow; and I have a good hope that he has entered into "rest." His wife died of the same complaint two days before he was taken ill. She had just come out, for the second time, from England.

* * * * * *

I hardly like to send you those pictures of my poor little boy. I would not; but that I like to send anything that may interest you, as I look for the same from you. It makes me sad to think that this picture of my dead child may be the only representative of me that may ever reach England, but who can tell? "Meliora speramus." . . . .

Your affectionate Brother, &c.

Lucknow, April 30, 1857.

MY DEAREST MOTHER,

THREE or four days ago, I received your letter, dated March 15th. . . . . You may all depend upon my not exposing myself more than is necessary. When I first came here, I thought that I could, with impunity, make sudden exertions, as I used to in England; but I know better now. I don't think the runs by the side of the buggy did me any harm; my doctors didn't think so; but I should not do it again. You forget that they were always after nightfall.

You are very kind to set such a value on my life. I hope I may be able, year by year, to make it more valuable to my fellow-creatures, by increased usefulness to them; but you all speak of me with far more esteem and affection than I deserve. I think I *do* receive all your letters. I am going to make all my English letters into books. You will have read, long ago, all about my journeys to Sultanpore and Seetapore. Last week I took another short trip to a place called Durriabad, forty-five miles from this, to baptize a child. . . .

Emmie is very brave about being left at night. However, the bearer sleeps, when I am out, just outside her door, in the verandah; the chokeedar is walking round and round the house all night; and Chloe is tied to the foot of the bed; so there is not much to fear under ordinary circumstances. I think I told you long ago that they say this house is haunted. I never saw the ghost; but I have killed a good many rats, which make ghost-like noises. Chloe and I slew one last night. They come in the evening from the well. Talking of ghosts reminds me of poor Wildig, of whom I told you in my last. He told me, a very short time before he died, that the natives say my house is haunted, and that no one but a Padré can live in it! Isn't it odd that they call us "Padrés"? The fact is, the first missionaries to India were Portuguese and Spaniards, Francis

Xavier, &c.... Pray give my kindest love to my dear old Uncle John. I must write to him. I know no one, out of our immediate circle, whom I love better. I often look at the daguerreotype I had done of him, and think of him with affection. I remember St. Chad's bells were going for Wednesday morning service as he sat to have it done; and the wind blew his grey hair up, and so it is in the picture. Thanks for Miss Ansell's letter. I had a very kind letter from Miss Jackson by the last mail. I take her writing to me most kindly; such a nice letter, too! She tells me of all the kind things that are said about me at St. Chad's; and that little Lizzie B. has begun to count up the time till my return.

 .... Fuzzl Ali is certainly killed. I had a visit this morning from Captain Boileau, the first cousin of the poor fellow who was murdered, and he told me all about it. He was out after Fuzzl, but Lieutenant Clarke caught him. He had intelligence, through spies, that Fuzzl Ali and his party were in a mango tope (or copse); and, as dense jungle reached close to it, Clarke's party were able to steal upon him unawares. All ran but four. They fired, and Clarke was shot through the right arm; but the whole affair didn't take three minutes. The four men were shot or bayonetted immediately. It really is a great relief; for travelling by palki was by no means safe while such a daring rascal was at large; and he was a rallying-point for the disaffected.

The Sepoys and natives generally are just now in rather a disagreeable state of feeling towards us. Perhaps you have read in the papers that two regiments mutinied, because they had cartridges served out to them which were said to be made up with bullocks' fat. . . . . One or both regiments are disbanded, and the soldiers are incapable of ever again serving the Company, and lose their pensions. Some of them had served thirty years, and therefore were entitled to large ones. It will be a good example to the other Sepoys; but, meantime, there is a good deal of disagreeable feeling. In proof whereof, the other day, because the doctor of the 48th here *tasted* in hospital a bottle of medicine which was to be given to native patients, the Sepoys, at least so it is believed, set fire to his bungalow. I think I told you this before. A friend of mine, also, the Adjutant of the 71st, found the other night in his garden an arrow, hidden under some leaves, and a bow by it. On the arrow was a bit of combustible stuff, which no doubt was intended to be lighted, and then shot into the thatch of his bungalow. Another was actually shot at the Brigadier's house, but missed. I have the advantage of living in a brick-built house, with a flat brick and plaster roof; so that they can't easily set me on fire. I expect there will be a bit of a row, when the natives know for certain that the King of Oudh is to be dethroned. They hug themselves with the idea that the Queen will reverse the decision of Parliament on this matter; but I don't think much harm will come of it. We have formed all the King's army into regiments in the Company's pay, and they like our rupees paid regularly once a month. With the King they were always in arrears. I have a servant, who was a bearer in one of the King's palaces, and he says he was almost always a year in arrears of wages! In the country they like British rule, because they don't get plundered now; but in Lucknow they want the King back, because so many of the King's tradesmen are out of employ, and hangers-on at court have lost their occupation. There, I don't think I have any more to say. . . .

Your affectionate Son, &c.

Lucknow, May 12, 1857.

My dearest Mother,

It wants several days to post-day; but, as I have nothing particular to do just now, I will begin a letter to you, which I can truly say is one of the greatest pleasures I have.

I always remember the 12th of May as a remarkable day. On this day, twenty-one years ago, when I was twelve years old, I went from Eton to Staines, in the front boot of a coach, to see a boat-race between Eton and Westminster. Eton won most gloriously. I remember coming back in the evening and telling it all to Edward, who, poor fellow, had been shut up in his tutor's pupil-room all day, " doing his verses ! " I believe I am just as great a boy about a boat-race now as I was then; for I am looking forward anxiously to see whether Oxford or Cambridge won the race which was pulled on the 3rd of April last. How much, and yet how little we alter! the worst of it is to find, not only our boyish tastes, but also our boyish faults clinging to us still.

. . . . . . Since I wrote to you last we have had a little excitement in this station. I told you about Dr. Well's bungalow being burnt down, and that it was supposed to be done by the Sepoys in revenge for his tasting a bottle of medicine in the hospital. Well, a day or two after I wrote, the whole of the huts of the Sepoys of the 13th Regiment were burnt, it was supposed by accident, but, from after events, that seems rather doubtful. You may imagine that huts with thatched roofs for a thousand men made a pretty good blaze. Last Sunday week it was my turn to take the evening service at cantonment church. There was an unusually thin congregation. Towards the end of the prayers a servant came into church, and spoke first to Major Bird, of the 48th, and then to Mr. Dashwood, of the same regiment. They both went out, and afterwards others were called away. I began to think that some more houses had been set on fire, but of course I went on with the service. The ladies began to look very uncomfortable; one or two went out of church; one or two others crossed over the aisle to friends who were sitting on the other side. Altogether, I had not a very attentive congregation. After service we found that the 7th Irregular Infantry, a thousand strong, quartered at the Moosa Bagh, had mutinied, and that the 71st, 48th, 7th Cavalry, and a troop of English Artillery, with six guns, had gone to quell them. This was the cause of the officers being called out of church. The 32nd Queen's, as I afterwards found, also marched to the Moosa Bagh, and an Irregular cavalry regiment, so that no less than 3,500 men marched to put down the mutiny. I felt very much inclined to ride down myself to see what was going on, but as the Moosa Bagh is seven miles from our house, and as I should have left my wife all alone, I stayed where I was. I thought of what William the Third said, when he was told that the Bishop

of Derry had been shot at the ford at the battle
of the Boyne—" What took him there?"
However, if so strong a force had not been sent
that the mutineers were completely overawed,
there might have been work for me to do. I
heard all about what took place from Sir Henry
Lawrence and one of the Artillery officers. Sir
Henry Lawrence went himself, as the highest
civil authority. When the troops arrived there
—somewhere about nine o'clock P.M., a bright
moonlight night—the mutineers were ordered
out; so out they came. They had gone to
their huts. Their mutiny consisted in refusing
to use some cartridges which had been given
them, because they thought they were greased
with English fat. They also threatened to shoot
one of their officers. Well, the mutineers were
drawn up in line, and Sir Henry Lawrence went
forward and harangued them, and then retired
to the neighbourhood of the six cannon, which
were drawn up in front of the mutineers. The
officer commanding the Artillery asked him if he
should give orders to load; he said, " Yes;" so
they loaded with grape. In loading, one of the
artillerymen anticipated the next order, and
lighted the match for firing the cannon. The
mutineers no sooner saw this than they imagined
that they were going to be fired upon, and
immediately they flung down their muskets, and

ran for their lives, and the 7th Cavalry after them, to bring them back. So ended the mutiny, happily without bloodshed; but this certainly would not have been the case, had not so strong a force been taken against them that they had no chance. Ninety of their muskets were found to be loaded. The Irregular regiments here were in the king's service before the annexation, and they are not, of course, in such a state of discipline as the Regulars. Sir Henry Lawrence told me that it was a mercy there was not a shot fired. If there had been, there would have been no stopping a fight, and the unfortunate mutineers would have been regularly massacred. Another most absurd story they have got hold of. This came out in the examination of some of the mutineers before Sir Henry Lawrence. They say that in consequence of the Crimean war there are a great many widows in England, and that these are to be brought out and married to the Rajahs in Oudh, and that their children, brought up as Christians, are to inherit all the estates! The natives are like babies—they will believe anything. However, Sir Henry looks very serious over the present state of affairs. No doubt the friends of the King of Oudh will make all the plots they can, and give the Government no end of trouble. I don't believe there will be a rising in Lucknow, but I know that the natives, many of them, wish it, and that our commanders here have prepared for it. The officers of the 32nd Queen's are not allowed to sleep away from the messhouse, as they formerly were, so that they may be ready at a moment's notice. Two cannon have been sent down to the city to strengthen the 32nd. If the Native Infantry and Cavalry regiments were to turn against us, we should be in a very ticklish position. We should have only the 32nd, and the Company's English Artillery, about 680 in all, and some three hundred civilians, against six Native Infantry regiments, three Regulars, three Irregulars, nearly six thousand in all, and two regiments, one Irregular, one Regular, of Cavalry, more than one thousand, besides the whole population of Lucknow, several hundred thousand men. And thus it is all over India. Our government in this country is the most wonderful thing in the history of the world. We are not one to a hundred of the inhabitants, nor anything like it. Our strength, under God—whose hand, I think, one may plainly see in our governing this immense country—lies in the disunion of its inhabitants, their being divided into Mahommedans and Hindoos, who hate one another with the deadliest of all enmities—the proverbial *odium theologicum*. If a Mahommedan makes a plot, a Hindoo reveals it to the English, and *vice versâ*. Besides, there are two parties among the Mahommedans, who hate each other nearly as much as if they were Mahommedans and Hindoos. Another chief reason of our keeping the country is the goodness and regularity of our pay.

All the people here have been in a regular fright, lest their bungalows should be burnt down; and they envy me my brick-built house, which would be very difficult to set on fire. Besides this, the natives have a superstitious reverence for a "Padré." They say, for instance, that my house is haunted, and that none but a "Padré" can live in it. I have often been asked, "whether I have seen the ghost," by English people. They say Mr. Beechey, who died here, haunts it. Did I tell you, that one night, hearing a strange noise at one of the doors, I went out with my revolver? No one was there, so I called the chokeedar, and asked him what it was. He looked very solemn, and said, "Beechey Sahib (or Mr. Beechey)." Next night, I heard the noise again; I sallied out, and killed a large rat, who, no doubt, was the "party" who caused the noise. So I showed him to the chokeedar, and told him I had caught "Beechey Sahib," which amused him prodigiously. . . . .

All this news is likely enough to have a bad effect on the disaffected here, and our Brigadier is taking means to prevent a surprise in case of the native troops mutinying. The Queen's regiment in the city has been reinforced by a troop of Native Artillery. It is unfortunate that they are so far from cantonments (five miles), and the natives might, by barricading Lucknow, make their progress here very slow, if not impossible. I asked the Brigade-Major, who is a friend of mine, why they had not sent the English Artillery to reinforce the 32nd? He said, "Because in case of mutiny they are all we have to defend us here." We think the Native Artillery will be true whatever happens, but, to provide against their treachery, a soldier from the 32nd has been appointed to each gun, who, if he saw anything going wrong, would give warning to the regiment, and they would instantly shoot the mutineers. It is also intended to have a company of the 32nd up here to protect the English Artillery in case of a row. If the Artillery are well protected, no doubt they would give a good account of the Sepoy regiments, should they mutiny; but, if not protected by English soldiers, they would be done for in case of a mutiny. There are only ninety of them. However, I don't anticipate any worse consequences than have already happened. The mutiny has spread from station to station, and, having been put down at each, has, I think, ceased. I think we have had our share here, and have reason to be most thankful that things were no worse; but time will show.

To change the subject, I am right glad to see that Oxford has beaten Cambridge so easily in the boat-race. It is now eleven years since I pulled in it.

Monday Morning.

Yesterday morning it was my turn to take the morning service at the 32nd Regiment, and in the city church. So I started in my buggy at five A.M. for the service at the barracks. I had not driven more than half a mile, before I met Mrs. Inglis and another lady and an officer, all three on horseback. I asked Mrs. Inglis what brought her to cantonments so early in the morning. She had already ridden six miles, and it was hardly five o'clock. She said, "Oh, we are all coming to take care of you; you will meet the regiment a little farther on." I drove on, and in five minutes met about 450 men of the 32nd, with Colonel Inglis at their head. "It's no use your going on, Padré," said he, "for we're all here." I said, "Very well; will you have service in the road?" He laughed; said that would not do, but that he would be obliged if I would come to them in the evening. It was no use going home again, as I had service in the city church at seven; so I drove slowly on, and presently met my brother Padré, Harris, coming up to cantonments to take the morning service. He had come from the Martinière, where he is living. We exchanged a word or two, and then I drove on to the Gubbinses, where I had a cup of tea, and some talk with Mr. Gubbins on the state of affairs. Foster Cunliffe was there also. He commands the artillery in the city.

I learned that in the night some natives had gone to Captain Hayes, the military secretary, and had told him that parties had been appointed in the three Sepoy regiments to go round to murder us all in our beds, and set the houses on fire. Captain Hayes, not knowing whether this was true or not, thought it wise to take all the precautions he could; so he sent to Colonel Inglis (as I understood) for help, and he sent at once a regiment of Native Cavalry, and the 32nd started from the city for cantonments before daybreak. Cunliffe also told me that the 32nd have completely left their barracks in the city, hospital and all. The sick have been brought to the Residency, so have the women, and the Residency is garrisoned by 150 men of the 32nd, and by the battery of Native Artillery. All the ladies, wives of civilians, who live in different parts of the city, have come into the Residency. Some are staying at Mr. Gubbins's, some at Dr. Fayrer's, some at Mr. Ommanney's, &c. By the Residency, I mean a piece of ground a good deal elevated above the rest of the city, allotted by the King of Oudh, when he first put himself under British "protection" some fifty years ago, to the British civil residents. It is walled round almost entirely; on one side native houses abut upon it, but on the other three sides it is tolerably clear. Roads without gates in some places connect it with the city, but it is not at all a bad place to make a stand, certainly the best in Lucknow, to which it is a sort of "Acropolis." The Residency contains the Chief Commissioner's house, Mr. Gubbins's, Mr. Ommanney's, Dr. Fayrer's, the post-office, city hospital, electric telegraph office, the church (last not least), &c. You will perhaps say, "Why did not all the 32nd garrison this place, and the rest of the English retire to it?" I'll tell you. We don't think the disaffected in the city are likely to rise, unless they know that they will be backed by the Native Infantry regiments. Now, if all the 32nd had gone into the Residency, there would have been no power to keep the three Native Infantry regiments in check. But now that the 32nd and English Artillery are in cantonments, the three Native Infantry regiments know that, if they mutiny, they will have to meet the 32nd and Artillery; and though they are five to one, and have artillery themselves (for there is an Irregular battery besides those I have mentioned), yet they have a wholesome dread of the English. They know that we have beaten them ten or twenty to one before now. Well, now, I don't think you need alarm yourself for us. You see, the Native Infantry, Cavalry, and Artillery are kept in check here by the 32nd and English Artillery, so that they cannot effect a junction with the city people without a fight for it, and they have no stomach for that, unless they are sure of being able to murder all before them, or are led by their English officers, who of course would all leave them. The English in the Residency are tolerably well protected by their position and garrison, and above all we must hope and trust that that over-ruling Providence which has so long enabled us, one to a thousand, to govern this country, will not desert us now. At church I said the Prayer in time of War and Tumults, and so, having in public and in private committed ourselves into God's hands, and taken all possible precaution, we calmly and fearlessly await the result. My opinion is that in a few days a terrible example will have been made of the Delhi insurgents, and this, and the precautions taken, will show the natives that it is their wisest plan to keep still. I had service in the city church: it was very fairly attended. After it was over, Schilling, the principal of the Martinière, asked me what I thought he had better do. The Martinière is a mile out of Lucknow, on the opposite side of cantonments. There are about eighty boys boarding there, eight masters, and two sergeants. There is a guard of six Sepoys, but the worst of it is, we don't know how soon our guards may turn upon us. I advised him as a matter of precaution to get some muskets and ammunition. We went first to Mr. Gubbins, who thought with me, and then I drove Schilling down to cantonments, and we went to Sir Henry Lawrence. He offered to give him a larger guard; but I said, "No; if we can't trust the guard, the smaller it is the better. We want to arm ourselves, lest they should turn upon us." So Sir H. Lawrence gave him an order for twelve muskets and ammunition, and gave him authority to command the guard, who previously were under one of their own men. So Schilling drove off in my buggy, and I have not heard from him since. He intended to have all the boys and masters in the main building, and distribute the six Sepoys as much as possible. The house is very strong. There is only one way to the upper part of the main building, up a narrow staircase, where half-a-dozen resolute men might defend themselves for a week. All this precaution may seem almost absurd, but what has happened at Meerut and Delhi shows us that it is necessary. Indeed, if there were anything like union among the natives, and a clever man at their head, all that we could do probably would not prevent our being cut off to a man, and the English would have to re-conquer the country.

My own precautions in self-defence are very simple. In case of a murdering party going about here as at Meerut, Emmie and I will go up to the roof of the house, and the baboo will go off for the nearest party of the 32nd. If they find out where we are, they must come up after us. The staircase to the roof is outside the house, and no one could attempt to ascend it without my having a shot at him with my revolver, and I should be protected by the parapet of the house. I could have at least four shots at them as they were coming up the staircase, and could not miss, and there are two doors on the staircase; so I have no doubt that I could hold out for ten minutes against almost any number, and in the meanwhile assistance would arrive.

I am uncommonly obliged to Edward for that revolver. I should be very sorry to shoot any one, but it is not likely that I am going to see my wife murdered before my face; if they do kill me, unless they get me at great disadvantage, depend upon it some of them, as the sailors say, "will lose the number of their mess."

Now you know my little arrangements in case of an attack. Things throughout India never looked so serious. It may all come to an end soon, and the country be more tranquil than ever, or we may all be murdered in a week. I think it will be the former. Whatever happens cannot be without the will of God, and "Heaven," as the old sailor said, "is as near us here as at home." To show you how serious people in authority think the state of affairs, the other day, after the mutiny in the 7th Irregulars had been put down, I said laughingly to Sir Henry Lawrence, "Why, Sir Henry, you may have some work cut out for you now before you go home." He said, very gravely, "I can assure you it is no laughing matter." I heard Colonel Inglis say the same thing to a man who was inclined to be too jocular yesterday.

Yesterday evening I went at six o'clock to the 32nd to give them Divine Service. I found them encamped in a mango tope about two hundred yards from my house. Poor fellows! there they had been in tents all day, the hot wind blowing, and the thermometer at 110°. Colonel Inglis had been to us in the afternoon to ask us to give up our house for the soldiers. Of course we consented, and had begun dismantling it, when there came a message that he had got them otherwise accommodated. He wanted my house because it has no thatch to be set on fire, and is near the artillery. The 13th have given up their mess-house for the soldiers; indeed, we ought all to turn out for them, if necessary, for the heat will soon knock them up. Five went into hospital yesterday, and they are, under God, our only hope in case of an outbreak. I gave the 32nd part of the Evening Service, and an extempore sermon on Deuteronomy viii. 11, bearing on the whole chapter. They stood in hollow square, muskets in hand. At seven was our regular Service at church. It was pretty well attended. Many, no doubt, were afraid to come. It would, of course, be very easy for the Sepoys to surround the church and murder us all; but it is of no use being afraid of anything, or our lives, under present circumstances, would be a burden to us. Sir H. Lawrence was there. Now, I have told you the exact state of things, because you would be sure to see in the papers something about it, perhaps an exaggerated account.

To say that we are in no danger of an outbreak would be absurd, but I do not think there will be one. Fancy how much worse than ours the position is of those, who are at stations, where there are no English troops! and this is the case with all except the large ones. When this is over, the Government must send us more troops, or we shall never be able to hold India. The Sepoys have never shown such a mutinous spirit before. There's no knowing what the cause is. I think it is a combination of circumstances. The immediate cause is perhaps the obnoxious cartridges. Agents have been at work (in whose interest it is impossible to say) persuading the Sepoys that they are all to be made Christians. Then I think the annexation of Oudh has had its effect. Some lay the blame on a colonel of a regiment at Barrackpore, who has been preaching Christianity in the bazaar of the station. The Sepoys could hear him if they liked. This may have had a bad effect; but I believe myself that the bad lives, which many Christians lead, has had at least as much to do with the mutinies as the preaching of Christianity. We may be sure that it has had the effect of making Him, who is above all, withdraw His protection. Our duty to preach the Gospel is plain; if it meets with opposition, are we to be astonished when we read what the Bible says? Perhaps it may not be wise at present for officers to preach; but how was Christianity spread in the West? Planted in spite of the most furious opposition, it throve because watered with the blood of martyrs.

Surely all missionaries are not to be muzzled, because the preaching of Christianity has roused opposition. No doubt we must be careful and wary; but we have God's commands to obey —"Go ye into all the world, and preach the Gospel to every creature." I do not believe He will allow our country to suffer, if she faithfully tries to carry this out. Had the Gospel been preached as it should have been; had Christians lived as Christians, perhaps this trouble would never have come upon us. I trust our rulers will not lose sight, whatever befalls, of the command, "We ought to obey God rather than man."

Emmie is very well, and has shown the greatest coolness and courage.

...... Fancy the 32nd out all yesterday with the thermometer 110°! Just make a room into an atmosphere of that kind, and try how you like it.

Ever your affectionate Son.

Lucknow, May 28, 1857.

MY DEAREST MOTHER,

I WRITE by the Calcutta mail, thinking it likely that the road to Bombay may be stopped before the 1st of June, when the mail goes out, to tell you that we are alive and well; as what you see in the papers may make you think the contrary.

..... Last week we heard from Mrs. Henry Salt, to the effect that she was safe at Meerut. She gave us no particulars, merely saying, that it was scarcely possible to conceive the horrors that had taken place at Delhi.

There is now again no mail between this and Meerut, owing to the mutiny of the 9th Regiment at Allygurh.

Lady Outram was living with her son at Allygurh. She, poor thing, naturally enough, fearing the fate of the ladies at Meerut and Delhi, when she heard of the outbreak, hurried out of her house with her son, to get to some place of safety; and in running along the road, I believe without shoes, cut her feet dreadfully. However, she got safely to Agra, where she now is with her son.

One night last week, while we were at tea, I heard a good deal of noise, and on going into the verandah, there was, apparently, a bungalow near our house on fire. We were told that the commencement of an outbreak would probably be the fires, and that in case of an alarm we were instantly to retire to the Residency in cantonments, it being guarded by a company of the 32nd Queen's. Well, there was a big fire, and no mistake; it lighted up my compound; so I thought, now's the time to be off; the next thing will probably be a rush of Sepoys into the compound, and then retreat will be cut off. Besides, at the Residency I should be of use as one of its defenders; at my own house I should probably in the end be killed. So I told Emmie she must come along with me directly. She was very cool, and wanted me to wait and go in the buggy; but I thought it better not. So off we went across the compound in the dark, I taking my revolver. It is only about a hundred yards across the compound; then there is the road between us and Sir Henry Lawrence's, the Residency bungalow aforesaid. A mud wall covered with tiles runs round our compound; it is about four feet high. I lifted Emmie on the top of this, got over myself, and then took her into my arms on the other side. I did not know that there was a ditch, lost my footing, and down we both came. "There now, you've gone and killed yourself," was all Emmie said, so it was plain that she was not hurt; neither was I. So I took my revolver and ammunition from the bearer who had come with us thus far, and we ran across the road to Sir Henry's. While we were crossing, the Cavalry picket dashed down the road on their way to the fire. Emmie got rather alarmed now, thinking they would turn upon us; but they did not. When we reached the Residency, we found twenty or thirty ladies there, and Dr. Brydon, the sole survivor of the Khyber Pass massacre of 1842, taking care of them. Sir Henry and all the other gentlemen had gone to the fire. However, it proved a false alarm so far as a rising was concerned.

..... On Friday a company, 100 men, of the 32nd Regiment, marched for Cawnpore in the middle of the night, Sir Henry Lawrence having had a requisition from Sir Hugh Wheeler, commanding at Cawnpore, in expectation of an outbreak. All the ladies there retire every night to the church to sleep! that being the only brick-built building in the place.

..... The band in the evenings was almost deserted; the only conversation, inquiries about Meerut and Delhi, and the probability of the Sepoys remaining faithful. Towards nightfall every one seemed to grow very nervous; doors were firmly secured, and officers, to say nothing of chaplains, slept with revolvers under their pillows. On Sunday morning it was my turn to take duty in cantonments. The 32nd and Artillery could not be allowed to leave their guns to go to church, but they were drawn up in hollow square; and I drove Emmie, who did not like to be left alone at home, to service on the parade ground. At a quarter past five A.M. I said part of Morning Prayers, and read the second lesson; and preached extempore on two verses of the Psalms for the day, the 24th of May:—" It is better to trust in the Lord than to put any confidence in man. It is better to trust in the Lord than to put any confidence in princes."* I gave them instances from Scripture of men who, putting their trust in God, had been delivered from great dangers; showed how many God's promises are to those who trust in Him; and then inquired who those are who have a right to trust in Him. I showed them that if they wished to have His help in adversity, they must serve Him in prosperity, and tried to prove to them the necessity of prayer, &c. &c.

I find I can get on very well now in extempore preaching, if I prepare beforehand; and it has a much better effect in the open air, and especially standing in the middle of a hollow square, where all can see what you have in your hand.

I had written a sermon on the same text, which I preached at seven A.M. at cantonments, and at seven P.M. at the city church, to two other and different congregations. I forgot to say that I told the soldiers in the morning how completely, under God, we trusted in them; that we feared no odds for the descendants of the men who won Plassy, and had themselves been tried

* See this Sermon at the end of the volume.

in many a hard-fought field. The 32nd were at Mooltan, Goojerat, and other battles. I cheered up the people in the churches as much as I could, and I hear that my sermon was considered appropriate and well timed.

On Monday morning, about half-past five, I was driving Emmie out, when at our gate we were met by Sir Henry Lawrence, who told us that, having heard a report which had caused him some alarm, he thought it would be better for us to go and stay for a day or two with the Gubbinses. We did not at all want to turn out, but having been told by Colonel Inglis of the 32nd, whom I afterwards met, that he had sent his wife to the Residency, I thought it would be better to take Sir Henry's advice. So about eight A.M. we left cantonments, having packed up some clothes, silver, and a few books. We left the house in charge of the baboo, and one or two servants whom we can trust. We found Mrs. Gubbins puzzled to know what to do with all the ladies in her house. As soon as I had seen Emmie safely housed, I went to the hospital, which is now in the Residency ball-room, a building detached from the Chief Commissioner's house. It is a beautiful room, or rather suite of rooms, and the men are doing much better there than they were in their own hospital. There were forty in hospital;

and three bad cases. Most of the forty could handle a musket, and would do it well, too, in case of an outbreak. I read and prayed with the men whose cases were worst, and talked to most of them. "It would be great odds, Sir, sure enough, if them Sepoys was to rise! 4,000 against 400; but we ain't afraid of them. We'd follow Sir Henry through fire and water; he's a good un; and a right good man to soldiers. Oh yes, Sir! we know what Jack Sepoy's good for; he'll fight well enough, if he's got an English regiment to back him, and English officers to command him; but I don't believe he'd be any use against *us*: about three rounds of grape would be enough for Jack!"

There was no swagger or bluster about what these men said. "By the help of God," many of them added, "we'll give a good account of them."

I found the hospital sergeant, a very good man and brave soldier, very ill. His wife, poor thing, was in sad, low spirits. She said, "I shouldn't care for the Sepoys, Sir, if only Knight was well."

On going back to breakfast, I found a large party assembled. We have here now, besides Mr. and Mrs. Gubbins, Mrs. Hayes, Mrs. Inglis and three children, (she is wife of the Colonel of the 32nd, and *such* a nice woman, and such a good mother!) Major and Mrs. Banks and baby, Mr. and Mrs. Thornhill, Mrs. Brydon, wife of the "sole survivor," and two children, Mrs. Couper and two children, and ourselves.

. . . . Mr. Gubbins has done what he could to fortify his house; he is a splendid shot, and then there are Major Banks, Thornhill and myself, with my revolver.

. . . . But I don't think the Sepoys will rise now; I think they would have done so, had not Sir Henry been too quick for them, in putting the place into a state of defence.

. . . . Last night I was awoke by a man coming into our room. I rushed out to seize him, when I was stopped by Captain Forbes, the husband of Emmie's friend, who commands an Oudh Irregular regiment of cavalry. He said, "Don't be alarmed; it's only my servant; I told him to take a note to Mr. Gubbins, and he thought yours was his room." He then told me that an electric telegraph message had just come from Cawnpore to say, that the Oudh Irregular Infantry had mutinied, and that Sir Hugh Wheeler had sent them away across the bridge over the Ganges, back again towards Lucknow. Forbes said he could not think why Sir Hugh Wheeler had not disarmed them. I suppose because he did not dare. Mr. Gubbins then came in, which put a stop to our conversation; and Forbes soon after went off, with the part of his regiment which is here, towards Cawnpore. This was at twelve, last night, and we have heard nothing of them yet.

Our forces are getting fast towards Delhi. Henry Salt will, I suppose, be in the affair, if one takes place; but I can hardly believe that the villains will stand, when they hear what's coming against them. If they do, a fearful revenge will be taken; for their cold-blooded murders, and the abuse of the English ladies, and other women who fell into their hands, have set the men's blood on fire.

. . . . . Very likely this will be my last letter for some time; it may be my last altogether.* I hope not; but come what may, I am prepared; and whatever you hear of me, it will not be that I have disgraced myself. Emmie sends her best love.

God bless you all.

Ever your affectionate

HENRY S. POLEHAMPTON.

* It was so.

EXTRACTS

FROM THE

DIARY OF THE REV. H. S. POLEHAMPTON.

Cantonments, Lucknow.

Ascension Day, May 21*st*, 1857.—I took service in cantonments, and Harris in the city. Here we had a congregation of sixteen, all ladies; of whom nine stayed to receive the Holy Communion. In the city Harris had only three persons for his congregation. He was very much disgusted, and no wonder; for, exclusive of the garrison, there are now more than two hundred people living within a stone's throw of the church. Many were, no doubt, wearied with a sleepless and anxious night; but surely even this ought not to have kept them away from the House of God at such a critical time as the present. At cantonments, I have no doubt, we should have had some officers at church; but Sir Henry Lawrence was holding a levée to announce his being appointed to command all the troops in Oudh, with the rank of Major-General. I do not suppose he could avoid holding the levée at that hour.

After church, I took Emmie for a short drive; and then, having put some books and papers into my buggy, I drove to the three bungalows, where the men of the 32nd Regiment are stationed. In Murray's bungalow was one company. Another, the sergeant told me, had gone away in the night, at twelve o'clock. This was to Cawnpore, as I afterwards found; whence had come a report of an uneasy feeling among the natives. This has weakened our garrison. We have not now more than 250 men here, exclusive of the Artillery (ninety more).

But what need we care for this, if we can only feel that "God is our hope and strength; a very "present help in trouble?" "Though an host "of men were laid against me, yet shall not my "heart be afraid; and, though there rose up war "against me, yet will I put my trust in Him." Oh that the present crisis may teach us all to strive more to *deserve* His help!

To return: one of the men at Murray's bungalow spoke most highly of the admiration of the regiment for Sir Henry Lawrence. "There is not a man of us, Sir, but what would be proud to follow Sir Henry through fire and water."

s

I left some books and papers with these men, and then went to where two other companies are quartered. With them is a man named Jones; an old parishioner of mine at St. Chad's. He was one of Yeoman's chair-men. I took him two or three "Eddowes' Journals," and Pidgeon's "Shrewsbury Guide;" with which he was much pleased. I then went to the hospital, talked to the men, and left them some books, religious and instructive. Then to the bungalow opposite the Residency (in cantonments), where the band and fifty privates are, and left them also some books; amongst others, a copy of the "Life of Hedley Vicars." Then I called at the Residency, hearing that Colonel Inglis was ill. Not much the matter. Couper told me that seven English regiments are fast closing round Delhi. At the band in the evening, Fayrer told me that his brother has a commission given him in the Irregular Cavalry, and that he had gone to Cawnpore with them. Came home to tea. We had not been at tea long, before I heard an unusual noise, and, going out into the verandah, I saw a bungalow, as I and the servants thought, on fire.

We had been told, and indeed knew from the experience of Meerut, that the natives always begin their atrocities by firing bungalows. We had been told, too, that as soon as a riot commenced, the best plan would be for us all to join at the Residency; because we should be there together, and so stronger for defence: and a company of the 32nd, quartered close by, would specially defend it. Thinking it very likely that the next thing might be a rush of mutinous Sepoys into the house, I thought it best to get Emmie away at once. So I got my revolver and ammunition, and told her to come. She was not at all frightened, and scarcely excited; and wished me to wait till the buggy should be got ready. I, however, felt that, if an outbreak had really begun, there was not a moment to be lost. We might be cut off from the Residency in a minute or two; and the buggy would, of course, show at once that we were English. So I said, "No; come along at once." Emmie then came; having first secured a little box containing daguerreotypes of our darling in Heaven.

My bearer followed. We went straight across the compound to the part of the wall opposite Sir Henry's back gate. I found it higher than I had expected. However, I took Emmie up in my arms, and placed her on the tiles on the top of it; then got up myself, and down on the other side. The fall was about six feet. I then called Emmie to drop into my arms, which she did; when, from the bank being very steep, I lost my footing, and we came down together into the ditch. However I held her up as well as I could; and we were neither of us hurt. We then went quickly across the road into the Residency garden. As we crossed, the Irregular Cavalry galloped by on their way to the fire. Emmie was rather frightened at them, as we had heard so many stories of native soldiers proving treacherous. However, they did us no harm; and we went on to Sir Henry Lawrence's. . . . (Nearly all the officers' wives, with their children, have been staying at the Residency ever since the news of the rising at Meerut came.) Sir Henry and all the officers had gone to the fire. It turned out not to be a bungalow, as I had supposed; neither was there any rising. A range of stables was burnt, and the fire at one time nearly caught Mr. Barwell's house. It seems very probable that this fire was lighted by some native for the purpose of drawing out the English troops. The authorities had had information which made them expect a fire this night; and they had sent particular orders to the Artillery and 32nd not to turn out till sent for. When we knew that it was a false alarm, we ordered the buggy, and returned.

Saturday, May 23d.—Up at five o'clock. Took Emmie for a drive, and then went to the Artillery Hospital (the occupants of which, however, have been removed to the Residency in the city); thence to the Artillery barracks, where I talked to many of the men; thence to the officers' mess, where I talked for some time with three of them. On my way home, called on Sir Henry Lawrence to ask if it is necessary for me to have a guard of Suwārs, when I go and come back from the church in the city to-morrow evening; and to ask Colonel Inglis to make arrangements about service for the soldiers to-morrow morning. During the day, wrote a sermon, on Psalm cxviii. 8, 9, one of the Psalms for the day: "It is better to trust in the Lord than to put any confidence in man: it is better to trust in the Lord than to put any confidence in princes."

Sunday, May 24*th.*—Up at half-past four. Service for three companies of the 32nd and the men of the Artillery at a quarter past five, near the guns on the parade-ground. The men were drawn up in hollow square, having their muskets ready loaded with them. Emmie went with me, and sat in the buggy near the square. I said part of the Morning Prayers, read the second lesson, and preached extempore on the same words, which I had chosen for my text for my written sermon. I, however, treated them differently. I was enabled to speak, as far as the time would allow, pretty fully, and without hesitation;

and I humbly trust that the Spirit of God may fix in the men's hearts some of the lessons which I endeavoured to teach. Service at six A.M. at cantonment church. A very fair congregation. In both my sermons I endeavoured to show how fully our present circumstances have taught us our dependence upon God.

* * * * *

Monday, May 25*th.*—As we were driving out at half-past five this morning, we met Sir Henry Lawrence. He told us that, as soon as we had breakfasted, we had better go down to the Residency in Lucknow, as they had had an alarm. So, after taking our drive, we packed up our valuables, and came to Mr. Gubbins'. We found seven ladies already here; and that Dr. Fayrer's and the Residency were full. Mr. Gubbins took us in. All day people were anxiously listening for the first sound of firing; but the day passed without anything. Mr. Gubbins has had a parapet made at the top of his house, pierced for musketry, and has all his guns loaded. He has six men (natives), on whom he thinks he can depend, of the Police Regiment. Besides these, in case of an attack, there are Mr. Gubbins, Major Banks, Thornhill, and myself, for the defence of the house. I have no doubt that we could hold out for a good many hours: but, in case of an attack from a large body of men,

I think it would be well to fall back to the Residency here.

Tuesday, Wednesday.—These days have passed much in the same way as the first on which we came. It is fearfully hot; much more so than at our own house. Every room here is full. There are in the house, Major and Mrs. Banks, Mr. and Mrs. Thornhill, Mrs. Inglis, Mrs. Couper, Mrs. Brydon, Mrs. Hayes. Emmie and I sleep in the drawing-room. As we should have to wait a long time for a bath-room here, we drive every morning to our own house at about six o'clock, have our bath and a sleep there, and come back to breakfast at ten. It is, no doubt, necessary that the ladies should be here; for, in case of a rising of the Sepoys, they would march on the city, and the 32nd and Artillery would follow them; and then the ladies must either shift for themselves, or a party of the 32nd must be left to guard them; so that their being here is all right; and, as all the sick have been moved into the Residency banquetting-hall, as a temporary hospital, this is clearly my place too. On Tuesday, there was an alarm of a rising at Cawnpore, which caused considerable excitement here. However, it turned out that there was not a rising; though there was very nearly being one.

On Wednesday, three men were taken, in the lines of the 13th Regiment Native Infantry, endeavouring to incite the men to mutiny. One of the Sepoys, whom they were trying to seduce, seized one of them. The man drew his knife upon him, when another Sepoy wounded him with a bayonet in the chest.

They were taken to Thornhill to be tried. He passed them on to Major Banks, who is trying them to-day. The general impression seems to be that they cannot be hanged, as the punishment for mutiny is transportation. However, they *may* sentence one to death for drawing his knife. I really think that the men ought to be hanged; but whether, in our present weak state, it will be wise to do so, is another thing. We have only about 600 men here altogether, if so many. Three companies are in cantonments, with the Artillery; about one and a half here in the Residency, with a battery of Native Artillery; and in a fort in the middle of the city is another company of the 32nd, with some Native Artillery. This place commands a great part of the city. Last night a telegraphic despatch came from Mr. Colvin, saying, that the Dooāb, a tract of country between the Ganges and Jumna, was in a state of anarchy. Sir H. Lawrence has sent them all the native troops, on which he can rely. No news from Delhi yet. We do not think we can hear before the 1st. News came this morning, that 200 of the Sappers and Miners, who revolted at Delhi, have been cut up by a faithful cavalry regiment. News came yesterday that Ferozeshore in the Punjab is in a state of mutiny; but that *there* also a faithful cavalry regiment charged and dispersed the mutineers. I am so sleepy from the heat that I can hardly write this.

Saturday, May 30*th.*—We drove this evening into cantonments, and to baby's grave. To-night, Emmie and I were going to bed, at a quarter past ten, in Mr. Gubbins' drawing-room, when he came into the room, looking rather excited, and said, "Polehampton, you had better get Mrs. Polehampton up to the roof directly: there is a row in cantonments; I have heard heavy firing there." We dressed, and were soon on the roof, which is reached by a cork-screw stone staircase. We found several ladies there before us, and in a short time the whole household was gathered there, children and all. We looked out towards cantonments, three miles distant, and saw that several bungalows were blazing. As we looked, one after another sprang up into flame. Then we heard rapid file firing—then the deep booming of four or five cannon—then all was still, except occasional dropping shots.

In the meantime, the fire seemed to spread wider and wider, till it was evident that nearly the whole of cantonments was in a blaze. The firing may have lasted an hour. When it began, or rather as soon as I heard it (for Mr. Gubbins had heard eight guns fired before we went on to the roof), I called those close about me on the roof together, and offered a few words of prayer that God would be pleased to make our cause his and give to us the victory. Those whom I asked to join with me readily consented, and ended with a hearty " Amen."

We expected every moment a rising of the townspeople; and Mr. Gubbins distributed guns and rifles to all of our little garrison, consisting of Major Banks, Thornhill, and myself. Besides ourselves, there were six of Weston's native police in the garden, on whom Mr. Gubbins entirely depended.

Presently Captain Carnegie, of the police, came up. He had been half way to cantonments, when he met Dr. Pitt in a buggy, with a Sepoy of the 13th, who, he said, had saved his life. Pitt gave the first information as to what had taken place; the whole account of which, as I afterwards gathered it, I give in this place.

About half-past nine o'clock, the men on guard at the guns saw parties of Sepoys steadily advancing up the road towards them, firing as they came. They immediately called the rest, and brought the guns to bear upon them. No one seems to know who gave the order to fire; but firing began from the right of the battery, and was taken up by gun after gun until all the eight were fired. The Sepoys immediately dispersed, and set on fire and plundered the bungalows. As soon as Brigadier Handscomb heard of it, he, with Barwell and Germon as aides-de-camp, galloped to where the firing was taking place. He came upon some of the 32nd, who were lying down to avoid the fire. They begged him not to go farther on, as they were sure that there were men concealed just ahead of them. He went, however: a regular volley was fired, and he fell. His body was at once rescued by the 32nd, but he was dead.

Poor Grant (71st Native Infantry) was on duty at the centre picket, close to the church. The men first fired on him, and wounded him. He fell, and some of the men, who were faithful, begged him to try to get away; but he said, "Oh, let me alone; let me alone!" and then some of the brutes, who had shot him, bayonetted him.

Ensign Raleigh had only joined the 7th Cavalry a day or two before. He was sick in his house, and when he discovered what was going on, ran out, and tried to escape; but the mutineers overtook, and murdered him.

We slept but little that night on the roof of the house.

Most of us leaned against the parapet, watching the fires in cantonments, until dawn. Having to take a funeral, I then went down to read the service. As I came back, boom, boom, went the guns again in cantonments. The 32nd and Artillery moved forward at dawn, and drove the mutineers before them out of cantonments. The wretches never let them get within musket range, but fled towards the cavalry barracks. When about half way there, the guns opened upon the mutineers with round shot. I cannot find out whether they killed many, but should think not, as they were much scattered.

Mr. Gubbins had, at day-break, ridden down to cantonments, with about eight Suwārs. After the guns had fired, he dashed after the mutineers, and pursued some of them into a village. Some of them stood, and fired at him, but missed him.

He fired his pistol at a man and wounded him in the heel and took him and seven other prisoners. The 7th Cavalry pretended to charge, but did nothing. A few hours after, they mutinied and joined the other fugitives.

It was impossible to have Church this morning; people were in such a state of excitement and alarm.

Nothing new occurred till towards two o'clock. Then Major Banks brought word that a rising was hourly expected in the city. He said that if he sent a Suwār with a message to cantonments he would take a very long time going, and that he could not trust one of them. He also said that he doubted whether the ladies ought not now to leave Mr. Gubbins' house, as he did not think it tenable, in case of a regular attack, by so few of us. I offered, if he liked, to drive down to cantonments, tell Sir Henry Lawrence of the intended rising, and ask Mr. Gubbins what he wished to have done about his house. Major Banks accepted my offer, but told me that I might get fired at from any house.

However, as it was clear that a messenger was wanted, I went. I fear I left poor Emmie in a state of anxiety; but it was a time when, if a duty came before one, it was to be done without fear of consequences. So off I drove, asking, as I went, the protection of God.

When I got to the top of the bridge, I saw a man riding towards me with a gun in his hand. He seemed very like a runaway mutineer. He looked hard at me with a troubled countenance, and brought the muzzle of his gun round towards me. I took up my revolver, keeping the muzzle pointed towards him, but without presenting it. He dropped the muzzle of his gun again and rode on. I fully expected that we should have exchanged shots.

On the road I met several suspicious-looking characters, armed; but they took no farther notice, than by staring at me.

I delivered my message to Sir Henry Lawrence—that a rising was immediately anticipated, and that some rioters had already sacked Mr. Mendes' house, and seemed flushed with success, and ready for more.

Sir Henry and the council of war, which was being held, seemed struck with this; but nothing was said to me.

Couper, the secretary, wrote to Brigadier Gray, to send more men to the Residency.

Mr. Gubbins said that the ladies had better go to the Residency, but that he should defend his own house.

I drove back; and when I came to the door of the Chief Commissioner's house, on my way to the Gubbins', I found the ladies flocking in, and was told that Emmie was already there. However, I was asked to go and fetch more ladies, which I did, till all were brought away. Major Banks, with much feeling, commended the care of his wife to me, saying that she would be well content to be where I was.

I forgot to say that in the night, on the housetop, he had asked me, as a Clergyman, what I should advise him to do, in case of its being certain that his wife would fall into the hands of the rebels, and that they would treat her as they had done the women at Delhi and Meerut. It was a difficult question: but I told him that, if I were certain that my wife would be so treated, I should shoot her rather than let her fall into their hands. (Colonel Inglis afterwards asked me whether I thought his wife would be justified in killing her own children, rather than let them be murdered by the natives. I said, no; for children could but be killed; whereas we had been told that at Delhi young delicate ladies had been dragged through the streets, violated by many, and then murdered.)

God forgive me, if I gave wrong advice! but I was excited; and I know at the time I should have killed Emmie, rather than have allowed her to be thus dishonoured and tortured by these bloodthirsty savage idolaters.

All the ladies from Fayrer's, Ommanney's, and Gubbins', were collected in the Residency, by about five. At half-past six, Harris and I had evening service in a large upper room in the Chief Commissioner's house. It was well attended. I preached extempore on the subject for the day; the office of the Holy Ghost. (It was Whit-Sunday.) I spoke of Him, with reference to present circumstances, as the convincer of sin, and the purifier. I was enabled to speak fluently, and, I trust, with good effect. The evening passed off without an attack. Emmie and I, Mrs. Inglis, Miss Dickson, the Harrises, and some others, took mattresses up to the roof of the house, and there we slept. I walked about for two hours. There was a little musketry in the city, but distant.

* * * * * *

From Sunday, May 31st, to Wednesday, June 3rd, nothing very remarkable occurred. The ladies who had come to the Residency from Fayrer's, Gubbins', and Ommanney's, returned to those garrisons. Active measures were taken to put the Residency in a state of defence. Every day drum-head court-martials were held on a large landing-place on the stairs of this house, to try Sepoys and other rebels. About twenty were hanged at the Muchee Bawn Fort.

About Thursday or Friday, sad news came in from Mynpoorie. Captain Hayes, Lieutenant Barbor, and young Fayrer, had gone out with a party made up of Gall's and Forbes' Horse, to restore tranquillity to the Dooāb. The men behaved very well, I believe, up to the day of which I am about to speak, and which must have been about June 1st or 2nd. In the morning, the Horse under Hayes marched out of Mynpoorie. When they had marched some miles, Fayrer got off his horse to have a drink at a well. Without any notice (so I understand from the account of the Sikh Rissaldar, who was one of the party and who behaved extremely well), a trooper came up behind Fayrer, and nearly severed his head from his body with one stroke of his sword. The Rissaldar, seeing that there was treachery, rode on to warn Hayes; but those, who were intent on murdering him, reached Hayes at the same time as the Rissaldar, and, before the latter could warn him, one of the mutineers plunged his sword into his side. He fell from his horse, and was killed.

Barbor and Carey, who were with the party, saw this. Carey galloped off towards Mynpoorie, and escaped. Barbor rode towards his own men of Gall's Horse, thinking that they would protect him; but, no—the villains turned upon him, and Forbes' men pursued him behind. He seems now to have made up his mind to sell his life as dearly as possible. He fired his pistol at one man, but only killed his horse. He then drew his sword, gave one man a terrible wound in the shoulder, and wounded another in the thigh; and then a shower of blows descended upon him from the rascals who hemmed him in, and he was nearly cut to pieces. One of the men, who had tried to warn him, now said, "Well! now it is all over: the Sahibs are dead: let us make common cause, Hindu and Mussulman, and march to Delhi." To this they all agreed, and began to start. But the Sikh Rissaldar had gone back, and had put Fayrer's and Hayes' bodies into the latter's palki gharree which had accompanied them. (It was the same carriage, by the bye, in which I took my little boy to be buried; and Hayes, poor fellow! helped to carry him to his grave.)

The mutineers asked the Rissaldar what he was doing with the gharree, and said that they wanted it for their own wounded, and that he must go with them. So they threw the bodies out of the gharree and rode off; and he with them. He soon, however, found a pretext for getting off his horse by the road-side, and, as soon as his companions were well ahead, he rode back to the place, where they had left the bodies. He found the head man of the village near which they were murdered putting them into a palki, and across a horse. He assisted him. The bodies were carried into Mynpoorie, and buried there.

Poor Hayes! He was a most kind-hearted fellow, and showed me great sympathy in my troubles; both in my own illness, and when our baby died. He has left a widow and five children. I had the painful task of announcing his death to his widow. She seemed quite stunned, and would not believe it for several days; but now that she knows the terrible truth, I know not how she bears it.

Mrs. Barbor, too, I had to tell. She had been married only three months. Poor Barbor was a fine stalwart-looking young man, of twenty-seven.

Young Fayrer had come from Australia, where he had been trying to make his fortune for a few years, with but little success. He had been unable, till within a few days of his death, to get any employment in India; when Sir Henry Lawrence gave him, with a hope of its being permanent, a commission in the Oudh Irregular Cavalry. He went away in overflowing spirits, rejoicing in what proved the cause of his death.

It was on or about Trinity Sunday that we heard that Sir Hugh Wheeler was attacked in his entrenchments at Cawnpore, by the four regiments quartered there, which had mutinied. He had with him about 250 men of different English regiments, which had been sent up from Calcutta, and one battery, I believe, of English Artillery. He had, as a precautionary measure, entrenched the barracks with a deep ditch and parapet of earth; and all the ladies had been sent in. He had not had time to secure the treasure, when he was attacked by the rebels. There were quartered there three Native Cavalry Regiments; about 3,600 men in all. After a day or two, they were joined by a Rajah. Intelligence of this was, I think, brought in by Captain Evans, the Commissioner of a place about ten miles this side of Cawnpore. He and a medical man came in together. Both their wives were in the entrenchment.

By the bye, I think we first had intelligence of the attack by electric telegraph, which was cut the day it began.

From that day to this, more than a week, we have been without certain intelligence from Sir Hugh Wheeler. The rebels, who seem to be pretty well commanded, have cut the bridge across the Ganges, and put guards at all the ghâts, to prevent our communicating with Cawnpore. From time to time natives have come in, saying that Sir Hugh continues to hold out, and that very few English have been killed. Some say that a Rajah has brought the rebels several guns; others, that they have only one. They have, it is said, hitherto kept well away from the entrenchment, preferring to fire from a distance —the cowards! when they are more than ten to one!

About June 2nd, news came of an outbreak at Seetapore. A messenger came in, saying that a number of fugitives thence were within fifteen miles of Lucknow. A party of volunteers went out, on horseback, to fetch them in. My buggy horse was borrowed for some one to ride for this purpose; but he was afterwards put into a buggy (when the volunteers met the fugitives) and brought in seven people. His back and shoulder were made raw in doing so, but it was in a good cause. The party met the fugitives about seven miles from this. They at first saw some men with muskets, in a mango-tope, and got ready to fight; but it turned out that these men, about thirty, were a party of the 41st Regiment, at Seetapore, which had remained faithful, and had carefully brought in those who had escaped. The party, who came in on the 4th, consisted chiefly of officers and ladies of the 41st, and some sergeants' wives and children. The 41st broke out into mutiny on the morning of the 3rd. They went, I believe, to the Treasury. Colonel Birch of the 41st (who was so attentive to us when we were at Seetapore), although advised not to do so, took the two rifle companies of his regiment, and went to try to bring the mutineers to a sense of their duty. They immediately shot him. On the alarm being given, all who lived at the end of the station, at which the Sepoy lines were, made their escape; and these were the party whom the volunteers went out to meet. They were part of two days and a night on the road (forty miles). The 41st guarded them most carefully, and would not let them rest at some suspected places.

The 9th Native Infantry were also quartered at Seetapore. They were on parade on the morning of the mutiny of the 41st, at seven o'clock. They were very orderly till they heard of this mutiny. On hearing of it, the quartermaster, Sergeant Abbott, went to two guns which they had prepared in case of a row, intending so to point them as to prevent the 41st from attacking the 9th; for neither he nor the officers seem to have suspected the 9th in the least. However, on getting to the guns, he found them surrounded by Sepoys, who forbade him to come near, on pain of death. He then returned to the place where he was before, where he found Captain Gowan (commanding the regiment), and the Adjutant. Gowan told him that the 41st had mutinied, and had shot Colonel Birch. The men then came clustering round them, as they often did, talking of all sorts of things. Captain Gowan began to address them, when, suddenly, a man levelled his musket and shot him. Another fired at the Adjutant, and killed his horse; and he, on falling, was killed by the men bayonetting him. Many of them then levelled their muskets at Sergeant Abbott. He told me that he escaped by being so near them. They had not fixed their bayonets; and he, with his arms, threw up the muzzles of their muskets, opened out a way for himself, and ran. Before he had got ten yards a volley was fired at him, but, as he said, God directed the bullets away from him. When he had got about twenty yards from them, a bullet hit him in the arm, and another afterwards grazed the same arm; and they continued firing at him till he was out of range. He ran to Mr. Christian's house, about half a mile from the parade-ground. At the gate of the compound he met Mr. Christian, and said to him, "For God's sake, Sir, send the ladies away while you have time: the 9th and 41st have mutinied." Christian told him not to be alarmed; that he had 200 men whom he could trust to defend his house (they were chokeedars, whom Christian had trained); and that they would avenge his wound.

Abbott said, "Don't let any such foolish notion enter your head, Sir, as that any native can be trusted. Get your horses out, and send the ladies away." Christian said, he was safer where he was, and intended to defend his own house. Abbott then asked him to lend him a horse, but he declined, saying that he would be safer there. He then asked to be allowed to go into the house to staunch his wound, which Christian told him to do, but not to go near the ladies. Mrs. Gowan, however, saw him, and asked him whether her husband was safe. Abbott bound up his arm with part of a sheet; and then ran down the high bank which is immediately below Christian's house, swam the river, and made off for the jungles. Before he had got very far, he saw Christian's house on fire.

He had not left it a quarter of an hour before the very men, whom Christian had trained, rose against him, murdered all whom they could get at before leaving the house, and, as the poor ladies and officers ran down the bank to escape from them, dropped on one knee and fired at them.

Mr. Lester, the Deputy Commissioner, made his escape through Christian's compound; and so did another sergeant. Lester told me that he saw Sir Mountstuart and the Misses Jackson amongst the fugitives, but that he crossed higher up the river, and more to the left, than they did. The sergeant of the —th told me that the bullets splashed in the water like hail. He said that he passed the ladies, when they reached the opposite bank of the river, and had got some distance on the other side. The gentlemen were helping and protecting them, but the poor ladies could not get along very fast, because their dresses were wet and clung to them. The gentlemen did not use their fire-arms much, because they were too much engaged in helping the ladies; but he saw one of them fire once or twice at Christian's mutinous guards, who had now crossed the stream, and, when he did so, the cowardly rascals threw themselves flat on the ground and remained there for a minute or two. The last persons he passed were Mr. and Mrs. Thornhill. He got away into the jungle, and was shortly joined by the quarter-master-sergeant of the 9th and Lester. I cannot give an *accurate* account of their further proceedings; but they were out seven days. I think, on the second morning they accompanied Lester to the head man of a village, whom he knew (he being in Lester's district). He helped them; and from him they went to a Rajah, who also knew Lester. This man had a fortified house, and 200 men to protect it. He put up Lester and the two sergeants, and two women, whom they found hiding in the jungles, for two days; giving them food, clothes, and money; and sent them with a guard into Lucknow. They all combine in saying that the country-people behaved very well to them. When they did not, it was from fear of the Sepoys. In fact, our rule has always seemed to be very popular in the country parts of Oudh.

The next rising was on June 9th, at Durriabad. We were first made aware of this by a clerk's coming in from that station. He had been fired upon, and had a wound in his side. In the evening came in Dr. Thompson, the apothecary in medical charge. He had been ordered at four that morning to proceed with the 5th Oudh Irregular Infantry with treasure, which they were to convey to Lucknow. The men started with apparent willingness; but before they had got a quarter of a mile from cantonments, they refused to go any farther, and turned back, and fired at Captain Hawes, their commanding officer. They also fired at Mr. Thompson, who at once rode straight off, and came in here, forty miles, for assistance, leaving his wife and children at Mr. Grant's house. Sir Henry Lawrence gave him fifty Suwārs; and he was starting for Durriabad at four o'clock the next morning, when he met Mr. Grant and his wife coming in, and they told him that they feared it was all over with the rest of the party. He came back in a fearful state of mind; but towards evening a messenger came in, saying that his wife and children, Mr. and Mrs. Fullerton, and several others were coming in, and were halting about ten miles from Lucknow. In the evening, they all came in safely. The Sepoys had overtaken and fired at them, about five miles from Durriabad; but, it seemed, more with a view to frighten than to kill them. When they fired, all the shots passed over the fugitives' heads; but they might afterwards have bayonetted them if they liked, as only two officers were with them. They, however, did them no farther harm, but let them go.

About the 7th, an alarm having come in that the regiment at Secrora was mutinously inclined, a party of volunteers, commanded by Captain Forbes, went out to bring the ladies in. They all came in safely on the 9th. As they came in, one of the Sepoys told the doctor that they should never get away from them; and Mrs. Forbes heard another of them talking unpleasantly about cutting throats.

On June 12th, about one o'clock, Captain Orr came in to say that the Military Police had mutinied. They had been on duty at the gaol. Those, who were there, left their post, and marched off to the barracks, where they were joined by the rest; and the whole regiment, 700 strong, after plundering the 32nd mess and a few other houses, marched in the direction of Sultanpore. . . . . It was at last determined to send after them a horse battery of artillery, a body of cavalry (composed of the Sikh troop of Forbes' Cavalry, which alone now remained faithful) and of volunteers, and about 200 men of the 32nd, drawn partly from the Residency, partly from the Muchee Bawn Fort.

This force started about two hours after the police had marched. It was a fiery hot day. The guns under Ashe, and the cavalry, overtook the police about eight miles from Lucknow, and four beyond the Dil Kusha Park.

The police, on seeing that they were pursued, ran, but kept pretty well together.

The 32nd, though they had done wonders in marching as they did, were nearly a mile behind the guns and cavalry, and could not get into action. The artillery opened upon the mutineers with round shot. The cavalry made a détour, so as to come out of a village on the flank of the mutineers. They made a charge which lookers-on have described to me as "splendid," but Forbes afterwards told me that the Sikhs did not charge *home*, nor use their swords. By the fire of the artillery, and by the charge of cavalry, about 40 of the mutineers were killed.

Thornhill, who went as a volunteer, rode at two men, and called to them to lay down their arms. One fired at him from a very short distance, but missed him. The other, seeing Thornhill coming at him in such a determined way, fixed his bayonet, and charged him. The mare which Thornhill rode, frightened by the report of fire-arms, suddenly checked, and thus threw the rider off his guard. He cut at the man, and, he thinks, struck him on the head; but he was unable entirely to ward off a bayonet-thrust which the man made, and he was wounded in the left breast and through the left arm. Captain Weston and some other officers were close at hand, and cut the man down.

Thornhill was the only Englishman wounded. Two Mahommedans, who were with the Sikh Cavalry, were killed; and the Rissaldar, who brought in the account of poor Hayes' death, was wounded. Two of the 32nd, and one of the Artillery, died from the effects of the sun.

Wednesday, June 10*th.*—This morning a letter came to Captain Orr from his brother; part of which I will transcribe, as it tells its own story, simply and forcibly.

"Jungle, near Mittolee, June 8th.

" I wrote to you on the 6th, but am afraid my
" letter has not reached you.

" On Sunday, May 31st, the 28th, at Shahjah-
" anpore, broke out into open mutiny; and some
" of the men rushed into church and murdered
" Collector Ricketts and wounded Spens of the
" 28th.

" James was killed on his parade-ground.

" The following made their escape :—Captains
" Sneyd, Lysaght, Salmon; Lieutenants Key,
" Robertson, Scott, Pitt, Rutherford; Ensigns
" Spens, Johnston, Scott; Quarter-master-
" sergeant Grant; Band-master; Drummer.
" Ladies :—Mrs. Scott, Miss Scott, Mrs. Lysaght,
" Mrs. Key, Mrs. Bowling, Mrs. Sheils, Mrs.
" Grant, Mrs. Pereira. Four children. Lieu-
" tenant Sheils, Veterinary Establishment. Mr.
" Jenkins, Civil Service.

" They ran away to Powaien; but the Rajah
" turned them out the next morning, and they
" came to Mohumdee.

"Thomason and myself, on hearing of this sad affair at Shahjahanpore, consulted together, and sent away Annie (his wife) to Mittolee, and went ourselves to the Fort, to protect the Treasury if possible.

"On Monday, at about noon, the party from Shahjahanpore arrived; and from that time the most alarming symptoms showed themselves amongst the men.

"I used every means in my power to pacify them, but in vain. By the most strenuous efforts, I persuaded them from hour to hour to come back to their allegiance.

"Every minute seemed to be our last.

"The men were civil to me to the last; but each one said he could not answer for what some of the bad characters would do.

"I succeeded in gaining some influence over them, and kept them quiet, till a detachment of fifty men came in on Thursday morning, 4th, from Seetapore, sent by poor Christian to escort the ladies in. These men brought with them a report that the whole of their light company at the Muchee Bawn had been cut up by the Europeans; and said that they were determined to take their revenge.

"Seeing the state of things, I sent for all the native officers, and told them to let me know at once, like men, what their intentions

" were; and, if reasonable, I would give my
" consent.

" They came to the resolution of marching on
" at once to Seetapore; and swore they would
" spare our lives, and take Thomason and me
" into Seetapore, and would allow the others to
" go away unmolested.

" I made them take a solemn oath, and they
" all put their hands upon the head of Lutchenun
" Jemindar.

" Well, we left Mohumdee at about half-past
" five P.M., on Thursday; after the men had
" secured the treasure (about one lac of rupees),
" and had released the prisoners. I put as many
" ladies as I could into the buggy, others into
" the baggage-carts; and we reached Burwan at
" about half-past ten P.M.

" Next morning, Friday, 5th, we marched
" towards Aurungabad.

" When we had come about four miles, the
" ' halt' was sounded; and a trooper told us to
" go on ahead, where we liked. We went on for
" some distance, when we saw a party coming
" along. They soon joined us, and followed the
" buggy, which we were pushing on with all our
" might.

" When within half a mile of Aurungabad, a
" Sepoy rushed forward, and snatched Key's gun
" from him, and shot poor old Sheils, who was

" riding my horse. Then the most infernal
" carnage ever witnessed by man began.

" We all collected under a tree close by, and
" put the ladies down from the buggy.

" Shots were firing in all directions, amid the
" most fearful yells. The poor ladies all joined
" in prayer, coolly and undauntedly awaiting
" their fate. I stopped for about three minutes
" amongst them; but, thinking of my own wife
" and child here, I endeavoured to save my life
" for their sakes. I rushed out towards the
" insurgents; and one of our men, Goordeen,
" 6th Company, called out to me to throw down
" my pistol, and he would save me.

" I did so; when he put himself between me
" and the men, and several others followed his
" example. In about ten minutes more they
" had completed their hellish work. I was at
" about three hundred yards' distance, at the
" utmost. Poor Lysaght was kneeling out in
" the open ground, with his hands folded across
" his chest; and, though not using his fire-arms,
" the cowardly wretches would not go up to the
" spot, till they had shot him. And then, rush-
" ing up, they killed the wounded and children,
" butchering them in a most cruel way. With
" the exception of the drummer-boy, every one
" was killed in the above list, besides poor good
" Thomason and our two clerks. They denuded

" the bodies of their clothes, for the sake of
" plunder. They had on them one thousand
" rupees, and Thomason one hundred. On our
" arrival at Aurungabad, some of the men pro-
" posed that I should send for Annie, and,
" marching on to Seetapore, put myself at the
" head of the regiment. To this I said I could
" do nothing, without knowing what the officers
" said. Fortunately, these men were not brutally
" inclined just then, and they explained to the
" men that it was only by the consent of these
" two companies that I had escaped; and there
" was no knowing what the rest of the corps,
" and the 41st and 10th, would say or do; and
" that, till their wish was known, it would be
" better for me to go to Mittolee.

" They let me have a horse and a few clothes.
" I persuaded a guard to bring me here, and got
" a letter from them, making me over to the
" Rajah. On reading this, the Rajah received
" me and sent me to the house, two miles off,
" where Annie was.

" We remained all Saturday there; and on
" Sunday morning, the Rajah's people, hearing
" of the mutineers coming to Mittolee, advised
" us to move into the jungle. Here we are;
" since yesterday morning, in a dense jungle,
" exposed to the most trying heat, without any
" shelter from the sun, except a few thin branches

"and a sheet we have put up. A few of our
"faithful servants are hovering about. Some of
"the Rajah's people feed us; but you can well
"fancy what our appetites are. My poor wife,
"as usual, is bearing up with her misfortunes
"like a saint; but is extremely weak. The
"Rajah sends word that he will do his best to
"protect us. The troops from Mohumdee and
"Seetapore are constantly marching forwards
"and backwards between Seetapore and Aurung-
"abad. We cannot find out their intentions.
"Perhaps they will go to Delhi. Some talk of
"going there—some to Lucknow. They cannot,
"I hear, decide about the distribution of the
"money, and might have a row. My opinion is
"that they will all, by degrees, walk home.

"You must have heard of the massacre at
"Seetapore. Three men, one lady, and one child
"are here also; but separate from us. The
"Rajah thinks it advisable to divide us, so as to
"have smaller parties. He is right. . . . .

"*June 9th.*—I managed to communicate with
"the other fugitives by letter to-day. Seetaram
"carried it.

"Their names are, Sir Mountstuart Jackson
"and sister, little Sophy Christian, Burnes, and
"Quarter-master-sergeant Morton, 10th Oudh
"Irregulars. I have a servant to cook for us,
"and he feeds the poor people.

"The troops are still at Mohoolie. They
"cannot make up their minds as to their move-
"ments. This morning they went some dis-
"tance towards Aurungabad with the intention
"of going to Delhi, but changed their minds
"again, and returned to Mohoolie, *en route* to
"Lucknow. They are constantly quarrelling
"about the division of their booty. A small
"party of Europeans could snatch their booty
"from them very easily. . . . . The natives all
"seem to think that Muchee Bawn is impregna-
"ble. The privations we are put to are inde-
"scribable; but the fearful heat beats all.". . . .

Such is Captain Orr's letter to his brother here. There is a good deal more, relating to private matters. It is a letter which does him the greatest credit; showing coolness, courage, and Christian faith: especially, written as it was in the jungle. Captain Orr sent an answer to his brother on the 14th by the servant who brought the letter. He required two days' rest, as his feet were much cut by walking ninety miles. He brought and took back the letters in a bamboo stick. I wrote to Sir Mountstuart Jackson; bidding him cheer up, and trust to the guardian care of God; and told him all the news I could.

I read Captain Orr's letter to Sir Henry Lawrence. He much wished he could send to bring them in; but a strong party of Europeans, not less than one hundred, would be necessary; and he could not spare them. A number of the officers of the Native Infantry Regiments, which have mutinied, volunteered to go, but Sir Henry would not allow it. He wrote to the Rajah, under whose protection Sir Mountstuart and the rest of the party are, and promised him exemption from one year's tribute if he would take care of them. A few days after this, the following letter came, inclosed in another from Captain Orr.

"Kutcheâna, near Matoli, June 23, 1857.

" My dear Polehampton,

" We have had wonderful news.* My sister
" and nine other Europeans are with T. Hearsey
" at Mutteeira, on the Korsāle. There are Mrs.
" Greene, Gonne, and Hastings, from Mullah-
" pore, the Sergeant of Police and wife, and a
" clerk and wife, and Mr. Bran and Mr. Carew,
" from Shahjahanpore. They are under the care
" of Rajah Anant Singh. Hearsey has commu-
" nicated with us. We all had extraordinary
" escapes. The Government has made a very
" generous offer to the Rajah for us, and he will
" most probably accept it. He must have had
" some news lately; as yesterday his karindar,

* See Mrs. Polehampton's Diary, p. 369.

"after treating us like dogs till now, became
"suddenly humiliated. Burnes has written
"a full account of the mutiny to Sir Henry
"Lawrence. I will just give you our own
"particular narrative.

"We were all most thoroughly deceived at
"Seetapore, fully trusting to the 9th, 10th, and
"police, to the last.

"I was with Lester, in his bungalow, when
"the troops turned out, as we thought, to fight
"the 41st. Captain Hearsey had 200 police in
"Barlow's compound, behind Lester's. Lester
"had a company of police in his garden. When
"he ordered them to advance to the front, they
"refused to move, and began looting his garden.
"We went over to tell Hearsey, and found him
"ready to receive the 41st.

"A good deal of firing was going on in the
"10th lines, and some of the police began to fire
"their muskets in the air. Hearsey was remon-
"strating with his subahdars, when some of the
"men called out to us to go to our bungalows.
"Lester and myself went back into Lester's
"compound, and were fired at by the police
"there. We ran right through the compound;
"and were then fired at by the 41st, who were
"in front of the house. We ran past a number
"of the 10th, who did not fire at us, and then
"got into Christian's bungalow. Everybody was

"collected there, except the officers and ladies of
"the 41st, and the officers of the 9th.

"As soon as we got there, the bungalow was
"set on fire, and shots were fired in at the back.
"We were nearly surrounded; but all went out
"at the back, down to the river. There was
"a bamboo bridge, not exactly behind Chris-
"tian's house, a little up the river, and a ford
"a little below the bridge.

"I went down to the river with my sisters
"and all the ladies; the gentlemen followed.
"I even then thought we should be allowed to
"walk off; but, on going down to the river, saw
"several of the police sitting about one hundred
"yards off, who began firing at us. The bridge
"was then clear; and I wanted to get all the ladies
"across. I took one of my sisters (having my
"gun in my other hand) towards the bridge,
"telling the others to follow. My sister ran
"across the bridge, and I looked round, and
"saw no one. They had all stopped behind at
"the ford. The police were then firing at us,
"and were running up to the bridge. If I had
"gone back, I should have lost both my sisters;
"so I followed the first. We went on towards
"a jungle, four of the police following; and
"saw the Thornhills and child, who had come
"through the river. They said that my sister
"was under charge of Lester, and had crossed

"the river. (This turned out a mistake.) We
"all went on to the jungle, followed by the four
"police, who were loading and firing. There
"was a cross fire of 41st Rifles, from lower
"down the river, that went over our heads. We
"got into the jungle and were pursued into it
"by the police for some distance.

"We heard them quite close; and the Thorn-
"hills were quite knocked up. I ran down a
"bank and pulled my sister through a small
"stream, up to my waist; the Sepoys firing as
"we crossed and ran up the bank. They did
"not follow farther. We went on and sat down
"in a very thick jungle, as I could not get my
"sister on in the sun, and thought it safer to
"hide than to run on, as there was firing on all
"sides. I saw no more of Thornhill. He may
"have got off; but we heard that he was killed,
"and my sister Georgina heard the same.

"We sat in the jungle for some time, and at
"last heard several people coming through the
"jungle. They were Pāsees, and stood talking
"just in front of us. One caught sight of me,
"and told us to sit still and we should get off.
"They got water for us and showed us a better
"place of concealment, and agreed to come at
"night and show us the road to Matoli, and
"we sat from eleven o'clock till sunset in the
"same place, the Pāsees occasionally appearing.

"They told us that the 'Burra Sahib,' his wife and child, had been all murdered by the side of the river. Burnes had left them there. They also said that the 'Chota Sahib' had been killed. Lester went by that name as well as myself. Probably the Sepoys had put me down as killed with Thornhill. The Pāsees told us that the 41st were in a strong party, lower down the river, and that nearly all the Sahibs had been killed. These Pāsees came after dark, and began by fixing their arrows and demanding money. Of course we had none; but I persuaded them to go on; and we left Seetapore burning behind us. We walked about half the night, having great difficulty with the Pāsees. I gave them a sword, to get us something to eat at a village, and they treated us to an elephant chupattie.

"Two other Pāsees came out, and they evidently followed me to get my gun. I had no shoes, my sister wearing mine; and I was tying up my foot, and my sister was holding the gun, when the Pāsees snatched it from her, and pointed their arrows and walked off. We went on towards the north-west, and crossing the Mohumdee Road, got into a bamboo enclosure, where we slept till the morning. Then we walked into the house of a zemindar. He was very civil, and gave us food and

" an out-house to ourselves. In the middle
" of the day, hearing that there were Sepoys
" in the village, they took us out into the
" jungle. There the Sepoys found us (three
" men). They demanded money and threatened
" to take our heads into the subahdars. They
" kept us in anticipation of this for some time;
" till, in the end, they contented themselves with
" robbing us of all pieces of metal we had about
" us. We left them, went through a stream,
" reached another village, and lay under a tree
" all day. The people here were very attentive,
" and told us of two Sahibs, about a kos off,
" under care of Saboo Singh. We started, and
" found Burnes, the sergeant and child. We
" then walked twenty miles, straight to Mattoli.
" Saboo Singh made arrangements for guides
" all the way. At Serkahā, a large body of
" thākoors turned out and escorted us. Farther
" on, my sister got a tattoo. This was lent us
" by Sheobuksh Singh, Havildar, 3rd Police.
" We made arrangements for a second tattoo
" farther on. At Mattoli the people tried to
" mislead us and keep us from seeing the Rajah.
" We found the fort. The gate was shut against
" us; but Burnes ran a-muck through all the
" guards, got under the gate, and sat down on
" the *inner* gate, where he was safe, according
" to their custom. He got one wound on the

"head, and another on the ribs. They then let
"us all in; and have since kept us alive with a
"very bad grace. We are now in one of the
"Rajah's serais, in a very thick jungle.

"My sister Georgina, whom I had given up
"for lost, escaped still more miraculously. She
"crossed the river at the ford, with nearly all the
"ladies, and was pulled out by Mrs. Greene;
"the Sepoys firing into them all the time, and
"as they ran up the bank. They sat down in a
"thick jungle close to the river, seeing the bun-
"galows burning. Some Pāsees looted them,
"and in the evening some Sepoys appeared, and
"levelled their muskets at them; but one of
"Hearsey's men took them under his protec-
"tion, fought about them, and took my sister,
"while another man took Mrs. Greene, by dif-
"ferent routes, to T. Hearsey. They all escaped
"in the evening, on Hearsey's elephant, with the
"sergeant and his wife, and a number of Sepoys.
"They went all night and the next day, and
"reached the Chanka river, where they slept in
"a bamboo fort. The two next days they went
"on, and then stayed four days near Buragaon.
"Hearing that Gonne was leaving Mullahpore,
"they went there; and all went down in a boat
"to Rampore, near Bhiram Ghât, where they
"heard of Sepoys coming up, and returned to
"Mullahpore. They then took up a position at

" Mutteora, on the banks of the river, under care
" of a first-rate man. They intend to remain
" there for the present.

" None of us expected to live through the
" massacre; and we have been most openly pro-
" tected by Providence, our escape being entirely
" through out-of-the-way circumstances.

"I suppose you have no mail going yet; but,
" on the first opportunity, will you kindly for-
" ward this letter to my relations? .... We have
" heard of two Europeans at Weyl; two, near
" this; and one at Kourera, to the east of this.
" The 41st officers, &c., were escorted by their
" grenadier company as far as Peernuggur. The
" colonel and two officers were killed at the
" Treasury; Hill and Gowan in their own lines;
" and Christian and Thornhill, we suppose, by
" the river. Christian's body was seen. Hoping
" I shall see you soon inside British lines,

"Yours sincerely,
"M. JACKSON."

* * * *

Between the 10th and 14th, news came in that a party of officers, who had been sent out at the beginning of the mutiny, commanded by Major Marriott, Pension Pay-Master, had been murdered. They had been sent by Sir Henry with detachments to assist Mr. Colvin, the Lieutenant-Governor of the North-West Provinces, to restore order in the Dooab. Soon after crossing the Ganges, Major Marriott perceived that the troops were in such a mutinous state that he thought himself justified in leaving them, and returning to Lucknow about June 10th. He reported that he had represented to the officers the state in which the troops were, and told them that, in his opinion, they would all do right to make their escape as soon as possible. Some of the officers wished to follow Major Marriott's advice, but were dissuaded by Captain Staples of the 7th Cavalry and others, who would not believe that a mutiny was likely to take place. Major Marriott told me that he put a cigar in his mouth and rode away after dinner, as if he were going for an evening ride; and came, sometimes riding, sometimes walking, the latter part of the way disguised in native clothes, to Lucknow. We hear that the other officers were murdered as they were sitting smoking after dinner. Their names were Captain Staples, 7th Cavalry; Lieutenant Farquharson, 48th Native Infantry; Cornet Martin, 7th Cavalry. Martin, when he saw what was likely to happen, jumped on his horse and rode off; but, after having been pursued some miles, he was overtaken and cut down.

On Thursday, June 11th, I met Dr. Partridge near the Residency. It was about seven in the evening. He told me that he and two other officers had been ordered to go, early the next morning, with some of Gall's Horse, to reconnoitre towards Seetapore. He felt perfectly certain, he said, that neither he, nor any other English officer, would ever come back. . . . . (This order was afterwards cancelled.)

While we were talking, several Sikhs of Forbes' Regiment passed us on horseback, and salaamed. One man, as he passed, made a much lower salaam than the others, which Partridge noticed. We went on talking, and presently the same horseman rode up, and said, "Partridge, I wonder you didn't return my salaam!" It was Major Gall, disguised as a Suwār, who had just had orders to go out with eighteen of his cavalry, to endeavour to get to Allahabad and Benares with despatches. He was, I believe, anxious to go out on this duty. He was out with his regiment at the time that Hayes, Barbor, and Fayrer were murdered by those of them, and of Forbes' Cavalry, whom Hayes commanded; and had a narrow escape of falling in with the mutineers. I spoke a few words to him, and wished him success in his expedition, and " God speed." He said, " God bless you both!" shook hands with us, and rode off. On Sunday, June 14th, his Madras Christian servant came in with the sad news that his master had been murdered, about forty miles from this, on Saturday morning. His story was that Major Gall stopped at a serai, and ordered him to prepare some food there. He begged his master not to stay there, as it was a bad place; but Major Gall said that, if he did not do so, the men would think he was afraid.

He had not been there long, before two companies of Sepoys arrived, probably from Allahabad; and some of them looked into the place where Gall was. He asked them what they wanted, whether they wished to kill him. They said "Yes," and immediately shot him. They debated whether they should kill the servant, because he was a Christian. However, they at last contented themselves with beating him, and sent him away.

On Monday, June 15th, came in a report that all the people at Sultanpore had been murdered, excepting the ladies, who had gone either to Allahabad or to a Rajah's house. Up to the present time, June 19th, we do not know the truth of this. It is also said that Mr. C. Cunliffe, Civil Service, has been murdered, in company with Lieutenant Longueville Clarke, in an attempt to cross the river, to come in from Bareitch.

On Tuesday, 16th, a sad affair happened here. There was a quarrel between the Quarter-master-sergeant and the Riding-master of the 7th

Cavalry; men of the best possible character in their regiment. The quarrel had begun between their wives, and was fostered by them ; and, after some words, the Quarter-master-sergeant, in a fit of passion, shot the Riding-master through the body. He died in a few hours, forgiving his murderer, with whom, up to that time, he had lived on terms of the greatest friendship. The Riding-master is a member of the Church of England, the other a Roman Catholic. Each has left a widow and three children. Thus two families are brought to grief, and perhaps to poverty, by an act done in a moment of passion.

Wednesday, June 17th.—In the evening I drove in the buggy to the Muchee Bawn Fort.

About a fortnight ago the cholera made its appearance in the Fort, where there are 230 men of the 32nd and 84th. I have buried nine, and the Roman Catholic priest several.

The Fort is about half a mile from the Residency. Just outside the gate, in the street, are three pairs of gallows, very simple in construction, not more than eight feet high. This morning, four men were hanged on them, for conspiracy. I forgot to say, that on Monday, 15th, Captain Carnegie, the head of the City Police, took twenty-one men ; some natives of Lucknow, some of Benares. They were all rich men, and most of them enormously fat. Fatness here is a sure proof of wealth. I saw them all sitting in a row under the verandah of the hospital, handcuffed together. These men had been plotting against us, and supplying the mutinous Sepoys with money. There was a drum-head court-martial held upon them. I don't know how many were found guilty; but the sentence was only confirmed on four of them, and they were hanged on the morning of the day I visited the Fort. One of them abused the "Feringhi pig-eaters" with his last breath, and exhorted the people to avenge his death on them in general, and on Captain Carnegie in particular.

At the Fort I found eleven men in hospital (four old cholera cases); all doing well. I went round to all the men, and talked to them. There are 230 in the Fort. It is a curious old place, built of brick; covers a large area, and is cut up into a great many quadrangles. In the centre one is the house of the Rajah who formerly occupied it, built in that nondescript style of architecture which prevails in Lucknow,—half French, partly Moorish, partly Indian,—painted a sort of yellow ochre, and ornamented with scrolls, leaves, &c. painted green.

The Fort must be a depressing place to live in; nothing to look at but stone walls. These walls are very rotten; the ramparts would all come down, if heavy guns were fired from them;

but the natives have a great idea of its strength.
It also commands the stone bridge (one of the
chief approaches to the city), and many streets.
It was, no doubt, wise to seize it at first; but I
cannot help thinking that it would now be wiser
to blow it up and abandon it, and to bring the
garrison in here. This, at least, if there is a
well-grounded fear of a siege; for we have a
mile of defences in the Residency, and only
about 400 men, including officers of the mutinous regiments and clerks, to defend it.

We can get no authentic news of what is
going on at Cawnpore. On the 16th came in a
letter from Sir Hugh Wheeler, dated the 14th,
saying that his losses had been cruel; but that
he was still holding out, and able to do so for
three weeks. He asked for reinforcements, and
said nothing about any having arrived, though
we know they have been sent up from Calcutta
and ought to have arrived ere this. I fancy
that they have found work to do at Benares and
Allahabad.

It is believed that Sir Hugh Wheeler is besieged by one cavalry and three infantry regiments, and that their artillery consists of two
24-pounders, lent by the Rajah of Bithoor, who
has also brought some troops. It is now more
than a fortnight since the siege of the entrenchments at Cawnpore began; 250, probably, to

5,000! On the day on which fighting began, June 4th, Sir Hugh telegraphed to Lucknow to say that two regiments had mutinied, and had gone to seize the treasure, which he had been unable to remove into his entrenchment. From that time to the present, only one letter has come from him or from any one in the place. The insurgents cut the telegraph wires, stopped the mails, destroyed the bridge of boats, and placed sentries at all the ghâts for several miles up and down the river.

We have learned, from what sources I hardly know, that their only effective guns are those lent them by the Rajah of Bithoor. In the entrenchment, they have, it seems, nothing larger than nine-pounders. We hear from natives who have come in, and from our spies, that the insurgents have only once endeavoured to storm the entrenchment, and that they were then beaten back with great loss. It has been decided that we cannot send reinforcements to the garrison. The only force we could spare would be the 200 men from cantonments, with two guns. The consequences to *us* of sending these would be, that the road would then be shut up in that direction, and that we should get no more supplies; and the Sepoys, hearing that we had sent away a part of our force, *might* summon up courage to attack us. The detachment would have great difficulty in crossing the river, and would have to fight its way into the entrenchment at Cawnpore. So we are not going to send help to the gallant little garrison who are holding out so nobly. It is a great pity; but those, who know how affairs stand far better than I do, say that it will not do to send away a man. Unless they have met with great opposition on the road up from Calcutta, reinforcements must be at hand.

I forgot to mention before, that I have benefited by the present state of things, to the extent of having gained by it a very good double-barrelled gun, in good order (flint locks, but very good); also another, without locks; a rifle, without lock; a gun-case, a powder-flask, and shot-belt. All these I got for nothing. Thousands of guns, rifles, &c. were taken from a store of the King's, and brought here for fear of their falling into the enemy's hands. All the rifles which were in good order were retained by Major Anderson, for the purpose of arming a rifle corps; but any Englishman, likely to be able to manage one, was allowed to take away a gun. Most of them were handsomely mounted with gold, at the touch-holes and in the pans. The soldiers were allowed to pick this out, and many of them got several rupees' worth. I heard one man say to another, "I say, Bill, ain't you going to the diggins?" The consequence of allowing the soldiers to pick out the gold was speedily seen, in one or two of them being drunk on duty.

Saturday, June 20*th.*—To-day Colonel Case told me that, in case of our being besieged and shut up, they should want one of the chaplains to live at the Muchee Bawn. He asked me whether I would give them a service to-morrow in cantonments.

* * * * *

Sunday, June 21*st.*—Up at half-past four. Drove to cantonments. The road perfectly quiet. Found about one hundred of the 32nd, half the company of Artillery, and ten or fifteen officers of the Native Infantry Regiments waiting for me, under a high flat-roofed tent, a sort of pavilion. I read Morning Prayers, and, at Colonel Case's request, gave them a sermon. I had not had time to write one, so I expounded part of the Second Morning Lesson,—the history of the miraculous draught of fishes, the cleansing of the leper, and the letting the lame man down through the roof to Jesus. It was a purely *extempore* discourse; but, I am thankful to say, I was able, in my judgment, to give a better exposition than I ever remember doing before. After service, I had tea with Colonel Case, in his tent. I asked him whether it would not be possible to detach part of our force to relieve General Wheeler at Cawnpore. He said, he feared not ; but, within four hours after I left, he volunteered to take a force, consisting of two hundred of the 32nd, and two guns, to do so. Sir Henry, however, would not let him go; saying that the engineers had reported the crossing to be impracticable. Any force from here would have to cross where the river is, they say, nearly a mile wide. Opposite Cawnpore, it is not more than half that breadth; but, if the troops crossed there, they would have to do so in the face of guns which command the crossing; and then, if our guns succeeded in driving the enemy from the opposite bank, our men would have to fight their way through the narrow streets of Cawnpore, for two or three miles, before they could reach General Wheeler's entrenchment. Besides this, we have intelligence from our spies that the enemy are closing in upon us, to the number of some 15,000, with sixteen or eighteen guns. At present they are in detached parties; but, as soon as Cawnpore falls—*quod Deus avertat!*—or if we were to weaken ourselves by sending away the force from cantonments, they would, without doubt, attack us.

After having tea with Colonel Case, I drove to our house. Found all right there: the baboo, Peter, and Nazir, ready to receive me. Chloe has four pups; two of them rather nice ones.

I took one in the buggy to show to Emmie. Got back to the Residency at eight o'clock. Had service in the large upper room. Sir Henry Lawrence was there. Harris had services at the hospital, and at Fayrer's garrison. Evening service in the open air, in Mr. Gubbins' garden. There may have been two hundred people there; I should think four hundred at least *ought to* have attended. Harris preached.

* * * *

Thursday, June 25th.—Up at half-past five. Went out to try to find a room for service next Sunday. I was offered a room in the Thuggee gaol, from which lately the prisoners have been removed, and it has been thoroughly cleansed and whitewashed, to be occupied by the English soldiers, in case of our being attacked and having to call in the two other detachments. I am glad to see that it will make good quarters for, I should think, three hundred men. But I did not like the idea of having Divine service here, so I went on to the place where the officers of the native regiments have their quarters. I found a very picturesque court, shaded by one fine tree. At one end of it is a handsome Mahomedan building,* now used by the officers as a mess-room, lofty, divided into three parts by two rows of Saracenic arches. It will make a capital

---

* Afterwards known as the "Brigade-mess."

church, and is capable of holding four hundred people. This court forms our most advanced out-post this way; the outer wall abuts on one of the streets of Lucknow; it is pierced for musketry, and an eighteen-pounder commands the street.

Friday, June 26*th.*—Up soon after five. There was a funeral at six; that of private Shawe, 32nd, who died of cholera last night. I had seen him four or five times. . . . After the funeral, drove to the Muchee Bawn. About eleven men in hospital; no bad cases, and nearly all Roman Catholics. Promised to send the men some books to read. On returning to the Residency, found that intelligence of the capture of Delhi had arrived, and that a salute was immediately to be fired from our eighteen-pounders. I was curious to know how I could stand the firing of heavy guns, so I took my station close to one. Found that I was not nearly so much affected by it as, apparently, many of the officers were. Twenty-one guns were fired; then the Muchee Bawn took it up, and then cantonments. No windows were broken by the concussion here, which was at one time feared would be the case.

A despatch came last night from Allahabad, saying, that, after some fighting, the fort, town, and cantonments are in the hands of the English; that the 1st Madras Fusiliers were there, and the 84th hourly expected; and that, as soon as they have arrived, succour will be sent to Cawnpore. This was written on the 20th, so that assistance from Allahabad cannot reach Cawnpore for a day or two more. If God gives them not his special help, our poor brethren there *must* fall into the hands of their enemies.

It is to be hoped that the news of the taking of Delhi may make them fear an army's marching down the country upon them, and so disperse them. What *ultimate* hopes of success they can have, one cannot understand. I heard to-day that government has offered a lac of rupees for the capture of the Nana, the Rajah who heads the insurgents at Cawnpore.

. . . . Went to the 32nd hospital. Saw —— who has been ill with sciatica, and, they say, suppressed small-pox, for some days. For the last few days I have read the Bible to him; to-day he said he was too weak. He has seemed to listen with great pleasure, but I have been unable to induce him to express himself at all on the subject of religion. Saw Knight, the hospital-sergeant (who is a trifle better), and Ellicott, and others. Altogether, the men are healthy here, considering all things. Went again to the mess-house, to see if it was being prepared for use as a church. Young Dashwood walked home with me. Came home, thoroughly tired, to breakfast. Prayers at eleven, in the large upper room. I afterwards had a bath, and then slept, without waking, for three hours.

Walked to the church with Emmie in the evening. It is full of grain, for the use of the garrison and their cattle. Much as it distresses me to see the church, where I have ministered for more than a year, and witnessed one of the most solemn scenes in my life (the Bishop of Madras' confirmation), so used, I prefer its being filled with grain to its being made a barrack-room, for obvious reasons.

Captain E. was at prayers to-night. I prayed especially for our brethren at Cawnpore; and he went away very quickly afterwards, I think to hide his emotion, poor fellow. His wife and children are in the entrenchment; so are those also of Darby and of another doctor, and also of Holloway, our regimental clerk.

They have been fitting elephants to the heavy guns to-day, which looks like an onward move. Johannes, a half-caste merchant here, who knows the natives well, says that the Sepoys will never try Lucknow: they have no leader, and are quarrelling about the money; and all the natives in Lucknow, who have anything to lose, would be against them.

A week ago, I engaged as khitmutgar an

African Christian, born at Boston, who speaks capital English. I gave him money to get some clothes made, expecting that he would return in two days. However, he did not come till to-day, when he excused himself by saying that he could not get a durzhee. This *may* be true; so I said no more, but told him to come and wait at tea to-night. He has not made his appearance. I cannot help fancying that the man is a spy. By his good knowledge of English, he could pick up a great deal, and a handsome reward from the Nana might induce him to betray us. We shall see.

Saturday, June 27*th.*—The African, Thomas Ramsay, came this morning, with a good excuse for not being here last night. I shall be careful as to what I say before him. News came to-day from Allahabad that all is quiet there, after hard fighting; and that part of the 1st Madras Fusiliers, and the 84th, a party of Sikh Cavalry, and two or four guns, started for Cawnpore on the 25th. They cannot get there before the 31st at the earliest; and it is very doubtful whether the brave little garrison can hold out till then. To-day a list of killed came. I believe it includes twenty-five officers. Sir Hugh Wheeler's son was killed by a round shot, while lying wounded by his mother's side. Many ladies have died from exposure to the heat.

Sunday, June 28th.—Up at half-past five, and got to the mess-house, our temporary church, by half-past six. In consequence of the heavy rain the officers had not expected service, and nothing was ready. However, I made the best arrangements I could. The rain held up just before church-time, seven o'clock; and we had a good congregation, considering the weather. (Harris was to have gone to cantonments and Muchee Bawn; but, in consequence of the rain, he only went to the latter.) I preached, extempore, on the Parable of the Marriage Feast and the Wedding Garment. I was able to speak freely and without hesitation, and I hope, so as to do good. Sir Henry and three of his staff were there; also, Captain Forbes, Dr. and Mrs. Brydon, &c. After service I went to the hospital. Saw Dr. ——, for whom we prayed in church this morning. He seemed very weak; but was glad for me to read and pray for him. Saw also Knight, and read and prayed for him; also Evans (from the Abbey Foregate, Shrewsbury), who was brought in last night with cholera. At eleven A.M. I had Communion Service in the Residency for those ladies who were unable to go to church this morning on account of the rain. Gave them an exposition of the Epistle. In the course of the day, fifty men of the 32nd and two guns went out to bring in treasure. Evening service at the mess-house at half-past six. It was very well attended. The Martinière boys sang very nicely. Harris preached on the verse, "Keep innocency, and do the thing that is right: for that shall bring a man peace at the last." After service I had prayers at the hospital; and saw and prayed with Evans. A doubtful case his recovery.

When I came in this evening, Dr. —— said to me, "Mr. Polehampton, with the best intention, you did —— harm to-day." I asked how; and he told me that he had rallied a good deal, but that, after I had been to him, his pulse became weaker. I told Dr. —— that I had said nothing that could possibly depress him. (I had read to him, in Hebrews, about the great High Priest, who can be touched with a feeling of our infirmities; and showed how our having Him in heaven encourages us to come *boldly* to the throne of grace.) Dr. —— has made a hasty jump to his conclusion, without any sufficient warrant.

* * * *

Monday, 29th.—Funeral—a cholera case from the Fort—at six o'clock. When it was over, as I was coming away, I met a man, who shocked me by telling me that poor Evans died two hours after I left him last night, and that his funeral was then on the way. Harris was there and would have taken it; but, being an old Shrewsbury man, I preferred to bury him myself.

Saw Dr. ——. He was much weaker, and wished to sleep; so I was unable to pray with him. At ten o'clock I heard that a report had come in, brought by one of Mr. Gubbins' spies, to the effect that Sir Hugh Wheeler had made terms with the Rajah; and that he had given up his position, and, I suppose, his arms, on the condition that he should be allowed to go down the river to Allahabad; that he and his garrison were allowed to embark, but that, when on the river, the enemy fired into and murdered them all. God grant that it may not be true! but I find all the officers believe it. Spies have also brought in intelligence that troops are advancing from the Seetapore side, and are now at Chinhut, ten miles from this. In consequence of this, the English are to be withdrawn from cantonments and brought in here. If the news about Cawnpore is true, we shall soon have the rebels from thence upon us.

At work for a great part of the day in putting our rooms to rights: no easy matter! Our baboo came to-day. As it is quite possible that this is the last, or *almost* the last, time we shall ever see him, I thought it well to ask him if he were now willing to be baptized. He was; and after much conversation with him, I baptized him in my room here; only Emmie being present. I could have wished that he should have been baptized in church, before many witnesses; but it is better as it is, under present circumstances. He says, however, that, if he is asked whether he is a Christian, he shall not deny his Lord. God give him grace to bear witness to Him! I believe him to have been long a sincere Christian at heart. He has Edward's address; and, in case of our dying here, or being killed, will write to him. I gave him fifty rupees to help him in case of our death. He could not take more, or I would have given him one hundred.

Walked out with Emmie at half-past six. A lady told her that the report about Cawnpore was now believed to be false; but Major ——— tells me that he believes it to be true. Just after prayers to-night, Major M. came to tell me that Mrs. H. (the wife of Lieutenant H. of his regiment), lately come in from Secrora, had died of cholera; having been taken ill only at three o'clock to-day. Went with him and got him a coffin, and saw her put into it—poor thing! Made arrangements about the funeral to-morrow. This evening I saw Sergeant ———, 52nd, who is ill with cholera. He is in a very desponding state of mind about his sins. I was able, I hope, to cheer him, on scriptural grounds. Good hopes are entertained for his recovery.

Tuesday, June 30*th.*—Out this morning by half-past five. Found that a force of about three hundred of the 32nd, an hundred and fifty Sepoys of the 13th, 71st, and 48th Regiments, Native Infantry, eight nine-pounders, and one eight-inch howitzer, drawn by elephants, had been sent out to meet the enemy. The Volunteer Cavalry and Sikhs, about a hundred in all, also went. Colonel Inglis commanded the expedition. They marched to Chinhut, a village about ten miles from Lucknow, where they found the enemy drawn up in force. But I will not give the particulars of the action; but relate what I saw myself. At about eleven o'clock I was looking out from the verandah outside our room, towards the direction whence we had been expecting all morning to hear firing, when I saw some horsemen galloping violently down the road. I did not see whether they came into the Residency compound or not; but the gates were immediately closed. There was evidently a great commotion; and I ran up to the top of the Residency to endeavour to discover what it was. The first thing I saw was an officer, evidently wounded, riding up, supported on each side by a Sikh. I ran down to the great door of the house to receive him, and found it to be Lieutenant Campbell, 71st Regiment, one of the Volunteer Cavalry. He was shot through the thigh, and was very pale and weak, and exhausted. From him I learned, to my dismay, that our men had been completely beaten, fearfully outnumbered; that they were coming in pell-mell; and that it was doubtful whether they would be able to save the guns. I helped to take him to the hospital, and had hardly done so, when there came in, in quick succession, James of the Commissariat, shot through the arm; Thompson, 32d, mortally wounded, and others; amongst them an artilleryman with both hands blown off. He and many other wounded came in on artillery-wagons. By about twelve o'clock the whole of the remains of our small force had come in, hard-pressed by the enemy, who had taken two howitzers and one nine-pounder. Colonel Case, Captain Stevens, Lieutenant Brackenbury, and about one hundred and twelve non-commissioned officers and men, were left on the field.

Within half-an-hour after the 32nd had come in, the enemy were at the bridge; and I could see their infantry lining the banks of the river and running down the bank opposite the Residency. Our eighteen-pounder at the Redan now opened upon them, and a party of about fifty men, who had been sent to retard their advance, disputed the bridge for a short time, but were soon obliged to fall back. They were sent there, chiefly, I fancy, to cover the retreat of the guns to the fort. Hardly had this party returned to the Residency, when the enemy began to open fire from the other side of the river. I was with the ladies, in the mess-room at the Residency, together with several officers who had no immediate duty. All had been ordered down from the upper story, as it was now considered unsafe. Sir Henry Lawrence and suite were in the next room to us. I was frequently at the hospital, where five men died of their wounds.

The Residency was struck several times by round shot during the day; but mostly in the upper story. A six-pound shot, however, at last passed through the staircase window and struck a corner of the room where we were. The ladies slept that night in an adjoining room. Awfully hot for them; no punkahs. I slept on the floor in the mess-room.

Wednesday, July 1st.—To-day two children died of cholera; Mrs. Watson's and Mrs. Soppitt's. . . . . Great difficulty in getting graves dug; the coolies had all run away. I got, at last, two native Christian servants of Mrs. Soppitt's, and my own man Peter, and Somerville, of the 32nd; and, with these, went at daybreak to dig a grave. Unable to get any directions in the proper quarter, as to the right place; was obliged, at last, to apply to Sir Henry Lawrence. He went down with me and pointed out a place beyond the church-compound, sheltered by a clerk's house, on which ten of our men were posted. I caught five stray coolies—they tried to run away, but I brought them back with my revolver—and we dug one large grave for seven bodies; I taking my turn at the work. As we were coming away, one of Mrs. Soppitt's servants was wounded in the arm by a musket-ball. .... The musket-balls were flying over us all the time, but high. To-day, while Sir Henry was sitting in his room with Captain Wilson, an eight-inch shell, from the howitzer captured from us, burst close to them; but providentially did no harm. We suffered much from the enemy's fire to-day; lost nine killed and wounded. At twelve o'clock at night, the remainder of our force stole a march on the enemy and came in from the Muchee Bawn, without the loss of a man. Immediately after their arrival the train was fired and the fort blew up with a tremendous explosion. We could not have held our own any longer without them.

After the shell burst in Sir Henry Lawrence's room to-day, it was not considered safe for the ladies to remain in the Residency any longer. Some went to the King's hospital; some to the Tykana. My wife begged me to ask Captain —— to get Sir Henry Lawrence to allow her to volunteer as a hospital nurse; and afterwards

Mrs. Gall and Mrs. Barbor joined in the request. Sir Henry was glad of their services, and we all moved to a room at the hospital, set apart for us, on the south side; with two windows open to the outside and two doors to the hospital-wards. It had been the room of the manager of the electric telegraph. I forget whether it was on Wednesday or Thursday that he was shot through the head with a musket-ball, immediately outside this house. His poor young wife, whom I had not long before visited, by his request, in a dangerous illness, was almost distracted.

But I cannot now write a minute account of what occurred between that time and the present date, July 15th; on which, for the first time, I have been able to write anything about the siege. I will only say how proud I was to see my dear wife going about the wards, on her message of mercy. I could not look at her without my eyes filling with tears.

Thursday, July 2nd.—Sir Henry Lawrence was wounded. A few days later, Mr. Ommanney was also mortally wounded. I do not quite know on which day Sir Henry died; but, if it please God to spare my life, I will fill up all this by and by. With him, a great and good man passed from amongst us. His death-bed was one of the most edifying scenes ever witnessed.

Wednesday, July 8th. (Ninth day of siege).—

Early this morning, I received a note from Miss ——, saying that her father was dead; and asking me to come and comfort her mother. I went. With much difficulty, and F. C.'s assistance, I got Mrs. —— to leave the room; and washed and laid out the body. Went home. Had just finished shaving and was stooping down to roll up our bed, when I felt a sudden stunning pain, and, after a second or two, knew that I had been shot. At first I thought it was a spent ball, from the smarting of the place; but, on looking, I saw a hole in the flesh. I then feared that the ball was still in; but Mrs. Barbor found it on the floor, to my great joy. Emmie made me lie down and brought in Dr. Boyd. He wanted me to be carried in to the receiving-room; but I felt as if I could walk without assistance. However, I soon found that I needed support on each side; and before I got into the receiving-room my eyes were dark. The examination was soon over; the wound pronounced not dangerous; and I was put to bed in the front ward of the hospital; next to Campbell, of the 71st. And here I have been ever since. For the first day I had a good deal of pain, but have suffered nothing since, except from restlessness at night. I trust it may be the last wound I shall ever have; but who shall say what is in store for us all, or who may be the next to go? God grant, that whoever of us it may be His will to take, away may be prepared! I have endeavoured to do my best to make my peace with Him; and, trusting in my Redeemer's merits, will endeavour to meet whatever may come without fear.

Rumours of reinforcements, without end. I believe none. I do not see how they can be here before August 10th, if then. If all India is as this place, none can come. But God can make a way of escape; and, if he do not, then through Christ " *Mors janua vitæ.*"

Tuesday, July 14*th.* (Fifteenth day of siege.)—This morning, about eight o'clock, the enemy opened a heavy fire of carcasses from the eight-inch howitzer and from nine-pounders; which they kept up, at intervals, during the day. Four or five nine-pound shot struck the hospital, but did no harm. Just outside the portico, however, a boy, of sixteen, belonging to the Artillery, had his leg taken off by a round shot. He called out piteously, "Oh Lord, my poor leg!" He soon, however, became very weak, too much so to endure amputation, and sank. This has been our heaviest day of casualties, I think; five killed and about eight or ten wounded, besides a fatal case of cholera.

Wednesday, July 15*th.*—Much refreshed by some sound sleep at intervals during the night. We had two alarms of attacks. A man rushed up to the main guard who sleep in the portico, close to my bed, and called out that the enemy were coming in. I started out of bed and took down my revolver; and, in doing so, hurt my wound a good deal. All the men stood to their arms; but it was a false alarm. About seven this morning, two round shots struck the south side of the hospital, but did no harm. Since then, till now, three o'clock, not a shot scarcely has been fired by either side to-day. One of the officers tells me that the enemy are getting guns into position all round; but not in positions where they can do much harm. (We have not, till this moment, when an eighteen has been fired, sent a shot at them.) My wound is going on, thank God! very well. I have been able to sit up nearly all day. Partridge came and gave me an account of the affair at Chinhut. A cool cloudy day. Altogether a great rest for us all. Firing continued very slack all day. Only one man wounded. He had his leg taken off, by a round shot, under the portico of the Residency, and is doing well, after amputation.

Thursday, July 16th.—Not much firing during last night; but a great deal of howling. This morning, at ten, we gave them, as far as I could make out, about twenty shells, in different places. The shells were, mostly, ill-directed: two fell into the river. One, only, that I could hear of, did much damage. They only fired one or two guns in return. None of them were to be seen anywhere, from the top of the Residency: except a party hard at work, throwing up a breastwork within about thirty yards of the garden-wall, and below the Treasury. What this is for, remains to be seen. They have also run two guns out of a house-wall opposite the King's hospital, not twenty yards distant. Unless these are taken or silenced, there will be mischief done.

A report is said to have come in to-day to Major Banks, brought by one of his spies, to the effect that the force sent to relieve Cawnpore (the 1st Madras Fusiliers, the 84th, some Sikhs, &c.; in all, about six or seven hundred), met a body of the enemy at Futtehpore, defeated them, and took four of their guns; but, being too weak to proceed, was waiting at Futtehpore for reinforcements. This seems likely. One man brought in to-day, wounded in the head; one shot dead close to the Chief Commissioner's house, just as he was eating his dinner.

The enemy kept up a heavy fire all night and howled a great deal; but did no other damage than wounding Captain O'Brien (84th Regiment) in the arm. He is a great loss, as he commands the detachment of the 84th; and there is only one other, a very young officer, with them.

. . . . Major Banks visited the hospital last night. He confirmed the report, that a spy of his had come in, and brought the above intelligence. . . . . The spy also said that the enemy here are very hard up for food; and that the Sikhs now with them, who deserted from us, would gladly come back if they could. Major Banks thought all this probable. I do not see how we are to get reinforcements, *via* Cawnpore, for a month. They *may* come from Delhi. But let us strive to curb our anxiety and trust that God will make a way of safety for us, as He knows best.

Friday, July 17*th*.—An Artilleryman brought in this morning at seven o'clock, wounded in the knee. Not much firing, as yet, to-day, on either side. In this ward are now—

Lieutenant Brown	Diarrhœa.
Myself	Shot through the body.
Lieutenant Foster	Wounded in the chest.
Lieutenant Farquhar	ditto through the jaw.
Lieutenant Smith	ditto in the hand.
Captain O'Brien	ditto in the arm.
Private—32nd	Leg amputated.
Private—32nd	ditto.
Private—32nd	Arm amputated.
Serjeant-Major Crook—32d	Cholera.
Corporal Green, Artillery	Wounded in the arm.
Captain Power	ditto.
Lieutenant Dashwood	ditto in the leg.
Lieutenant Campbell	ditto in the thigh.
Lieutenant Charlton	ditto in the head;

the ball not out. He is perfectly sensible; and yesterday I talked to him—the first I have seen since I was wounded—and am going again to-day. Yesterday I walked the length of the ward for the first time. My wound going on very well; health very good. Thanks be to God for his merciful preservation of me and my darling Emmie thus far!

This morning, as Clare Alexander was loading a mortar at his battery, through the negligence of the man who ought to have stopped the vent, the mortar went off, and knocked him and Captain Barlow over. Alexander is severely injured; and not likely to be of any use for weeks. Barlow is only hurt in the arm. Mr. Brown, a clerk, was brought in also, with his foot smashed by a musket-ball.

Saturday, July 18*th.*—Very heavy fire of musketry for two hours last night, beginning at twelve o'clock. Not a man of ours, however, was hit. I had the best night I have as yet had. This morning, early, a sergeant of Artillery was shot dead, as he was shifting a sand-bag at the Redan, and a 32nd man was wounded. Since that, two others have been brought in; one wounded in the leg, the other in the arm. We have kept up a heavy fire from an eighteen near the hospital to-day. To-day we hear that the rest of the bungalows in cantonments are on fire. Talked a good deal to Charlton to-day and prayed for him. . . . .

* * * * *

LETTERS AND DIARY

OF

MRS. HENRY STEDMAN POLEHAMPTON.

LETTER I.

To Mr. Polehampton's Mother.

MY DEAR MRS. WOOD,

Not much more than a year ago, I had, as I then thought, almost the hardest possible task to fulfil; that of writing to tell you of the very severe illness of my precious husband. And yet, when I then wrote, it was to announce his partial recovery. But my present task is one mingled with sorrow such as the heart only can conceive; it is impossible to speak about it; and joy, such blessed fathomless joy, that eye hath not seen, nor ear heard, neither hath it entered into the heart to conceive its fulness. Oh, dear Mrs. Wood, had you been with me to watch the entrance of that blessed soul into the glory that awaited it, to see the perfect serenity and peace that was his through that last short but

painful illness, you would not think it strange
for me to say that I have never known what it is
to have one repining thought since he was taken
away from me. It was *impossible* to feel anything but *rapture* in the thought of his having
entered into his Master's joy.

. . . . He had not the least fear of death.
He said to those who came to see him on his
deathbed, "I am not in the least frightened, and
I know exactly how I am." And his beautiful
fearless smile must have proved to them how
little dread there was for him in the prospect of
death.

. . . . I cannot tell you what a strange
unearthly sort of peace I had at the time of his
death. Through that last day and night of his
life, up to the moment that he died, a marvellous
kind of triumphant feeling came over me. I
cannot explain it, but I felt as if I were watching his entrance *into the joy of his Lord;* and
I seemed to *feel the joy myself.* This feeling
continued for days after, in a greater or less
degree, and only became less radiant as the
death-like blank in my own life became more
apparent.

. . . . And think, too, of all the pain and
anxiety and uneasiness of heart that he was
saved by being called at the time that he was,
to rest from his labours. Our really *troublous*

times had scarcely commenced then; he was indeed taken away from the evil to come. There is a passage, which it always seems to me may be so well applied to him, in the twenty-second chapter of the Second Book of Kings, " Because " thine heart was tender, and thou hast humbled " thyself before the Lord, when thou heardest " what I spake against this place, and against " the inhabitants thereof, that they should become " a desolation and a curse, and hast rent thy " clothes, and wept before me; I also have heard " thee, saith the Lord. Behold therefore, thou " shalt be gathered into thy grave in peace; and " thine eyes shall not see all the evil which I will " bring upon this place." ·

. . . . I had the great satisfaction of being able to put up a stone over his grave shortly before I left Lucknow. One of the soldiers procured me a slab of white marble from one of the king's palaces, and this I had laid upon a plain brickwork which he made for me. He engraved upon it the following inscription, with a small plain cross at the head:—

HENRY STEDMAN POLEHAMPTON,
CHAPLAIN OF THIS STATION,
BORN FEBRUARY 1, 1824.
DIED JULY 20, 1857.

"Enter thou into the joy of thy Lord."

... I trust I shall see you all before very long, but I do not yet know when I shall be able to sail.

May God comfort you all.

Ever yours most affectionately,

EMILY A. POLEHAMPTON.

LETTER II.

To the Rev. Edward Polehampton.

MY DEAR EDWARD,

You ask me to write my recollections of the siege; but as I kept no journal during our residence in hospital, in the early part of the siege, it would be impossible for me to give, at this distance of time, any detailed account of my life there; but I will mention a few of its incidents, which were omitted in Henry's diary.

He and I shared a small room at the back of the hospital with Mrs. Gall and Mrs. Barbor, in which we had to sleep, dress, and have our meals. As this room was on the most exposed side of the building, we were obliged to be very careful in arranging ourselves, both at night and also at our meals, so as to avoid the bullets which were constantly coming into the room. There were two windows, and we took out all the glass from them, to prevent the danger of being struck by the flying splinters. We all slept between the windows, under the protection of the wall, and we seldom woke in the mornings without finding several musket balls near us; once or twice they lay within a few inches of where our heads had been.

We were fortunate in retaining amongst us about six servants. Three of these were Mrs. Gall's Madrassees. Ours were the Baboo; Ramsay, the African kitmutgar; and Peter, our native Christian Church Chuprassi. About a week after the siege commenced, Peter asked us to let him go outside the intrenchments. He said that he felt confident he could do so in disguise, and return in safety. He went out, and returned to us in a day or two, bringing some tidings of our house in cantonments, which he had managed to visit. He said that it was still standing, but had, of course, been sacked by the enemy. The books were scattered about on the ground, the pictures had been broken and thrown into the well. He discovered that the old Mehter had taken Chloe into the city, for safety, as he supposed.

When we had been about a week in hospital, we were joined by Miss Birch, the daughter of Colonel Birch, who commanded the 41st Native Infantry, and who was murdered at Seetapore. She proved a most kind and energetic assistant, but unhappily her health was not strong, and she had not been with us many days, when she was taken ill with fever and ague; and Dr. Boyd preferred her returning at once to Mr. Gubbins', of whose garrison she had previously been an inmate.

About the time Henry was wounded, the atmosphere throughout the hospital was daily becoming more poisonous. Bullets were flying so constantly through various parts of the building, that it was necessary to have all the doors and windows closely barricaded, excepting only those of the front ward. Consequently, the heat being at this time very oppressive, the wards low and much crowded, the wounds of all kinds and in all stages, it may not be difficult to form some idea of the state of our *inner* atmosphere. Those who came in from the *comparatively* pure air outside, often said that they could hardly endure to pass through the inner wards. The flies, too, at this time were one of our chief annoyances. It seemed impossible in any degree to thin their numbers; they literally swarmed throughout the wards, and of course much aggravated the sufferings of the wounded. But our poor sufferers, in this, as in other hardships, showed such marvellous patience and powers of endurance, as can be imagined only by those who have witnessed the same sufferings under similar circumstances. Various expedients for purifying the air were adopted, such as burning camphor, &c. in the different wards, but the good effects were very transient. During this part of the siege, the upper rooms of the buildings were unused (with the exception of one, which for a time was converted into a cholera ward), as they were far too much exposed to shot of all kinds to allow of their being occupied.

On the 1st July, Miss Palmer (the daughter of the Colonel of the 48th Native Infantry) was wounded in the leg by a round shot, which passed through the window of the room she occupied in the Residency. The leg was amputated, and, as in all like cases at that time, no hope seemed to be entertained of her recovery from the first. Henry went to see her, and found her perfectly calm and resigned. Her father seemed to be her only care; and repeatedly during Henry's visit she entreated him to take care of her father when she should be gone. She only survived the amputation for a day or two. Poor girl! she had come out from England but a few months before, and was then, at bright seventeen, looking forward with vivid hopefulness to her Indian life. During the first week of the siege, Maggie Macdonough, a little girl about twelve years old, the child of an English sergeant in the 71st Native Infantry, came one day into the hospital, saying that she had been struck in the head by a bullet. She was able to tell her own story with perfect calmness, and little thought, poor child, how serious an injury she had sustained. The ball was lodged in the head, and it was necessary to perform a painful operation, and to remove a portion of the skull, in order to extract it. She bore her sufferings with wonderful patience, and for a time appeared to be going on well; but in less than a fortnight she was seized with fits, her whole body becoming paralysed, and shortly after these came on she sank rapidly. She was one of Mrs. Barbor's especial charges, and was most kindly and carefully tended by her up to the time of her death. She was a beautiful child, and had been one of Henry's special favourites amongst the children in the Artillery School in cantonments, which she had regularly attended in old times. Poor Mrs. Macdonough, after her child's death, made herself most useful in attending upon the sick and wounded.

.... On the evening of Henry's death, July 20, the day on which the rebels made their most serious attack upon us, the doctors insisted upon my leaving the hospital, which I was very reluctant to do. Mrs. Gall and Mrs. Barbor (the widows of Major Gall and Lieut. Barbor, killed just before the siege) accompanied me, and Colonel Palmer took us all to an empty room in a house called the Begum Kotee, which we were allowed to keep to ourselves, with the exception of a fourth part, divided from the rest by purdahs. This partition was occupied by Captain Thomas, Madras Artillery, and his little girl. His wife had died of small-pox, a few days before we came to the house. Two rooms beyond opened out of ours, in one of which the Grahams lived; the other was occupied by Mrs. Bartrum, Mrs. Benson, Mrs. Clarke, and Mrs. Kendal. The whole of this party had come into Lucknow from several out-stations in the district, shortly before the siege commenced. We never went out of our room excepting at night, when I always took advantage of the darkness, and walked to and fro upon a little narrow pavement outside our doors, which was bordered on the other side by a drain, the unhealthy qualities of which by no means improved our situation. But at the time of which I write, we were not allowed to go beyond this, and I used to take a strange pleasure in walking here alone at night, and listening to the bullets that were constantly flying overhead; especially in the starlight nights, when all looked so calm and peaceful above. It was difficult at such times to help longing for one's summons to that blessed home.

At this time, Colonel Palmer and Mr. Harris were our most constant visitors, and they did indeed show us the kindness of true friends. Mrs. Gall, Mrs. Barbor, and I were the only three in the garrison who, under the same circumstances (having all lost our husbands), lived alone together. There being thus no gentleman in our party, we were of course thrown entirely upon our own resources in every way. But Colonel Palmer and Mr. Harris were always, by their unwearied kindness, trying to lessen in some degree the sense of our utterly lonely position. From them we learned the daily reports, and all the tidings concerning the garrison. But I think we cared little for what was going on, and, as far as we alone were concerned, looked forward with small interest to the prospect of "relief." The only occurrences, which at this time varied in any way the usual course of things, were the occasional attacks of the enemy. There was something very grand and exciting about these, when they suddenly commenced in the dead of night; or rather, *after* their commencement, when the firing was just at its height. We used to jump out of bed, and run out into the verandah, and stay there during these attacks, until sometimes warned back by a stray bullet falling near our feet, or striking the wall or doorway above our heads.

Until the 23rd of August, we did not leave our room at all, except, as I said, to walk up and

down in front of our doors. On Sunday, the
23rd, Mrs. Barbor and I went with Colonel
Palmer to Dr. Fayrer's garrison, where we had
afternoon service with the Holy Communion.
Five of our small congregation were newly-made
widows.

From this time we were no longer afraid to
venture farther beyond our own precincts than
we had hitherto done, and we extended our
evening walk rather more each day, under Colonel
Palmer's escort. One evening he took Mrs.
Barbor and me to the Residency, which we had
been longing to visit. We went all over the
house, and into the rooms on the highest story
that we had occupied just before the siege. I
found the room, in which Henry and I had lived,
in a complete state of ruin. Part of the walls
had fallen in, the floor was covered with bricks
and mortar, and several round shot were lying
there. The whole of the verandah outside the
windows, in which Henry and Mr. Harris used to
take "chota haziri" (early breakfast) together,
during that month of our residence here, before
the siege, had been loosened by the constant
firing, and had fallen to the ground. I found
the large earthen bath, that we had left in the
bathroom adjoining, shattered by round shot,
several of which had entered the room. We
went up to the roof to look out, but it was not

considered safe for us to remain there. The panoramic view of the city and surrounding country appeared more beautiful now than ever to us, who had for so long been confined to our own limited quarters. I strained my eyes to catch a glimpse of the church in cantonments, but it is not quite visible from the Residency. But I knew the adjacent country well, and it made my heart sick to look at it, and to think of my own dear home, which was hidden amongst the trees. . . . . Our poor Baboo made himself most useful to me for a month after I went to the Begum Kotee. He did not refuse to do anything that I wanted, and even washed my clothes regularly. I would not have allowed him, however, to do this work, had it been possible to get it done otherwise. But I did so only at his own special request. One day he came to me, looking very faint, with his white cap and dress saturated with blood, but with a strange expression of pleasure on his face. On my asking what was the matter, he said, "I am very glad; I have been shot in the head." I had noticed for some time past that he had showed perfect indifference as to his safety, and seemed quite fearless when walking about under fire. But his present apparent joy rather startled me. I sent him at once to the European hospital, as I knew that Dr. Thompson would attend to him for me. He

examined the wound, and found that it was only
a slight one, as the ball had not entered deeply,
but had struck him, and glanced off. He bandaged it, and sent him to lie down for the rest of
the day. The next morning, to my astonishment, he returned to me, looking pulled down by
the loss of blood, but otherwise all right again.
Soon after this, he grew so anxious to go outside
the garrison to see what was going on, and to
find out what had become of our house in cantonments, that he insisted on going out disguised as a common coolie, and said that he was
almost certain he should not be recognised, but
should come back to me in three days. I tried
hard to persuade him not to venture, and told him
that, if he went, I should never expect to see him
again. However, he had set his mind upon it,
and went out leaving me the following note:—
"My dear madam, I have been to Mr. Harris."
(I had told him that I could not consent to his
going without his first consulting Mr. Harris.)
" He said to me some Christians have gone out,
" and he heard they are all killed; their blood
" scattered about the ground. I think myself to
" death as a dream. 1 am not the least frighted
" of it. If I die, I will see Mr. Polehampton. Is
" it not a good thing for me? I hope God will
" protect me, if I put my trust in Him."

This was the last I ever heard of him, and

I have not the least doubt he was killed at once, as soon as the Sepoys saw him; for he was well known to them as being with us, and he had attended church regularly for many months. Not long before the siege, Henry baptized him, and he then told us that he had made up his mind to profess himself openly as a Christian, without fear of consequences, if the time should come for him to be tried. Even all our servants, who ran away just at the commencement of the siege, were killed outside. Every one, who was known to have done any sort of service for the Christians, was put to death. I feel so happy in thinking of the Baboo's death: I know he was so true to his Christian profession, and he seemed to me to be almost longing for an opportunity of bearing witness to his Lord. How soon, too, *his* desire was granted to him of rejoining his earthly master and best friend!

.... I had now no servant of my own left, excepting the African, and he would do nothing but wait at meals, and fill my bason with fresh water; so I had to wash my own clothes, and keep my portion of the room clean. These were, however, the only hardships that any of our party ever had to undergo in the siege, and we were, therefore, more fortunate than many others. Poor Mrs. Bartrum, for instance, undertook the cooking for her party, and she found the gun-bullock beef so tough that she had always to beat it with a heavy stick for half-an-hour, in vain attempts to make it tender, and then to cut it up with *nail-scissors* into shreds, before stewing! I had laid up a good store of soap just before the siege commenced, so I did not find much difficulty in washing the clothes; only in the hot, damp weather it was very exhausting work.

.... A day or two after General Havelock relieved us, September 25, I went to the hospital and asked the doctors to let me return there, to help to nurse. They at once gave me leave to do so, and I continued at it until the end of the siege, about the end of November. Mrs. Gall also soon joined us; Mrs. Barbor was not well enough to do so. I cannot tell you what delight I took in it, but I was able to do very little, and latterly I had no help, as neither Mrs. Gall nor Mrs. Barbor were strong enough for it. I had such marvellous strength and good health during the siege; scarcely an ailment except a day and night, a little before Henry's death, when I felt very ill with fever.

.... The whole of the hospital building was now occupied, the danger from shot in the upper story being not so great as formerly. The rooms up-stairs, two of which were very spacious and lofty, were appropriated to the 32nd Regiment and Artillery of our own original garrison. This was a delightful change for these men, many of whom had lain for nearly three months in the dark, ill-ventilated wards below, where, during the whole above-mentioned time, they could only see to read for an hour in the day, and hardly that. They had now, not only the benefit of the pure fresh air which was allowed to come freely in upon them, but also the refreshment for their weary eyes of the beautiful view of the country towards cantonments. Some portions of these upper rooms were at this time occupied by about twenty wounded officers (some of them convalescents); most of these were soon afterwards removed to a large room in the Begum Kotee, which was from that time used exclusively as a hospital for the officers.

The lower wards were now entirely given up to the wounded of the new regiments that came in with General Havelock, and were, of course, much crowded. But, happily, the extreme heat of the weather had now abated, and there was no longer the same necessity as in former times for the close barricading of all the doors and windows.

.... My own private life was so unvaried and uniform, that there is nothing in it worth relating. If I give you a sketch of one day, you will have an idea of what it was during a great portion of the time, that is to say, after the reinforcements came in; before that, from the time of Henry's death, I had no employment of any sort. We used to pass the day in our gloomy room as well as we could, in reading, and writing, and working. After this, I used to go to the hospital after breakfast, spend as many hours there as I found necessary, and return to dinner. In the evening I only spent an hour in the hospital, and then, when it got dark, my time of *rest* came; the most precious hour I had in the day; and that I spent at my darling Henry's grave. I often wonder now, in looking back at that time, how I escaped as I did on these occasions, for the bullets were constantly flying thickly, close over my head as I was sitting at the grave, and several times shells burst within a few yards of me there. It seemed so strange that I should be one to escape.

.... It has certainly been through the most wonderful interposition of Providence that the remnant of our garrison has been brought out safely, and more marvellous still that we were enabled to hold out as we did, with our limited supply of provisions and medicines. At one time I had so completely given up all hope of ever seeing any of you again in this world, that I wrote a long letter to my mother with this idea, intending it to be sent to her in case of my death.

I cannot tell you what a strange feeling it is to think that I have lost everything I had in the world in the way of property, with the exception of the few *precious* things I managed to put into small compass to bring away with me. The day before we left Lucknow (and we had only this one day's notice to leave), orders were given that we were to have no means of carriage except for ourselves; and I could bring away nothing in the shape of baggage, but must leave all my property behind. Accordingly, we set to work to destroy *everything*, except such things as we most valued, and could put into carriage-bags and pillows, &c. I burnt all my books, clothing, papers, and letters,—in fact, *all* I had in the world, save a few things that I kept in our overland box, on the chance of bringing it away. All my husband's sermons that I cared most about I wore in a large pocket round my waist; his gown and surplice, hood and stole, and baby's clothes, I sewed into a pillow; and several small things, likenesses, &c., I put into my carriage-bags. I managed to secure far more than I ever hoped for in this way, and, to my great joy, found that I might bring my overland box away. You will imagine how much vexed I was the next morning, when it was too late to save all my other things, to hear that each lady was to have a camel for her own use; I might then have brought away all the books and other things that I prized so much. The only thing left that I cared about was my harmonium, which I valued very much, because it was given us by the 52nd Regiment (Queen's); it had been lying in the church uninjured throughout the siege, and this I have managed to save, and, as you know, have brought home with me.

Twenty of us have become widows in the siege; this, of course, does not include those among the soldiers, clerks, &c.; and of these twenty only a few are older than myself, and one or two are only nineteen years old.

On our arrival at Cawnpore, we found it besieged by the Gwalior rebels. It seemed like old times to have shells bursting about us again, as they did when we were on the other side of the river, within a few yards of us. I forgot to tell you that I was twice struck by musket balls during the siege; once on the arm, and once afterwards on the ankle.

I inclose you a meagre kind of diary I kept on my way from Lucknow to Calcutta; I do not think there is much to interest you, but you can make what use you like of it.

Ever your affectionate Sister,

EMILY A. POLEHAMPTON.

DIARY.

Lucknow, Wednesday, Nov. 18, 1857.

EARLY this morning we received notice that we were all to leave Lucknow, probably within a few hours.

. . . . Went to the churchyard and spent some time there. To-day for the first time I have been able to see the stone and inscription by daylight. What would I not give to be resting there with him! God only knows how I have longed to die where he has died, and there to be buried!

Thursday, 19*th.*—At about three o'clock we started in our buggies, with cavalry horses provided for us by Captain Barrow. I was thankful that we had not to pass by the old well-known roads. Outside the Baillie Gate, the buildings all deserted and in ruins; whole plains covered with dead horses, camels, bullocks, &c. Our horse, faint and weak from want of food, lay down two or three times from exhaustion; at one time the soldiers were obliged to cut the traces. Mrs. Gall and I walked the greater part of the way. We found our walk in the heat very trying, as we were told to *run* fast now and then, the enemy seeing us from various points, and firing upon us. Arrived at Secundra Bagh (three miles from the Residency) at about four o'clock. This morning, only a few hours before we started, an order came for us all to be allowed camels to bring away our things. I thus managed to save my harmonium and overland trunk, all the other things being destroyed. Found detachments of regiments at Secundra Bagh; 93rd Highlanders, Naval Brigade, Sikhs, &c. The smell through the buildings and garden almost unendurable, our troops having killed 1,700 of the enemy inside the walls, two days ago; and the bodies have, many of them, only just been buried, others burnt; some are unburied still; we remained in this place all day. The officers brought us tea, with milk and sugar, and bread and butter, the first we had tasted for nearly five months! As soon as it was dark, doolies were provided, and we went on. I attempted to go on in my buggy, but, as soon as the horse was put in again, he fell down and broke the shafts, so that I was obliged to leave the buggy on the road, and take a doolie. We were sent on under a strong escort of cavalry and infantry, and skirmishing parties constantly went out to reconnoitre. Arrived at the Dilkoosha Palace about ten o'clock; about three miles from Secundra Bagh. Found tents prepared for us, the Palace being crowded with sick and wounded of all regiments. After a little trouble I found Mrs. Gall, and we went together to a large tent, where we settled ourselves next to Mrs. Inglis and her party. Brigadier Little brought us tea, bread and butter, and meat, and lent us coverlets. We lay on the ground in our clothes and slept pretty well, for we were almost tired out. About sixty people slept in the tent.

Friday, 20th.—Mr. Freeling came to us this morning, bringing several officers of the 8th Queen's, who asked us to breakfast. When we were at their mess, they made arrangements for us to come and live in their quarters. They gave us up their own sleeping tent, pitched close to the mess tent, and made it very comfortable. We breakfast and dine at mess, and they send us everything else that we want to our tent. Mrs. Gall, Mrs. Barbor, Mrs. Graham, and I are together. Mrs. Banks, Mrs. Couper, and Mrs. Aitken dine and breakfast with us.

Saturday, 21st.—We walked, escorted by four or five of the officers, to the Muchli Bagh, afterwards to the top of the palace. Saw some of the enemy's Suwārs in the distance, at the Galls' house.

Sunday, 22nd.—Directly after breakfast, an attack was made upon the outskirts of the camp. The bugle sounded and all the officers and men were called out. We ran out too, and went to the top of the palace, where we could see what was going on. Some infantry and a small party of horse artillery of ours advanced, and the enemy soon retreated, having done no greater harm than cutting up about twenty grass-cutters. After this I went to see the wounded men in the 78th hospital tents. To-day the whole garrison leave the Residency, and join our camp here. The tidings of the prisoners in the Kaiser Bagh are, that Sir Mountstuart Jackson is hanged and his sister also killed. Nothing known of the rest. Charlie Dashwood died to-day in the Dilkoosha Palace.

Monday, 23rd.—Brigadier Greathed breakfasted at mess. He told us that they all came in safely last night, and now the Residency is wholly abandoned! Our old kitmutgar came to see me to-day. I asked him to try and get me tidings of Chloe, and promised him a good reward if he would bring her to me. He said, the old mehter (sweeper), who took care of her, had been killed, and he thought Chloe had probably been killed also. We went to the post-office tent; no letters for me. I took possession of those for Sir M. Jackson and his sisters. General

Havelock died this morning of dysentery. He died indeed the death of a Christian hero.

Tuesday, 24th.—Captain Hinde lent me a bullock cart for the harmonium, as it is too large for the camel, having fallen off several times. Left the Dilkoosha at half-past eleven—Mrs. Graham, Charlie Palmer, and I—in a bullock cart. We had a very wearisome drive; the road crowded with conveyances and baggage of every description. Our whole *cortége* covers seven miles of ground. Passed numerous dead bodies, said to be those of the grass-cutters killed in the attack the other day. Arrived at Alum Bagh a little before five (seven miles). After waiting a long time in the cart, Mrs. Graham and I sent the servants to look for the rest of our party, but they could not find them. At last we tried to find our way to the 8th lines; the lines, however, were far off, and the officers had not arrived, their regiment being rear-guard. So we made up our minds to stay in the cart all night. We had fortunately brought cold meat and bread with us. After roaming about the tents, in search of Mrs. Gall and Mrs. Barbor, we returned to the cart and managed to sleep in it; Mrs. Graham and her child and Charlie and I had a very uncomfortable night, as we were fearfully cramped.

Wednesday, 25th.—Captain Hinde came early

this morning, and brought us tea and bread; the Madras servant having gone to tell him how we were situated. He went to look for Mrs. Gall and shortly returned with her. She and Mrs. Barbor, after a long search for us last night, had also returned to their cart and slept in it. We all dressed as well as we could in the open air. . . . .

Thursday, 26th.—Mr. Jackson came to see us this evening. He is in wretched spirits about his nephew and nieces (Sir M. Jackson and his sisters), but says that he has still *hopes* of their safety, having now heard that they have been removed from the Kaiser Bagh to the Dowlut Kana, probably for safety. He has had one letter from them, which he says was evidently written under dictation by Sir Mountstuart, as he speaks in it of being unable to write upon family matters in "this business letter." It is signed by "Mountstuart and Madeline Jackson."

Saturday, 28th.—Marched at seven. Heavy firing heard in the direction of Cawnpore. Passed Bushirat Gunge, the scene of one of Havelock's battles; also Unao. The plains strewed with skeletons. The villages all in ruins; the walls of the houses loop-holed. Arrived within two miles of Cawnpore at seven P.M. (twenty-eight miles). A heavy day's march, and the men much fatigued. Took up four of them for the latter part of the way, two on the box and two behind. Several of the regiments are sent on into Cawnpore to-night; it being again besieged by the Gwalior force, 17,000 strong, commanded by the Nana. Had we not made this forced march, or had we even arrived a few *hours* later, we could not have relieved the garrison, as the enemy would have destroyed the bridge of boats, and we should have been cut off. A bitterly cold night.

Sunday, 29th.—At three o'clock this morning heard orders given for marching. Saw the bungalows burning in cantonments. After breakfast the regiment was ordered into Cawnpore. We reached our encampment at twelve, about a mile from Cawnpore, and in full view of it. The bungalows, bazaars, &c., all in flames. A very good encamping ground, the turf clean and soft. Captain Green came in the evening and took us on to his advanced picket on the brink of the river, the order having been given for us all to march into Cawnpore in the night, and this picket was on the way to the bridge. We dined on the open ground by moonlight. A quiet night; only a little musketry now and then.

Monday, 30th.—As we were waiting for orders this morning, Mrs. Barbor began to sketch Cawnpore, the church, &c., she and I sitting on the box of the gharree (or small carriage). While we were there, the enemy began to fire round shot upon us from the other side of the river. They must have seen us plainly, as we were in a very conspicuous place. The officers took us away in haste; and when we had gone a few yards in the rear, another round shot struck the very spot where our gharree had been. They took us back to the lines of the 5th brigade (32nd, 23rd, &c.). The firing soon slackened, and we returned half-way and breakfasted. Sat on the grass all morning. Marched at three; arrived at the barracks in Cawnpore in about half an hour. A good deal of round shot fired at us as we drove, but we crossed the bridge safely. It was quite like old times again in the midst of shot and shell. We could not cross the river without a feeling of horror, as we thought of all that had happened there, within a few yards of where we were crossing. We were *close* to the place, where Sir H. Wheeler's garrison went into the boats, according to their treaty, and then were immediately fired on, and men, women, and children, to the number of some eight hundred, all slaughtered, most of them on the spot, the rest soon afterwards. There were only four survivors of that fearful tragedy. Our three carriages were the last to cross. One of the soldiers on guard at the bridge looked in at the gharree as we reached the other side, and said, "Thank God, the sepoys haven't got at *you!*" When we arrived at the barracks, three of the 8th officers came and said they had been looking for us all day. They took us to their lines, and we dined with them. The Nana has just issued a proclamation in Cawnpore that he intends to have a second massacre here, similar to the first. Several round shot were fired into the 8th camp, just as we were driving away. It is wretched to see the utter ruin and desolation of this place; the gardens a wilderness, and all the houses burnt and broken down, only the outer walls standing. I am almost glad that I was not able to see our own dear old cantonments at home in their present state.

Wednesday, Dec. 2d.—Captain Green came early this morning to look after us; all our meals are sent us from his mess. We had Mr. Fisher's tent pitched outside the barrack, and moved into it after breakfast. Captain Hinde and Major North came to see us. We went in the evening with Captain Green and Mr. Plowden to see the old intrenchments. It is impossible to describe the wretchedness of the places where those unhappy creatures were besieged until the day that they left them for the river, according to the Nana's agreement. The chapel is close by, in which, at one time, many of the women and children lived. Only its outer walls are now standing. Mrs. Barbor and I wandered through all the rooms searching for relics. I found some pieces of music amongst the ruins, and some torn drawing-paper, &c. Mr. Plowden says that he has now a long, beautiful plait of a lady's hair, torn out by the roots, which he found in the room, where the women and children were killed. We are not able to see *that* room, as that part of Cawnpore is now again in the hands of the enemy. We were told to draw eight days' rations today, and to be ready to march at a moment's notice, as we should probably have to do so in the night. However, it passed without disturbance.

Thursday, 3rd.—This evening Mrs. Gall and I walked down to the river, and went through one of the ruined bungalows. The floors are all dug up by the natives, in search of treasure. Marched at ten o'clock.

Friday, 4th.—Arrived at the halting-place (twenty-eight miles from Cawnpore) at eleven A.M. The heat very great for the last three hours. We have no tent, and have therefore to lie under the shade of trees, and manage as we can, without even a bathing-room. A poor woman is lying close to us, who had her hand shot almost off this morning by a gun, which was lying loaded in her cart. Dr. Fayrer has just taken off the thumb; he thinks the rest of the hand may be saved. She is only twenty-one; her husband was killed in the siege, having only been married three months, and she expects her confinement next month. She is very quiet and patient, but I fear this wearisome march must tell upon her fearfully. There is the same black *leaden* look about her face that one always sees in amputation cases. The worst of it is, not a doolie can be procured for her, and the shaking of a bullock-cart would almost certainly be fatal.

Saturday, 5th.—Reached the encamping ground at eight this morning. As yesterday, we had to manage as well as we could on the open ground. We chose a raised puckha platform, built round a large neam tree; spread our beds there, and made a little bath-room, by putting a coverlet round the branches of a tree. Marched at seven P.M.

Monday, 7th.—Arrived at Chimia, where the railway begins, at about six this morning. Part of the 23rd are encamped there, on their way to Cawnpore. One of the soldiers brought me some tea and bread and jam from his own store. Great confusion in getting into the train. The soldiers all came to see us off. Just as we began to move away, they cried out, "Vengeance for the daugh-"ters and babes of England, slaughtered at

"Cawnpore! And we shall have it too!" They then cheered loudly as our train moved away. When we arrived at Allahabad, we found the station *crowded* with the residents, officers, soldiers, ladies, &c.—in fact, almost all the inhabitants seemed to be here to receive us, arranged on both sides of the train, and there was a burst of cheering as we came up. We found large, comfortable tents prepared for us inside the Fort. To-day's parole " Heroine," in honour of our arrival.

Tuesday, 8th.—Mrs. Spry (wife of the chaplain at Allahabad) asked Mrs. Harris and myself to help her to distribute the contents of a box sent up by Lady Canning for the Lucknow ladies. It contains shoes and boots, brushes, stockings, handkerchiefs, soap, &c. People seem to have expected us to arrive in utter destitution, as is indeed nearly the case. Mrs. Spry and others have been commissioned to buy in stores of all the things that we most need, at the expense of the Relief Fund. Mr. Gubbins is very ill, dangerously so, Dr. Fayrer says. Mrs. Gubbins looks quite worn out. She says that the fever is just like what my husband's was last year, and that he is constantly delirious. He has been ill ever since he left Cawnpore, and I never heard of it until last night. I hope it may please God to spare his life, and let him see England again.

He was one of the bravest and most gallant men we had in the siege.

Walked in the evening with Mrs. Barbor and Mrs. Lewin to the European shops, about a mile from the Fort. On our way home, we met Mr. Edmonstone, the judge, who put us into his buggy, and walked back with us. He said that we had done a most rash thing in walking outside the Fort alone, and begged us never to do so again, as there are no European troops near the shops, and a great many natives, who would think nothing of insulting or shooting us.

Wednesday, 9th.—Tidings came in that a fight took place yesterday at Chimia, the railway-station. Our Sikhs drove the rebels back into the villages, and in one of them they found the clothes of Europeans, covered with blood. The English mail came in this evening; not a letter for any of the Lucknow garrison, except one for Mrs. Brydon. It is supposed that we were entirely given up for lost by those in England, as it is only thus that the failure can be accounted for. The rumour of our walk to the shops last evening has made quite a sensation throughout the place. It seems that it was a far more rash proceeding than we had any idea of. We are told that the officers never venture outside the Fort walls without loaded revolvers. Mr. Gubbins a little better to-day.

Thursday, 10*th*.—To-day I had the address of Mr. Erskine's friends. I must write to his uncle first, and inclose a letter for his mother, as she may not have heard of her son's death. His last words were, "Tell my dear mother that my last thought was of her." Mrs. Inglis called this evening. She heard from the Brigadier to-day. He has received a highly complimentary letter from the Governor-General, expressing his admiration of the conduct of our garrison. There seems still to be much uncertainty as to the safety of the roads for dâk travelling; 10,000 of the enemy are still within five miles of us here.

Friday, 11*th*.—There are a great many widows and children of soldiers here, and Mrs. Harris and I are going to try to get up a school ourselves for them, and teach them for an hour or two daily. A notice came round this evening to say that the *Madras* steamer is expected soon, and that the sick are to go down the river on the "flat" accompanying it. I want, if possible, to accompany the sick either by this or the next steamer. Dr. Thompson tells me that he thinks 100 of our sick here must die.

Saturday, 12*th*.—Mr. Gubbins much better. Mrs. Inglis heard from the Brigadier to-day. He is left in command of the Cawnpore garrison, having taken it with the stipulation that he should be allowed to keep his own Lucknow garrison with him. Went to Mr. Spry, the chaplain here, with Mrs. Harris, to ask him about our getting up a school in the barracks. He told us to take possession of any empty room we liked. I spoke to him about my going down as nurse with the sick, and he promised to try and arrange it for me. Went to the barracks to arrange about a Sunday class for to-morrow. Wrote to Dr. Kay. This is the first letter that I have been able to write.

Sunday, 13th.—To-day Mr. Harris had a thanksgiving service, with the Holy Communion, for the survivors of the Lucknow garrison, in the Fort chapel, at 'eleven o'clock. The Psalms he selected were the thirty-fourth, seventy-first, and ninety-second; the Lessons, Exodus xv. and Romans xii. We had a very large congregation. The alms at the offertory to be given to the Lawrence Asylum, as a sort of tribute to Sir Henry's memory. It was the first time that I had been at service in any sort of church since May 24th, when I was with my own dear husband at church at cantonments, and in the city. The sight of the Communion-table, and everything as in old times, was almost more than I could bear. What would not this service have been to me, if *he* had been here to celebrate it! I have always such a *craving* for his presence at these times of service; and yet I well know how selfish this is. God grant that it may not be long before I may join him in the services of the Church above! "I trust I shall see thee shortly, and we shall speak face to face."

Went with Mrs. Harris to the barracks at two o'clock, and had school there for an hour. The children far less wild and unmanageable than we had expected, and all very clean and nicely dressed.

Monday, 14*th.*—Mr. Spry thinks that I had better get a place on the "flat" with the sick, if I can, and said he would speak to the captain about it. Dr. Hutchinson told me this evening that he is going down in charge of the sick and wounded by the first steamer. He says that none of the bad cases are going yet, and that he thinks a nurse will scarcely be required. I am going with him through the hospital-tents this morning, and shall then find out more about it.

Tuesday, 15*th.*—Went at eleven this morning to the hospital-tents with Dr. Hutchinson; there are a great many of them, and the regiments all mixed up together. Went through almost all, and saw the old Lucknow cases. Some of them have died on the way. They are looking much better on the whole, but some have been so shaken by the journey that they are far worse than when in our old hospital. They are in very good spirits.

The Lucknow cases are those in the 32nd, Artillery, 78th Highlanders, Madras Fusiliers, 1st Fusiliers, a few of the 84th, and 90th. Went to the school at two for an hour and a half. The list of passengers for the first steamer has been sent round to-day. The committee have put down my name as nurse to accompany the sick. However, as I find that only convalescents are going now, I have withdrawn my name, and given my place to Mrs. Barlow, who is particularly anxious to go at once. Went to the barracks in the evening to find out all the women who have not yet had relief.

Thursday, 17*th*.— .... School from half-past two to half-past three P.M.

Saturday, 19*th*.— .... School from two to half-past three P.M.

Sunday, 20*th*.—Mr. Harris preached from the epistle, " Rejoice in the Lord always." No school to-day, as Mrs. Inglis asked me to let the 32nd children go to her, as they used to do on Sundays in former times. A letter from Dr. Kay to-day. Mr. Spry preached in the evening from the text, " Our light affliction, which is but for a moment."

Monday, 21*st*.—Received a very kind letter from the Archdeacon of Calcutta. School from two to half-past three. The Archdeacon says that there is going to be a " thanksgiving service" in the cathedral for our garrison, and they are anxious that we should all be there to join in it.

Tuesday, 22nd.— .... School from two to half-past three. Walked on the ramparts in the evening. We heard from some Artillery officers that the enemy are seen plainly from four miles down the river, and that they have fifteen guns. An order issued that no one is to travel down country by dâk at present. Heavy firing heard in the direction of Benares.

Wednesday 23rd.— .... School as usual. Mrs. Thornhill took a class.

Thursday, 24th.—Mrs. Inglis came to our tent to-night, and told us about the account that Mrs. Case's ayah gives of what was going on in Lucknow, outside our intrenchments, during the siege.

Sunday, 27th.— .... A very large congregation. We hear that the sepoys have taken up their quarters in cantonments at Lucknow; and that they have colonels, majors, captains, &c., as in our regiments.

Tuesday, 29th.—This morning at two o'clock the horse letter-dâk from Cawnpore was stopped by the enemy, seven miles from this place. They wounded eight of our men, and took away the horses; but one man managed to secure the bags, and ran in here with them. School as usual. Heard this evening that Mr. Inglis (13th Native

Infantry) died and was buried to-day. I had never even heard of his wound, or should have gone to see him long ago; but Mrs. Lewin tells me he was wounded in leaving Lucknow (he fought all through the siege), and has been ill ever since.

Wednesday, 30th.— .... Our baby's birthday! This morning I heard from Dr. Kay. He asks me " especially to take Phil. iv. 4—7, and repeat " it, when any despondency approaches." His letter seems to have come just when I most needed it.

Thursday, 31st.— .... No news yet of the Residency and burial-ground. School as usual. Wrote to Mr. Jackson, and inclosed a copy of Sir Mountstuart's letter.

Saturday, January 2nd, 1858.— .... Received a letter from Mrs. Wood, written to Henry in October. They seem to have been more anxious in England then, than when they wrote in November.

Tuesday, 5th.— .... Heavy firing heard here this morning and in the night. The enemy have attacked a rajah, who is friendly to us, within a few miles of this, on the other side the Ganges. One thousand two hundred of our troops went out at three this morning, with several guns. We killed two hundred of the enemy, and hanged twenty prisoners. Only one of our men wounded.

School at two P.M. Walked with Mrs. Harris on the ramparts. She says that a letter has been received from Captain Hearsey, who is in Nepaul. He says that he knows nothing of Georgina Jackson's fate, as she did not escape with him, as was supposed. It is believed, however, that she is in the care of some rajah; whereabouts, I do not know. The last news of the prisoners in Lucknow is, that Maun Singh, in whose care they were, was trying to effect their release, and that they were going to escape in native disguise, when it was discovered by a sepoy. The men were then given up to the sepoys, and the ladies sent back to their former place of confinement, said to be with the rajah's own women.

Wednesday, 6th.—The steamer has arrived which is to take us down; and I have written to ask Mrs. Bartrum to share my cabin with me. Captain Edgell called while we were at breakfast, to tell us about the steamers.

Heard from Mr. Jackson in answer to my letter. He thinks that the copy I sent him may be of use in helping them to trace Georgina Jackson. He seems to have given up all hopes of Sir Mountstuart, but speaks of the probability of rescuing the ladies very soon.

Saturday, 9th.— . . . . Received letters from home, and from Edward, written in June!

Monday, 11th.—Preparing for the steamer.

Sent the harmonium on to the boats by coolies. Heard of a terrible report about the burial-ground at Lucknow. I can scarcely endure to think about it; but fear it must be true.

.... Reached the steamers about seven P.M.

.... The European women and children are placed on flats, each of which a steamer tows. We are to reach Calcutta in a fortnight.

Wednesday, 13th.— .... Passed Chunar about four P.M. I was greatly disappointed at not stopping there, as I could have gone to see the stone that French has prepared for my darling baby's grave. The scenery is beautiful about this station—green banks sloping down to the river, &c. The port something like that at Allahabad; the ramparts covered with Europeans, come to see us pass.

Thursday, 14th.—Arrived at Benares about eight A.M. .... Dr. Fayrer tells Mrs. Thornhill and myself he does not believe in the report of the desecration of the burial-ground; but there is no doubt about the church having been razed, and a bazaar built over its ruins. On Sunday evening I had a long talk with Mrs. Orr about her sister and the other prisoners in Lucknow. She tells me that she and Madeline Jackson are suffering wretched discomfort, though not treated with actual cruelty. They are kept in a small room, in which it is not possible for them to stand upright, and they have never been allowed to stir out of this room during their confinement. They are not allowed to wear English clothing, but have had each of them *one* set of native clothing given them in November, which they have had to wear ever since. Maun Singh's Vakeel appears inclined to treat them kindly. It is through him that they have been able to communicate with Captain Orr, and he managed to send, through the Vakeel, some arrowroot and medicines for Mrs. Orr's little girl, who was very ill.

Friday, 15*th*.—Sailed at eleven A.M. and went on shore at Ghazeepore. We went to her Majesty's 37th lines, and rested in the soldiers' barracks. They seemed much delighted to see us, and looked at us with great curiosity, and wanted to bring us beer, &c.

Saturday, 16*th*.—Left Buxar early this morning, and arrived at a very narrow part of the river, called the Boliah Flats. Here we stuck fast, and here we have remained all day, in spite of the vigorous efforts of all hands on board to get us off. Even as I now write, at nine P.M., the natives are working hard at the capstan, and keeping up the wild song they have been singing all day. Mrs. Bartrum, Mrs. Thornhill, and I had a long talk together to-night upon deck. There is a chain of sympathy between us, which very few can understand. Captain Edgell told me to-night that he remembers Henry and Edward at Eton quite well. Edward, he says, was his senior. When he first came to Lucknow, on seeing Henry he recollected him at once, and was remembered by him.

Sunday, 17*th*.— .... Captain Edgell read the Morning and Evening Service; Captain Boileau reading at night that beautiful Sermon of the Bishop of Oxford upon Prayer.

Tuesday, 19*th*.—Reached Dinapore at twelve. Brigadier Christie, who is in command here, and Mr. Burge, the chaplain, called upon us. The latter asked Mrs. Thornhill and me to dine at his house, and the Brigadier drove us there in his buggy. Mrs. Burge says, that she knew Mrs. Wood as a child, when she was living at Salt Hill, and that she remembers my husband and his brother Edward very well, and that Edward and a brother-in-law of hers are great friends. Mr. Burge told me what *he* believes to be the true account of Mr. ——'s death, which he had heard from a soldier who had lost both arms, and who had been in ——. The account given to him by a native was this: that, after joining in prayer with the others, he was not killed, as was reported, when they were all fired upon, but only wounded .... and that he was afterwards taken through the bazaars, and at last crucified; nailed to his own pulpit, which was then set on fire. . . . .

Wednesday, 20th.— . . . . The Brigadier and the Burges stayed with us till just before we sailed, at eleven A.M. Mr. Burge ran back to the ship, just as we were starting, to bring me a beautiful bouquet of English flowers.

Sunday, 24th.— . . . . Captain Edgell read prayers this morning, and Captain Boileau read the Bishop of Oxford's Sermon on "Time."

Wednesday, 27th.— . . . . Sailed early, and continued our course till eleven at night, there being bright moonlight, when we reached Coolna. I lay at the ship's head for nearly an hour to-night, with my head over the side of the ship, resting upon the anchor, talking to Mrs. Inglis and Mrs. Watson.

Thursday, 28th.— . . . . Sailed to-day through the "Sunderbunds." The scenery is very beautiful; the river winding in all directions, sometimes very narrow, and again becoming so broad as to appear like a lake: the banks on both sides covered with dense jungle. Numbers of alligators of all sizes on the banks. The officers shot several. The captain says that rhinoceroses infest these jungles, and that in his two last voyages he has seen them close to the steamer. The jungles also abound with tigers. . . . .

Friday, 29th.—To-night a native fell through

one of the holds, and his leg was struck by some machinery beneath, and broken so badly as to require amputation below the knee. Dr. Fayrer is now taking it off, just outside the saloon door.

Saturday, 30th.— . . . Arrived in Calcutta about four P.M., entering by the Hooghly. The captain took us, by our special request, to a ghât, where he knew we might land quietly. Consequently, we found very few people awaiting us. I had several invitations to people's houses, but I had previously settled to go with Mrs. Bartrum to one of the "Houses of Refuge" provided for us by the Relief Fund. Mr. Moultrie brought me letters from Edward and Mr. Alfred Williams, both written in November. Mrs. Bartrum (whose husband was shot through the head just outside the Residency in Havelock's attack, after behaving with the most devoted courage) came with me to "3, Harington-street," where we found everything very comfortable. Mrs. Bartrum's little boy (her only child) is very ill, and I fear will die. She and I and her little boy are to go to England in the *Himalaya* Government troop-ship, if we can possibly get ready in time.

Monday, February 1st.— . . . . Henry's birthday! . . . . In the evening we went to see the *Himalaya*. She is a most splendid vessel, and the largest that has ever been to India. Lady Canning, the Archdeacon, and Dr. Kay, called.

Wednesday, 3rd.—Went to Government-house. Lady Canning was very kind, and made many inquiries about the hospitals, &c. She wishes very much that I should be with the invalids on the voyage, and offered me books for them. She made us pay a long visit.

Thursday, 4th.— . . . . Mrs. Bartrum's child weaker. Dr. Kay called; he brought me his own Hebrew Bible, the one he used to lend me in the *Pera*, two years ago!

Monday, 8th.— . . . . Mr. Hogg, the Administrator-General, called, and settled our papers, &c. He remembered Edward and Henry at Eton.

Tuesday, 9th.— . . . . Received a letter from Lady Canning, inclosing one for Miss Nightingale, whom she wishes me to know.

Wednesday, 10th.—Mrs. Bartrum's baby very ill. He has been looking worse daily lately, but now there is a decided change for the worse. Went on board the *Himalaya*.

Thursday, 11th.—The poor little boy died at about two this morning. Mrs. Bartrum called me at about half-past one. She seemed much terrified by the change in him, scarcely knowing what it was. I, however, knew only too well. But she was very good, and I persuaded her to keep quite quiet, so as not to disturb the dear little child in his last moments; and he died in her arms, without much previous suffering, except from difficulty of breathing. I washed and dressed him, and laid him upon her bed, and in the morning we gathered roses and other flowers from the garden to lay around him. He had his picture taken as he lay (with buds of orange blossom upon his pillow, and such a sweet smile on his face), by a daguerreotypist, in the middle of the day. The portrait was most successful; the poor little thing lay with its head a little on one side, and he looks as if he were smiling in sleep. The portrait was slightly tinted, to take off the pallor of the effect. We took the little coffin with us in the mourning coach, Dr. Fayrer accompanying us. The Moultries were there, and took Captain Boileau in their carriage. The Wylies also met us at the grave. Poor Mrs. Bartrum kept up very well, until the handful of earth was cast upon the coffin, and that was almost too much for her. Mr. Moultrie was most kind, and she will never forget the kind tender sympathy he showed her *so silently*. All this brought back my own losses too vividly to my mind! . . . .

. . . . Mrs. Bartrum has had a stone put up to her husband and child, with this verse, "Is it well with thy husband? Is it well

" with the child? And she answered, It is "well." ....

And now we are both of us alone in the world; but it may be, that, through God's mercy, not a very long time may intervene before we shall again "see all the blossoms of our earthly hopes blooming in a brighter world."

Dr. Kay called in the evening, and brought a copy of the "Sheltering Vine" for Mrs. Bartrum.

Friday, 12th. — Came on board the *Himalaya* at nine A.M. The Moultries and Dr. Kay were busy for an hour in arranging my cabin, which is very large and comfortable. Dr. Kay had fastened up his print of "Hagar and the Angel," and brought me an arm-chair for my cabin. Nothing can exceed his sympathy and kindness, and that of the Moultries. They all stayed till just before we sailed, which we did at eleven.

Saturday, 13th.—Dr. Bremner took me round to see the men; there are about 137 sick and wounded, some very bad cases; 7 or 8 consumptive, 2 now requiring amputation. There are perhaps about 10 of the Lucknow cases, several of the 32nd.

This is the last entry in the Journal. Mrs. Polehampton landed at Plymouth, June 8, 1858, after a long, though pleasant, voyage. About twelve of the men had died on board. One of the editors, who met her at Plymouth, can bear good testimony, from what he saw and heard on board the ship, that she proved indeed a "ministering angel" to the poor wounded fellows whose sufferings and deathbeds she comforted and relieved.

EXTRACTS

FROM

SERMONS PREACHED IN INDIA.

From his first Sermon in India, preached in Calcutta Cathedral on the 4th Sunday in Lent, 1856.—(See Letter of March 8, 1856.)

. . . . DOES our love show itself in our endeavours to extend the Church of God? Do we give of our substance for the spread of the Gospel? Especially, are we doing what we can to extend its influence in this land? From its inhabitants, whose rulers God has allowed us to become, we derive great temporal advantages. Rich as we are in spiritual things, we reap from them an abundant harvest of the good things of this life. What are we doing for them in return? We have given them a more equitable code of laws: we instruct them in many branches of worldly knowledge. But are we giving them, to the extent which Christ requires of us, that instruction in the science of divine things, without which knowledge, though "knowledge is power," is a power which will be wielded, not for the good, but for the hurt of mankind? *How* the knowledge of God is, as it ought, to be far more widely extended among the heathen inhabitants of this land, it is not for me, new comer among you as I am, particularly to point out. But, sure I am that *there must be a way*, when I remember that God never orders men to perform impossibilities, and recal to my mind his express command, "Go ye into all the world, and preach the gospel to every creature." One way there is, which is open to all; the way of teaching *by example*. It is well known that there is no such stumbling-block in the way of the heathen, as the profligate and immoral lives of those who call themselves Christians. Let us then, brethren, be careful of this, that none of us put a stumbling-block, an occasion of falling, in the way of our heathen fellow-men; especially before those who, having been illuminated with some rays of truth, are feeling their way, amid the darkness of doubt and difficulty, towards the source of light—the fountain-head, from which streams down the river of eternal truth. Not merely by abstaining from grosser sins, but by cultivating every grace, which the Gospel requires in those who would be true followers of Christ, by showing forbearance and gentleness, and that "not only to the good and gentle, but also to the froward," let us show that we are true disciples of Him, who, having it in his power to call to his aid innumerable legions of angels, yet allowed himself to be reviled without reviling again, and, " when He⋅suffered, threatened not;" in all this "leaving us an example, that we should follow his steps." . . . .

. . . . " For lack of knowledge and judgment, many are so wanting in love for their heathen brethren, that they despair of their conversion, and thus deprive the Church of Christ of those energies which, if used actively in his cause, might, by the blessing of God, materially tend to hasten the time when his kingdom shall come, and his " will be done on earth, as it is in heaven." If they would strive to obtain more knowledge of the character of those, whom it is our bounden duty to bring to Christ, and, having obtained it, would act with sustained vigour, tempered by judgment, surely we should soon be enabled to thank God that there " were added to His Church daily" many of "such as should be saved." . . . .

From the last Sermon preached before H.M. 52nd Regiment, at Lucknow, December 28th, 1856.

PSALM CXIX. 96.

" I see that all things come to an end, but thy commandment is exceeding broad."

OFTEN as I have stood before you, my brethren, to address you on the subjects which most nearly concern your welfare both here and hereafter; and solemn as every such occasion is, because on each is delivered to you a message from God; still, never has it been my lot to speak to you at a time which brings with it, to every thinking mind, a feeling of such solemnity as the present. For we are standing, as it were, between two of these great periods of time by which our life and the history of the world is marked off. But three days more, and then (unless it please God that eternity shall first begin) the old year will have ended

—the history of the new year will have begun. There may be some among you, brethren, who take but little heed of the ending of one, the beginning of another year, further than so far as is necessary to make up your worldly accounts. But depend upon it, whether you heed it or not, as year after year comes to an end, the all-seeing God is noting in his book the improvement or the falling away of every one of us. *He is* making up our accounts for eternity, whether we do so or not. . . . .

Such being the case, and since this, my brethren of the 52nd Regiment, is, in all human probability, the last time of my addressing you—almost certainly the last time of my addressing *all* of you—I beseech you to give me your most earnest attention. . . . . " The days of our age are threescore years and ten." But, even if God should allow us to remain upon earth the full measure of our days, we shall find it little enough for the work we have to do. What is that work? It is not to be all for *ourselves* and our *own* good. The Word of God bids us provide for ourselves and those dependent on us: but besides this there is a work which every one of us has to do for God. *Sin* is the one thing above all others which grieves Him. . . . . Sin is the thing which God most hates. As the only return we can make Him for the blessings of life, and health, and preservation from evil, and the high station which, as a Christian, every one of us enjoys above the other inhabitants of the earth, above all for the blessings of eternal life which may be ours, if it be not our own fault, through Jesus Christ our Lord, He expects us to endeavour to fight against *sin* in ourselves and others. . . . .

.... And while, my brethren, in looking back upon the past, you consider, repent of, and make resolutions to amend your conduct towards God, forget not to thank Him for his many mercies to you and to your country. To your country God has again given the blessings of peace. And though, alas! even at this time of year, when the multitude of the heavenly host proclaimed "Peace on earth," at the birth of the Prince of Peace, the sound of warlike preparation again is heard; let us hope that, in answer to our prayers, its horrors may yet be averted.

It is natural for you, as soldiers, to wish to add another honour to those of which this regiment has already gained so many. But, oh! my brethren, when we think of the fair fields which must be wasted, of the treasure which must be squandered, treasure which might be spent in civilising the world and spreading the Gospel of Christ; when we think of the happy wives and children who must be made widows and orphans, before these honours can be gained, would you not, if you could make the choice, rather still remain without the medal on your breasts, or the victory on your flag, than that they should be gained by the infliction of such miseries at home and abroad? I am sure, if this regiment ever is called to face an enemy again, it will do its duty nobly, as it did of old; but I will tell you *who* will do their duty best—the men that keep from *sin;* the men who are not ashamed of reading their Bible, and saying their prayers; whose peace is made with God through Christ: *these* are the men that are not afraid to die.*
I know that many a hardened sinner is a daring

* See Letter of July 18, 1856.

soldier; but it will generally be found to be the other way, and that that is true which the poet has said,

'T is conscience that makes cowards of us all.

With regard to the mercies which God has shown to this regiment, and to ourselves individually. It pleased Him to send upon you that fearful scourge, the cholera. You are leaving behind you many a dearly-loved wife and child, many a gallant comrade, whose names upon our church-walls will long remain as a record of your stay in this station. But how many are there here whom God in his mercy spared, when He smote the rest? And why did He spare you? Was it for your righteousness? No! but through his great mercy, that you might still have time to make your calling and election sure. What return can you make Him, brethren, but by an amended life?

Others there are of us, brethren, but we are but few, whom our Creator, having smitten us with deadly sickness, and having brought us to the very gates of death, mercifully has restored us again to health and strength. What were our feelings, when death stood full in view? Had we a good hope that for our Saviour's sake our sins were blotted out, or did we fear to die, because our evil lives witnessed against us; because the Saviour, never sought in health, was a stranger to us in sickness? What vows did we make that we would forsake our old sins, that we would endeavour steadfastly to walk in God's ways, if He should be pleased to spare us? How are we keeping these vows? Two passages of Scripture let us take for our warning. " When the unclean spirit is gone out of a man, he walketh through dry places seeking rest: and, finding none, he saith, I will return to my house, whence I came out. And, when he cometh, he findeth it empty, swept, and garnished. Then goeth he and taketh seven other spirits more wicked than himself: and they enter in and dwell there; and the last state of that man is worse than the first." And let us remember our Saviour's warning to the man whom he healed of a disease of thirty-eight years' standing, "Behold, thou art made whole; sin no more, lest a worse thing happen unto thee." . . . .

. . . . I have now to thank you for the kindness and attention, with which I have been received by you all, from the colonel to the private. I shall always be able to give good testimony of the quiet and orderly behaviour of the regiment, while at this station. I trust you will never lose that good name, which in this respect you possess. But try to be something better than even *orderly* and *respectable* men. Be *Christian* men. Be not only soldiers, but " good soldiers of Jesus Christ." With many such, so far as man can judge, I have met in this regiment. I pray that you, my brethren, may be kept steadfast in the course upon which you have entered. All those, who will endeavour to serve Christ faithfully, must encounter opposition, and ridicule, and sneers, wherever they may be placed. But these you will disregard, feeling that you would indeed be guilty of folly, indeed deserving of ridicule, if you were to give up those principles which alone can stand the test of "the hour of death and the day of judgment." Such of you as are members of the Church of England will, I trust, remain firm in communion with that Church. Those who are not, will, I trust, live in concord and union with those who are: knowing that you serve one common Master, Christ: who will at the end join together in the Church triumphant in heaven all who have believed in Him, loved Him, and striven earnestly to walk in his commandments.

And now, my friends of the 52nd Regiment, I must bid you farewell. We may not meet again in this world; but, by the mercy of God, we shall in that better land, where there will be no more need of soldiers, either of the cross or of the crown; when our last battle shall have been fought, our last victory won, through faithful fighting under his banner, who is now the Captain of our salvation, but whose enemies then will all have been put under his feet, never more to rise again; and Him we shall serve under his everlasting reign, who is King of kings, Lord of lords, and Prince of Peace.

Last written Sermon. Preached at Christ Church, Lucknow, when tidings came of the Mutiny of Sepoys, and the Massacre at Delhi and Meerut. Sunday, May 24, 1857.

PSALM CXVIII. 8, 9.

"It is better to trust in the Lord than to put any confidence in man. It is better to trust in the Lord than to put any confidence in princes."

"What is there," says the excellent Hooker, in the fifth book of his "Ecclesiastical Polity," "what "is there necessary for man to know which the

"Psalms are not able to teach? Heroical mag-
"nanimity, exquisite justice, grave moderation, exact
"wisdom, repentance unfeigned, unwearied patience,
"the mysteries of God, the sufferings of Christ, the
"terrors of wrath, the comforts of grace, the works
"of Providence over this world, and the promised
"joys of the world to come, all good necessarily
"to be either done, or known, or had, this one
"celestial fountain yieldeth. Let there be any grief
"or disease incident into the soul of man, any wound
"or sickness named, for which there is not in this
"treasure-house a present comfortable remedy, at all
"times ready to be found." *

I was, brethren, forcibly struck with the truth of this well-known passage, when, on looking yesterday into the services of this Sunday, in search of words upon which to found my present discourse, I lighted, in the Psalms for the Morning Service, upon the words of my text:—"It is better to trust in the "Lord than to put any confidence in man. It is "better to trust in the Lord than to put any con- "fidence in princes." What words could be more suitable to our present circumstances? What more calculated to give us true courage and solid comfort than such assurances as these?

And this assurance is given us by a man who had often been placed in such circumstances, yea, in circumstances more full of danger and anxiety than ours. He felt its truth, when he prevailed over the giant with a sling and a stone. It was the stay and comfort of his heart, when, constrained to dwell at the court of Saul, that monarch at one moment

* Eccl. Pol. Book v. chap. 37.

caressed him, at another sought his life. Nor less deep was its consolation, when he fled for his life from Saul, "like a partridge on the mountains;" nor again, when, driven from his kingdom by the unnatural conduct of his son Absalom, and the treachery of his trusted friend Ahithophel, he spoke, in the bitterness of his spirit, words which at once expressed his own condition, and were a prophecy of that which should in later days befal his antitype, the Messiah:—" It is not an open enemy that hath done " me this dishonour, for then I could have borne it; " neither was it mine adversary that did magnify " himself against me; but it was thou, my companion, " my guide, and mine own familiar friend." It would be easy to multiply quotations from his writings to show how perfect and entire was David's trust in God; equally easy would it be to show from history the truth of his own saying,—"Thou, Lord, hast never failed them that seek Thee."

Nor does the experience of David alone, but that of all the eminent persons, whose lives are recorded in Scripture for our instruction, teach us the self-same lesson. Why need I remind you of Israel, triumphing by the sea-shore over that mighty host, which, if their trust had been in themselves alone, had speedily glutted itself with their slaughter, or driven them back as slaves? Who remembers not Daniel in the den of lions? or the three servants of God in the burning fiery furnace, where the fire burned them not, because there walked with them another in the midst of the flame?—" and the form of the fourth was like the son of God." What humble servant of God is not cheered by remembering how, when the king of Syria sent horses and chariots and a very great army, and compassed the city in which Elisha and his servant were concealed, and the servant cried out with fear, "Alas, my master, what shall we do?" he answered :—" Fear not, for they that be with us " are more than they that be with them. And the " Lord opened the eyes of the young man, and he " saw; and behold, the mountain was full of chariots " and horses of fire round about Elisha." Let these few instances, out of many which might be brought forward, suffice as proofs of the doctrine of my text. To these we might add many instances from the history of the Church of Christ since the closing of the canon of Scripture, in which the hand of God has been manifest in the deliverance of his people, though these instances lack that positive proof which Scripture alone can furnish.

But why need I say more? He who believes in God, and in Holy Scripture as the Word of God, believes also, as an infallible truth, that now, even as in the times of the patriarchs, and prophets, and apostles of old, He, who is the same yesterday, to-day, and for ever, appoints his guardian angels to " tarry " round about those that fear Him, and deliver " them."

But, brethren, have all, who call themselves Christians, a right to use the language, and to take to themselves the confidence, furnished and implied by my text, and such like passages? He, for instance, who makes self his god, who spends his day solely in the pursuit of wealth and fame, or in the enjoyment of pleasure, either criminal or frivolous; who knows not the meaning of self-denial, either to mortify his own sinful lusts and passions, or that he may benefit others; he who thus lives, when all things are quiet about him, a stranger to God, a worshipper of *self*, and all that may gratify *self*, has such an one any right to take to himself, as belonging to him, the comforting assurances of God's Word, when troubles arise from within or from without? It is true, we hear many persons, who at other times scarcely ever mention the name of God but to take it in vain, confidently express their trust in Him, when, and not until, they can see deliverance nowhere else; and then, as soon as the danger is over, they return to their old habits, and forget Him in prosperity, whom they had been only too glad to reckon their friend in time of trouble. But can such persons have *true* confidence in God? You, my brother or sister, whose conscience tells you that, although your conduct may be outwardly decent, you have yet, as far as any real acquaintance with God is concerned, been living without Him in the world, answer this question to yourself.

The last few days must have caused great "searchings of heart" to all of us. It has been impossible for the wisest among us (whatever his *opinion* may have been), impossible for the wisest among us to say with certainty whether, in almost any given hour, the fate of those, who in other places in this land have met with unexpected and cruel deaths, might not have been his fate also. Now, it is clear that such circumstances as these, in which we undoubtedly have been placed, and which may, for anything we know, still be our condition, ought to have a very serious effect upon us. They have plainly taught us that, after all we can do, there is but little confidence for safety to be placed in man. They ought also to have taught us, if we knew it not before, that we can securely place that confidence alone in God. They ought, farther, to lead us carefully to ask ourselves whether we feel that that confidence is ours. I am not an alarmist. I am sure we all feel that everything, which political wisdom could suggest, or military skill execute, has been carried out for our safety. In this place we are more favoured than our brethren at many other stations. We are not without a well-tried, though it may be a small band of brave defenders, of our own countrymen, prepared to shed their heart's blood for our safety and the honour of our country; the descendants of those who from age to age, in every portion of the globe, have gained victories for England, often against fearful odds; many of them the very same men who, in this country and in Europe, have added lustre to our arms. Far are we, I am sure, from thinking, brethren, that if the worst we can dread were to happen, our case is desperate. What Englishmen have done, Englishmen can do; but what they have done was by the help of God; and for whatever they may have to do, they must ask, with humble hearts, for the same gracious assistance, or their efforts will be in vain.

But suppose—I will not say, that we had been overcome—but that we had been surprised, as others, by those treacherous foes, of whom too many lurk about us in the guise of friends, before our preparations were complete, or we even feared the presence of danger. Had those wretched creatures been the permitted instruments of our death, who at other places have spared neither sex nor age, what would have been our feelings in those last awful, inevitable moments? Should we have felt that we had not only a cruel death to face, but also, far more terrible, to go forth without a friend, without the only friend whom the disembodied spirit can claim, into that vast unknown future, or could we have felt and said with David, "Yea, though I walk through the "valley of the shadow of death, I will fear no evil; "for thou art with me: thy rod, and thy staff, they "comfort me"?

Although, brethren, these considerations are obvious, and such as must have suggested themselves, one would think, to every heart, they are yet such as it is my bounden duty to bring before you. May the Spirit of God carry them home, for the use of all our future lives, to all our hearts!

We know not, brethren, what trials may yet be in store for us. I think I am correct in saying that those, who have the best means of information, have the fullest confidence that all will be well. But let us not therefore suffer the present trying time to pass away, without striving to fix deeply in our minds the lessons it ought to teach. In every day and hour of our common life, we have need to learn and practise them, as much as, nay more than in the present unusual state of affairs. We have need to practise these lessons, because death is ever near us; we cannot tell how near: "in the midst of life we are in death" is God's truth, not merely man's wisdom; and to practise them more than at present, because, when our lives are rolling on in their usual course, we are off our guard. And how great a mercy is it from our God, that we know not the day of our death; that we are not kept all our lives, as we have lately been, in a state of apprehension! For it is impossible to contemplate death, the parting of the soul from the body, without some apprehension; such is a part of the punishment due to our own and our first parents' sins. Our utter ignorance of the time of our death frees us, in the usual course of our lives, from fear of it. It is only when we see it close at hand that we fear; and all that fear, excepting such portion of it as God wills that we should feel, may be taken away, if, instead of placing confidence in man and earthly things, we will put our trust in the Lord.

But this trust will not be blind, unthinking reliance in the mercy of God, that all will come right at last. As under present circumstances, those who are in authority here, while they place, as I am sure they do, their reliance upon God for wisdom, yet neglect no human measures for ensuring our safety; so we, brethren, in our every-day trial for life and death, eternal life and death, must give earnest heed to the commands of the great Captain of our salvation. We must "work out our own salvation with fear and trembling," while yet we trust for eternal life only to Him, "who worketh in us both to will and to do."

These are among the most striking of the commands of our great Captain, Jesus, which I have already mentioned: "Watch and pray, lest ye enter "into temptation—what I say unto you, I say unto "all; Watch. Watch ye therefore, and pray always, "that ye may be counted worthy to escape all these

"things which shall come to pass, and to stand
"before the Son of Man." And for what are we to
watch? For his coming:—"lest coming suddenly,"
either in the hour of our death or the day of
judgment, "He find us sleeping." "Take heed to
"yourselves, lest at any time your hearts be over-
"charged with surfeiting and drunkenness and cares
"of this life, and so that day come upon you un-
"awares."

But it is not sufficient to watch. "Watch and
pray," says our Saviour. Aye, brethren, without
prayer, heartfelt prayer, all our watching will be in
vain; all our resolutions of amendment will be worse
than useless; we shall but add sin to sin in the shape
of broken vows, unless we get, through prayer, the
help of the Holy Spirit of God.

If then, brethren, the present crisis, by placing
the fear of death before us, has taught us that we are
not prepared for it, oh let this consciousness bring us
to our knees! Our shame it is that we have not
hitherto served God from love; but fear will bring
about in us that love to God, without which we
cannot serve Him aright; if only we seek in earnest
the help of his Spirit, that this blessed result may
be produced.

Our fear has taught us, surely it has taught us all,
our *entire* dependence on God. Surely we must
come to love Him, Who thus allows us, evil as we
are, to depend on Him from day to day!

And when we really love Him best—when we
"seek first the kingdom of God and his righteousness," then, brethren, and only then, shall we really
feel the confidence expressed in our text: "It is

"better to trust in the Lord than to put any con-
"fidence in man. It is better to trust in the Lord
"than to put any confidence in princes."

Having first sought, in humble confession of the past, and with steadfast resolution for the future, to deserve that help on which we see we so entirely depend; we shall be prepared, my brethren, to go on our way through this world towards the next, fearing nothing—prepared for all things. On this head, and to conclude, let me quote the words of the pious Archbishop Leighton—words which I have quoted here before, but which need no apology for their repetition.

"Well, choose you: but, all reckoned and examined,
"I had rather be the poorest believer than the
"greatest king on earth. How small a commotion,
"small in its beginning, may prove the overturning
"of the greatest kingdom! But the believer is heir
"to a kingdom that cannot be shaken. The mightiest
"and most victorious prince, who has been gaining
"new conquests all his days, is stopped by a small
"distemper in the middle of his course; he returns
"to his dust, and then his vast designs fall to nothing.
"In that very day all his thoughts perish. But the
"believer in that very day is sent to the possession
"of his crown; that is his coronation-day: in that
"very day all his thoughts are accomplished.

"How can you affright him? Bring him word
"that his estate is ruined. 'Yet my inheritance
"is safe,' says he. Your wife, or child, or dear friend
"is dead. 'Yet my Father lives.' You yourself
"must die. 'Well, then, I go home to my Father
"and my inheritance.'

"Would you be quiet, and have peace within in "troublous times? Keep near unto God; beware of "anything that may interpose between you and your "confidence.

"This is the blessed and safe state of the true "Christian. Who can think that he leads a sad, "heavy life? Oh! it is the only lightsome, sweet, "cheerful condition in the world. The rest of men "are poor, rolling, unstayed things; every report "shaking them, as the leaves of trees are shaken "with the wind.

"But the man who trusts in God, and he alone, "can look the grim visage of death in the face with "an unappalled mind; death, which damps all the joys "and defeats all the hopes of the most prosperous "man of the world.

"But to the righteous there is hope in his death. "Though riches and honour and all the glories of "the world are with a man, yet he fears: fears the "more for these, because here they must end.

"But he who trusts in God looks death out of "countenance; and over him the second death shall "have no power;" for, my brethren, he knows in Whom he has believed; and is confident that through His merits he shall be found at last, washed in His blood, without spot before the throne of God.

APPENDIX.

BRIGADIER INGLIS'S NARRATIVE OF THE DEFENCE OF LUCKNOW.

"*From Brigadier Inglis, commanding Garrison of Lucknow, to the Secretary to Government, Military Department, Calcutta.*

"Dated Lucknow, Sept. 26.

"SIR,—In consequence of the very deeply-to-be-lamented death of Brigadier-General Sir H. M. Lawrence, K.C.B., late in command of the Oudh Field Force, the duty of narrating the military events, which have occurred at Lucknow since the 29th of June last, has devolved upon myself.

"On the evening of that day reports reached Sir Henry Lawrence that the rebel army, in no very inconsiderable force, would march from Chinhut (a small village about eight miles distant on the road to Fyzabad) on Lucknow on the following morning; and the late Brigadier-General therefore determined to make a strong reconnoissance in that direction, with the view, if possible, of meeting the force at a disadvantage, either at its entrance into the suburbs of the city, or at the bridge across the Gokral, which is a small stream intersecting the Fyzabad road, about half-way between Lucknow and Chinhut.

"The force destined for this service, and which was composed as follows, moved out at six A.M. on the morning of the 30th of June:—Artillery: four guns of No. — Horse Light Field Battery, four ditto of No. 2 Oudh Field Battery, two ditto of No. 3 ditto ditto, and an 8-inch howitzer. Cavalry: Troop of Volunteer Cavalry; 120 troopers of detachments belonging to 1st, 2d, and 3rd Regiments of Oudh Irregular Cavalry. Infantry: 300, her Majesty's 32nd; 150, 13th Native Infantry; 60, 48th Native Infantry; 20, 71st Native Infantry (Sikhs).

"The troops, misled by the reports of wayfarers—who stated that there were few or no men between Lucknow and Chinhut—proceeded somewhat further than had been originally intended, and suddenly fell in with the enemy, who had, up to that time, eluded the vigilance of the advanced guard by concealing themselves behind a long line of trees in overwhelming numbers. The European force and howitzer, with the Native Infantry, held the foe in check for some time; and had six guns of the Oudh Artillery been faithful and the Sikh Cavalry shown a better front, the day would have been won in spite of an immense disparity in numbers. But the Oudh artillerymen and drivers were traitors. They overturned the guns into the ditches, cut the traces of their horses, and abandoned them, regardless of the remonstrances and exertions of their own officers, and of those of Sir Henry Lawrence's staff, headed by the Brigadier-General in person, who himself drew his sword upon these rebels. Every effort to induce them to stand having proved ineffectual, the force, exposed to a vastly superior fire of artillery, and completely outflanked on both sides by an overpowering body of infantry and cavalry, which actually got into our rear, was compelled to retire with the loss of three pieces of artillery, which fell into the hands of the enemy, in consequence of the rank treachery of the Oudh gunners, and with a very grievous list of killed and wounded. The heat was dreadful, the gun ammunition was expended, and the almost total want of cavalry to protect our rear made our retreat most disastrous.

"All the officers behaved well, and the exertions of the small body of Volunteer Cavalry—only forty in number—under Captain Radclyffe, 7th Light Cavalry, were most praiseworthy. Sir Henry Lawrence subsequently conveyed his thanks to myself, who had, at his request, accompanied him upon this occasion (Colonel Case being in command of her Majesty's 32nd). He also expressed his approbation of the way in which his staff—Captain Wilson, Officiating

Deputy Assistant Adjutant-General; Lieutenant James, Sub-Assistant Commissary-General; Captain Edgell, Officiating Military Secretary; and Mr. Couper, Civil Service—the last of whom had acted as Sir Henry Lawrence's aide-de-camp from the commencement of the disturbances —had conducted themselves throughout this arduous day. Sir Henry further particularly mentioned that he would bring the gallant conduct of Captain Radcliffe and of Lieutenant Bonham, of the Artillery (who worked the howitzer successfully until incapacitated by a wound), to the prominent notice of the Government of India. The manner in which Lieutenant Birch, 71st N.I., cleared a village with a party of Sikh skirmishers, also elicited the admiration of the Brigadier-General. The conduct of Lieutenant Hardinge, who, with his handful of horse, covered the retreat of the rear-guard, was extolled by Sir Henry, who expressed his intention of mentioning the services of this gallant officer to his Lordship in Council. Lieutenant-Colonel Case, who commanded her Majesty's 32nd Regiment, was mortally wounded whilst gallantly leading his men. The service had not a more deserving officer. The command devolved on Captain Stevens, who also received a death-wound shortly afterwards. The command then fell to Captain Mansfield, who has since died of cholera. A list of the casualties on this occasion accompanies the despatch.

"It remains to report the siege operations.

"It will be in the recollection of his Lordship in Council that it was the original intention of Sir Henry Lawrence to occupy not only the Residency, but also the fort called the Muchee Bhawun, an old dilapidated edifice which had been hastily repaired for the occasion, though the defences were, even at the last moment, very far from complete, and were, moreover, commanded by many houses in the city. The situation of the Muchee Bhawun with regard to the Residency has already been described to the Government of India.

"The untoward event of the 30th June so far diminished the whole available force, that we had not a sufficient number of men remaining to occupy both positions. The Brigadier-General, therefore, on the evening of the 1st

July, signalled to the garrison of the Muchee Bhawun to evacuate and blow up that fortress in the course of the night. The orders were ably carried out, and at twelve P.M. the force marched into the Residency, with their guns and treasure, without the loss of a man; and shortly afterwards the explosion of 240 barrels of gunpowder, and 6,000,000 ball-cartridges, which were lying in the magazine, announced to Sir Henry Lawrence and his officers, who were anxiously waiting the report, the complete destruction of that post and all that it contained. If it had not been for this wise and strategic measure, no member of the Lucknow garrison, in all probability, would have survived to tell the tale; for, as has already been stated, the Muchee Bhawun was commanded from other parts of the town, and was, moreover, indifferently provided with heavy artillery ammunition, while the difficulty, suffering, and loss which the Residency garrison, even with the reinforcement thus obtained from the Muchee Bhawun, has undergone in holding the position, is sufficient to show that, if the original intention of holding both posts had been adhered to, both would inevitably have fallen.

"It is now my very painful duty to relate the calamity which befel us at the commencement of the siege. On the 1st July an 8-inch shell burst in the room in the Residency in which Sir H. Lawrence was sitting. The missile burst between him and Mr. Couper, close to both, but without injury to either. The whole of his staff implored Sir Henry to take up other quarters, as the Residency had then become the special target for the round shot and shell of the enemy. This, however, he jestingly declined to do, observing that another shell would certainly never be pitched into that small room. But Providence had ordained otherwise, for on the very next day he was mortally wounded by a fragment of another shell which burst in the same room, exactly on the same spot. Captain Wilson, Deputy-Assistant Adjutant-General, received a contusion at the same time.

"The late lamented Sir H. Lawrence, knowing that his last hour was rapidly approaching, directed me to assume command of the troops, and appointed Major Banks to succeed him in the office of Chief Commissioner. He lingered in great agony till the morning of the 4th July, when he expired, and the Government was thereby deprived, if I may venture to say so, of the services of a distinguished statesman and a most gallant soldier. Few men have ever possessed to the same extent the power which he enjoyed of winning the hearts of all those with whom he came in contact, and thus insuring the warmest and most zealous devotion for himself and for the Government which he served. The successful defence of the position has been, under Providence, solely attributable to the foresight which he evinced in the timely commencement of the necessary operations, and the great skill and untiring personal activity which he exhibited in carrying them into effect. All ranks possessed such confidence in his judgment and his fertility of resource, that the news of his fall was received throughout the garrison with feelings of consternation, only second to the grief which was inspired in the hearts of all by the loss of a public benefactor and a warm personal friend. Feeling as keenly and as gratefully as I do the obligations that the whole of us are under to this great and good man, I trust the Government in India will pardon me for having attempted, however imperfectly, to portray them. In him every good and deserving soldier has lost a friend, and a chief capable of discriminating, and ever on the alert to reward merit, no matter how humble the sphere in which it was exhibited.

" The garrison had scarcely recovered the shock which it had sustained in the loss of its revered and beloved general, when it had to mourn the death of that able and respected officer, Major Banks, the officiating Chief Commissioner, who received a bullet through his head while examining a critical outpost on the 21st July, and died without a groan.

" The description of our position and the state of our defences when the siege began are so fully set forth in the accompanying memorandum, furnished by the garrison engineer, that I shall content myself with bringing to the notice of his Lordship in Council the fact that when the blockade was commenced only two of our batteries were completed, part of the defences were yet in an unfinished condition, and the buildings in the immediate vicinity, which gave cover to the enemy, were only very partially cleared away. Indeed, our heaviest losses have been caused by the fire from the enemy's sharpshooters stationed in the adjoining mosques and houses of the native nobility, the necessity of destroying which had been repeatedly drawn to the attention of Sir Henry by the staff of engineers; but his invariable reply was, 'Spare the holy places, and private property too, as far as possible;' and we have consequently suffered severely from our very tenderness to the religious prejudices and respect to the rights of our rebellious citizens and soldiery. As soon as the enemy had thoroughly completed the investment of the Residency, they occupied these houses, some of which were within easy pistol-shot of our barricades, in immense force, and rapidly made loopholes on those sides which bore on our post, from which they kept up a terrific and incessant fire day and night, which caused many daily casualties, as there could not have been less than 8,000 men firing at one time into our position. Moreover, there was no place in the whole of the works that could be considered safe, for several of the sick and wounded who were lying in the banqueting-hall, which had been turned into a hospital, were killed in the very centre of the building, and the widow of Lieutenant Dorin and other women and children were shot dead in a room into which it had not been previously deemed possible that a bullet could penetrate. Neither were the enemy idle in erecting batteries. They soon had from twenty to twenty-five guns in position, some of them of very large calibre. These were planted all round our post at small distances, some being actually within fifty yards of our defences, but in places where our own heavy guns could not reply to them; while the perseverance and ingenuity of the enemy in erecting barricades in front of and around their guns, in a very short time rendered all attempts to silence them by musketry entirely unavailing. Neither could they be effectually silenced by shells, by reason of their extreme proximity to our position, and because, moreover, the enemy had recourse to digging very narrow trenches about eight feet in depth in rear of each gun, in which the men lay while our shells were flying, and which so effectually concealed them, even while working the gun, that our baffled sharpshooters could only see their hands while in the act of loading.

APPENDIX. 403

"The enemy contented themselves with keeping up this incessant fire of cannon and musketry until the 20th of July, on which day, at ten A.M., they assembled in very great force all around our position, and exploded a heavy mine inside our outer line of defences at the Water-gate. The mine, however, which was close to the Redan, and apparently sprung with the intention of destroying that battery, did no harm ; but as soon as the smoke had cleared away, the enemy boldly advanced under cover of a tremendous fire of cannon and musketry, with the object of storming the Redan. But they were received with such a heavy fire, that after a short struggle they fell back with much loss. A strong column advanced at the same time to attack Innes's post, and came on to within ten yards of the palisades, affording to Lieutenant Loughnan, 13th Native Infantry, who commanded the position, and his brave garrison, composed of gentlemen of the Uncovenanted Service, a few of her Majesty's 32nd Foot and of the 13th Native Infantry, an opportunity of distinguishing themselves, which they were not slow to avail themselves of, and the enemy were driven back with great slaughter. The insurgents made minor attacks at almost every outpost, but were invariably defeated, and at two P.M. they ceased their attempts to storm the place, although their musketry fire and cannonading continued to harass us unceasingly as usual. Matters proceeded in this manner until the 10th of August, when the enemy made another assault, having previously sprung a mine close to the brigade mess, which entirely destroyed our defences for the space of twenty feet, and blew in a great portion of the outside wall of the house occupied by Mr. Schilling's garrison. On the dust clearing away, a breach appeared, through which a regiment could have advanced in perfect order, and a few of the enemy came on with the utmost determination, but were met with such a withering flank fire of musketry from the officers and men holding the top of the brigade mess, that they beat a speedy retreat, leaving the more adventurous of their numbers lying on the crest of the breach. While this operation was going on, another large body advanced on the Cawnpore Battery, and succeeded in locating themselves for a few minutes in the ditch. They were, however, dislodged by hand grenades.

At Captain Anderson's post they also came boldly forward with scaling ladders, which they planted against the wall; but here, as elsewhere, they were met with the most indomitable resolution, and, the leaders being slain, the rest fled, leaving the ladders, and retreated to their batteries and loopholed defences, from whence they kept up, for the rest of the day, an unusually heavy cannonade and musketry fire. On the 18th of August the enemy sprung another mine in front of the Sikh lines, with very fatal effect. Captain Orr (Unattached), Lieutenants Mecham and Soppitt, who commanded the small body of drummers composing the garrison, were blown into the air, but providentially returned to earth with no further injury than a severe shaking. The garrison, however, were not so fortunate. No less than eleven men were buried alive under the ruins, from whence it was impossible to extricate them, owing to the tremendous fire kept up by the enemy from houses situated not ten yards in front of the breach. The explosion was followed by a general assault of a less determined nature than the two former efforts, and the enemy were consequently repulsed without much difficulty. But they succeeded, under cover of the breach, in establishing themselves in one of the houses in our position, from which they were driven in the evening by the bayonets of her Majesty's 32nd and 84th Foot. On the 5th of September the enemy made their last serious assault. Having exploded a large mine, a few feet short of the bastion of the 18-pounder gun, in Major Apthorp's post, they advanced with large scaling ladders, which they planted against the wall, and mounted, thereby gaining for an instant the embrasure of a gun. They were, however, speedily driven back with loss by hand grenades and musketry. A few minutes subsequently they sprung another mine close to the brigade mess, and advanced boldly; but soon the corpses strewed in the garden in front of the post bore testimony to the fatal accuracy of the rifle and musketry fire of the gallant members of that garrison, and the enemy fled ignominiously, leaving their leader—a finelooking old native officer—among the slain. At other posts they made similar attacks, but with less resolution, and everywhere with the same want of success. Their loss upon this day must have been very heavy, as they came on

APPENDIX.

with much determination, and at night they were seen bearing large numbers of their killed and wounded over the bridges in the direction of cantonments. The above is a faint attempt at a description of the four great struggles which have occurred during this protracted season of exertion, exposure, and suffering. His Lordship in Council will perceive that the enemy invariably commenced his attacks by the explosion of a mine—a species of offensive warfare for the exercise of which our position was unfortunately peculiarly situated, and had it not been for the most untiring vigilance on our part in watching and blowing up their mines before they were completed, the assaults would probably have been much more numerous, and might, perhaps, have ended in the capture of the place. But by countermining in all directions we succeeded in detecting and destroying no less than four of the enemy's subterraneous advances towards important positions, two of which operations were eminently successful, as on one occasion no less than eighty of them were blown into the air, and twenty suffered a similar fate on the second explosion. The labour, however, which devolved upon us in making these countermines, in the absence of a body of skilled miners, was very heavy. The Right Honourable the Governor-General in Council will feel that it would be impossible to crowd within the limits of a despatch even the principal events, much more the individual acts of gallantry which have marked this protracted struggle. But I can conscientiously declare my conviction, that few troops have ever undergone greater hardships, exposed as they have been to a never-ceasing musketry fire and cannonade. They have also experienced the alternate vicissitudes of extreme wet and of intense heat, and that too with very insufficient shelter from either, and in many places without any shelter at all. In addition to having to repel real attacks, they have been exposed night and day to the hardly less harassing false alarms which the enemy have been constantly raising. The insurgents have frequently fired very heavily, sounded the advance, and shouted for several hours together, though not a man could be seen, with the view, of course, of harassing our small and exhausted force, in which object they succeeded, for no part has been strong enough to allow of a portion only of the garrison being prepared in the event of a false attack being turned into a real one. All, therefore, had to stand to their arms and to remain at their posts until the demonstration had ceased; and such attacks were of almost nightly occurrence. The whole of the officers and men have been on duty night and day during the eighty-seven days which the siege had lasted, up to the arrival of Sir J. Outram, G.C.B. In addition to this incessant military duty, the force has been employed in repairing defences, in moving guns, in burying dead animals, in conveying ammunition and commissariat stores from one place to another, and in other fatigue duties too numerous and too trivial to enumerate here. I feel, however, that any words of mine will fail to convey an adequate idea of what our fatigue and labours have been; labours in which all ranks and all classes—civilians, officers, and soldiers—have borne an equally noble part. All have together descended into the mine, all have together handled the shovel for the interment of the putrid bullock, and all, accoutred with musket and bayonet, have relieved each other on sentry, without regard to the distinction of rank, civil or military. Notwithstanding all these hardships, the garrison has made no less than five sorties, in which they spiked two of the enemy's heaviest guns and blew up several of the houses from which they had kept up the most harassing fire. Owing to the extreme paucity of our numbers, each man was taught to feel that on his own individual efforts alone depended, in no small measure, the safety of the entire position. This consciousness incited every officer, soldier, and man to defend the post assigned to him with such desperate tenacity, and to defend the lives which Providence had entrusted to his care with such dauntless determination, that the enemy, despite their constant attacks, their heavy mines, their overwhelming numbers, their incessant fire, could never succeed in gaining one single inch of ground within the bounds of this straggling position, which was so feebly fortified that had they once obtained a footing in any of the outposts the whole place must inevitably have fallen.

"If further proof be wanting of the desperate nature of the struggle which we have, under God's blessing, so long and so successfully waged, I would point to the roofless and ruined houses, to the crumbled walls, to the exploded mines, to the open breaches, to the shattered and disabled guns and defences, and lastly to the long and melancholy list of the brave and devoted officers and men who have fallen. These silent witnesses bear sad and solemn testimony to the way in which this feeble position has been defended. During the early part of these vicissitudes, we were left without any information whatever regarding the posture of affairs outside. An occasional spy did indeed come in with the object of inducing our sepoys and servants to desert; but the intelligence derived from such sources was of course entirely untrustworthy. We sent our messengers daily calling for aid and asking for information, none of whom ever returned until the twenty-sixth day of the siege, when a pensioner named Ungud came back with a letter from General Havelock's camp, informing us that they were advancing with a force sufficient to bear down all opposition, and would be with us in five or six days. A messenger was immediately despatched, requesting that, on the evening of their arrival on the outskirts of the city, two rockets might be sent up, in order that we might take the necessary measures for assisting them while forcing their way in. The sixth day, however, expired, and they came not; but for many evenings after officers and men watched for the ascension of the expected rockets, with hopes such as make the heart sick. We knew not then, nor did we learn until the 29th of August—or thirty-five days later—that the relieving force, after having fought most nobly to effect our deliverance, had been obliged to fall back for reinforcements; and this was the last communication we received until two days before the arrival of Sir James Outram on the 25th of September.

"Besides heavy visitations of cholera and small-pox, we have also had to contend against a sickness which has almost universally pervaded the garrison. Commencing with a very painful eruption, it has merged into a low fever, combined with diarrhœa; and although few or no men have actually died from its effects, it leaves behind a weakness and lassitude which, in the absence of all material substances save coarse beef and still coarser flour, none have been able entirely to get over. The mortality among the women and children, and especially among the latter, from these diseases, and from other causes, has been perhaps the most painful characteristic of the siege. The want of native servants has also been a source of much privation. Owing to the suddenness with which we were besieged, many of these people who might, perhaps, have otherwise proved faithful to their employers, but who were outside the defences at the time, were altogether excluded. Very many more deserted, and several families were consequently left without the services of a single domestic. Several ladies have had to tend their children, and even to wash their own clothes, as well as to cook their scanty meals, entirely unaided. Combined with the absence of servants, the want of proper accommodation has probably been the cause of much of the disease with which we have been afflicted. I cannot refrain from bringing to the prominent notice of his Lordship in Council the patient endurance and the Christian resignation which have been evinced by the women of this garrison. They have animated us by their example. Many, alas! have been made widows, and their children fatherless, in this cruel struggle. But all such seem resigned to the will of Providence, and many, among whom may be mentioned the honoured names of Birch, of Polehampton, of Barbor, and of Gall, have, after the example of Miss Nightingale, constituted themselves the tender and solicitous nurses of the wounded and dying soldiers in the hospital."

The Brigadier then enters into specific details of the services rendered by the most distinguished officers, &c., whether living or dead, among whom Mr. Polehampton is mentioned. He also bears testimony to the unsurpassed courage and loyalty of the native troops; expresses the deep and grateful sense entertained by the garrison of the services rendered by Sir James Outram and General Havelock and their troops in effecting the relief of Lucknow at so heavy a sacrifice of life, and concludes with these words:—" We are also repaid for much suffering and privation by the sympathy which our brave deliverers say our perilous and unfortunate position has excited for us in the hearts of our countrymen throughout the length and breadth of her Majesty's dominions."

APPENDIX.

THE GOVERNOR-GENERAL'S REPLY TO SIR J. INGLIS.

"Fort William, December 8th, 1857.

"THE Right Hon. the Governor-General in Council has received from Brigadier Inglis, of H.M.'s 32nd Regiment, lately commanding the garrison in Lucknow, the subjoined report of the defence of the Residency in that city, from the first threatened attack upon it on the 29th of June, to the arrival of the force under Major-General Sir J. Outram, G.C.B., and the lamented Major-General Sir H. Havelock, K.C.B., on the 25th of September.

"The divisional order of Major-General Sir James Outram upon the report accompanies it.

"The Governor-General in Council believes that never has a tale been told which will so stir the hearts of Englishmen and Englishwomen as the simple, earnest narrative of Brigadier Inglis.

"It rightfully commences with a soldier's testimony, touchingly borne, to the chivalrous character and high deserts of Sir Henry Lawrence, the sad details of whose death are now made known.

"There does not stand recorded in the annals of war an achievement more truly heroic than the defence of the Residency at Lucknow described in the narrative which follows.

"The defence has not only called forth all the energy and daring which belong to Englishmen in the hour of active conflict, but it has exhibited, continuously and in the highest degree, that noble and sustained courage which, against enormous odds and fearful disadvantages, against hope deferred and through unceasing toil and wear of body and mind, still holds on day after day and triumphs.

"The heavy guns of the assailants, posted almost in security, within fifty yards of the intrenchments—so near, indeed, that the solicitations, and threats, and taunts, which the rebels addressed to the native defenders of the garrison, were easily heard by those true-hearted men; the fire of the enemy's musketry, so searching that it penetrated the innermost retreat of the women and children, and of the wounded; their desperate attempt, repeatedly made, to force an entry, after blowing in the defences; the perpetual mining of the works; the weary night-watching for the expected signal of relief; and the steady waste of precious lives, until the number of English gunners was reduced below that of the guns to be worked—all these constitute features in a history, which the fellow-countrymen of the heroes of Lucknow will read with swelling hearts, and which will endure for ever as a lesson to those who shall hope by treachery, numbers, or boldness in their treason, to overcome the indomitable spirit of Englishmen.

"A complete list of the brave men who have fallen has not yet reached the Governor-General in Council; but the names mentioned in Brigadier Inglis's report are, in themselves, a long and sad one.

"Amongst those who have nobly perished in this protracted struggle, Sir Henry Lawrence will occupy the first place in the thoughts of his fellow-countrymen. The Governor-General in Council has already given expression to the deep sorrow with which he mourns the loss of that distinguished man. But the name of Sir Henry Lawrence can never rise up without calling forth a tribute of honour and admiration from all who knew him.

"The Governor-General in Council has also to deplore the loss of Major Banks, an officer high in the confidence of the Government of India, and who, with the full approval of the Governor-General in Council, had succeeded to the charge of Chief Commissioner upon Sir Henry Lawrence's death; of Lieutenant-Colonel Case, her Majesty's 32nd Regiment, who was mortally wounded while leading on his men at Chinhut, on the 29th of June; of Captain Radcliffe, whose conspicuous bravery attracted the attention of Sir Henry Lawrence on that occasion; of Captain Francis, who was also especially noticed by Sir Henry Lawrence for his gallant conduct while in command of the Muchee Bhawun; of Captain Fulton, of the Engineers, whose indefatigable exertions are thankfully recorded by Brigadier Inglis; of Major Anderson, the chief engineer, who, contending against deadly sickness, did not cease to give his valuable aid to his commander; of Captain Simons, Artillery, mortally wounded

APPENDIX. 411

at Chinhut ; of Lieutenants Shepherd and Arthur, 7th Light Cavalry, killed at their posts ; of Captain McCabe, her Majesty's 32nd, who fell while leading his fourth sortie; of Captain Mansfield, of the same corps, who fell a victim to cholera.

" The Governor-General in Council laments also to find in this melancholy record the names of Mr. Lucas, a traveller in India, and of Mr. Boyson. These two gentlemen, acting as volunteers, received charge of one of the most dangerous outposts, and held it at the cost of their lives.

" The good services of H.M.'s 32nd Regiment throughout this struggle have been remarkable.

" To the watchful courage and sound judgment of its commander, Brigadier Inglis, the British Government owes a heavy debt of gratitude ; and Major Lowe, Captain Bassano, Lieutenants Edmonstoune, Foster, Harmar, Lawrence, Clery, Cooke, Browne, and Charlton, and Quartermaster Stribbling, of this corps, and Captain O'Brien, of H.M.'s 84th regiment, are praised by their superior as having severally distinguished themselves. Of the 7th L.C., Colonel Master, to whom was entrusted the command of a most exposed post, Captain Boileau, and Lieutenant Warner are entitled to the thanks of the Governor-General in Council.

" The Governor-General in Council recognises with pleasure the distinction accorded to Major Apthorp, Captains Kemble and Saunders, Lieutenants Barwell and Kier, of the 41st N.I., as well as to Captain Germon and Lieutenant Aitken, of the 13th N.I., the latter of whom commanded an important position in the defences with signal courage and success ; to Captain Anderson, of the 25th, and to Lieutenant Graydon, of the 44th N.I.

" His Lordship in Council desires to acknowledge the excellent service of Captain Dinning and Lieutenant Sewell, of the 71st N.I., and of Lieutenant Langmore, of the same regiment, who held continuously a post open to attack, and entirely without shelter for himself or for his men by night or by day ; as well as of Lieutenant Worsley, of the same corps ; of Lieut. Tulloch, 58th N.I. ; of Lieut. Hay, 48th N.I., who was placed under the Engineers, to assist in the arduous duties of that department ; and of

Ensign Ward, of the same regiment, who, when the officers of Artillery were mostly disabled, worked the mortars with good effect; also of Lieutenant Graham, of the 11th N.I., and of Lieutenant Mecham, of the 4th Oudh Irregulars.

"Of the native officers and men of the 13th, 48th, and 71st Regiments of Native Infantry, who have been amongst the defenders of the Residency, it is difficult to speak too highly. Their courageous constancy under the severest trials is worthy of all honour.

"The medical officers of the garrison are well entitled to the cordial thanks of the Government of India. The attention, skill, and energy evinced by Superintending-Surgeon Scott; Assistant-Surgeon Boyd, her Majesty's 32nd foot; Assistant-Surgeon Bird, of the Artillery; Surgeon Campbell, 7th Light Cavalry; Surgeon Brydon, 71st Native Infantry; Surgeon Ogilvie, Sanitary Commissioner; Assistant-Surgeon Fayrer; Assistant-Surgeon Partridge, 2nd Oudh Irregulars; Assistant-Surgeons Greenough and Darby, and of Mr. Apothecary Thompson, are spoken of in high terms by Brigadier Inglis.

"To Dr. Brydon, especially, the Governor-General in Council would address his hearty congratulations. This officer, after passing through the Cabul campaign of 1841-42, was included in the illustrious garrison, who maintained their position in Jellalabad. He may now, as one of the heroes of Lucknow, claim to have witnessed and taken part in an achievement even more conspicuous as an example of the invincible energy and enduring courage of British soldiers.

"The labours of the officers of Engineers—Lieutenants Anderson, Hutchinson, and Innes; and of the Artillery—Lieutenant Thomas (Madras) and Lieutenants Macfarlane and Bonham, receive, as they deserve, honourable mention, which the Governor-General in Council is glad to confirm by his cordial approval.

"The services rendered by Mr. McRae, Civil Engineer; Mr. Schilling, Principal of the Martinière, and by Mr. Cameron, a gentleman who had visited Oudh for commercial purposes, merit the especial thanks of the Government of India.

"The Governor-General in Council has read with great satisfaction the testimony borne by Brigadier Inglis to the sedulous attention given to the spiritual comforts of his

APPENDIX. 413

comrades by the Rev. Mr. Polehampton and the Rev. Mr. Harris. The first, unhappily, has not survived his labours.

"The officers of the staff have rendered excellent service. That of Lieutenant James, sub-assistant commissary-general, calls for the especial thanks of the Government of India. This officer, although severely wounded at Chinhut, resolutely continued to give valuable aid to the Brigadier; and it is mainly owing to his forethought and care that the supplies of the garrison have sufficed through the hardships of the siege.

"Captain Wilson, 13th Native Infantry, deputy-assistant adjutant-general, has evinced courage, activity, and sound judgment, in a very high degree.

"Lieutenant Hardinge, officiating as deputy-quartermaster-general, as well as commanding the Sikh cavalry of the garrison, has proved himself worthy to bear his soldier's name.

"Lieutenant Barwell, 71st Native Infantry, fort-adjutant, is honourably mentioned; and Lieutenant Birch, of the 71st Native Infantry, who acted as aide-de-camp to Brigadier Inglis throughout the siege, has discharged his duties in a manner which has called forth emphatic praise from his commander.

"The officers of the civil service have not been behind their military brethren in courage and zeal. The assistance rendered by Mr. Couper to Brigadier Inglis, as previously to Sir Henry Lawrence, has been most valuable.

"Messrs. Thornhill and Capper were wounded during the siege; and Mr. Martin, deputy-commissioner, and Captain Carnegie, assistant-commissioner, have earned the special thanks of Brigadier Inglis.

"To all these brave men, and to their brother officers and comrades of every rank and degree, European and native, who have shared the same dangers and toils with the same heroic spirit, the Governor-General in Council tenders his warmest thanks.

"The officers and men of her Majesty's regiments must receive their full measure of acknowledgment from a higher authority than that of the Governor-General in Council; but it will be the pleasing duty of his Lordship in Council to express to her Majesty's Government, and to the Honourable Court of Directors of the East India Company, in the strongest terms, the recommendation of them to that favour for which Major-General Sir James Outram so justly pleads.

" Meanwhile, it is a gratification to the Governor-General in Council to direct in a general order of this day, that the rewards and honours therein specified shall be at once awarded to the officers and men of the two services and to the civilians respectively.

"This notice must not be closed without mention ot those noble women who, little fitted to take part in such scenes, have assumed so cheerfully and discharged so earnestly their task of charity in ministering to sickness and pain. It is likely that to themselves the notoriety of praise publicly given may be distasteful, yet the Governor-General in Council cannot forego the pleasure of doing justice to the names of Birch, Polehampton, Barbor, and Gall, and of offering to those whose acts have so adorned them his tribute of respectful admiration and gratitude.

"The history of the defence of the Residency of Lucknow does not end with the narrative of Brigadier Inglis. But no full reports of the course of events at Lucknow subsequently to the junction of Sir Henry Havelock's force with the defenders, or of the final and effectual relief by the advance of the Commander-in-Chief, have yet been received. It is known, however, that the success which has carried joy to so many aching hearts has been clouded by the death, within the last few days, of one of the first soldiers of India, Major-General Sir Henry Havelock.

"The Governor-General in Council deeply deplores the loss of this able leader and truly brave man, who has been taken from the service of his country at a time when he can least be spared, though not before he had won for himself lasting renown, and had received at the hands of his Sovereign the gracious and prompt recognition of his merits.

"R. J. H. BIRCH, Colonel,
Secretary to the Government of India,
Medical Department."

CPSIA information can be obtained at www.ICGtesting.com
Printed in the USA
BVOW010957131011

273558BV00004B/4/P